YOUR MONEY MENTORS

YOUR MONEY MENTORS

Expert Advice for Millennials

**Russell Robb and
Katharine Robb Meehan**
with David Tabatsky

ROWMAN & LITTLEFIELD
Lanham • Boulder • New York • London

Published by Rowman & Littlefield
An imprint of The Rowman & Littlefield Publishing Group, Inc.
4501 Forbes Boulevard, Suite 200, Lanham, Maryland 20706
www.rowman.com

86-90 Paul Street, London EC2A 4NE, United Kingdom

British Library Cataloguing in Publication Information Available

Library of Congress Cataloging-in-Publication Data

Names: Robb, Russell, author. | Meehan, Katharine Robb, 1992- author. |
  Tabatsky, David, author.
Title: Your money mentors : expert advice for millennials / Russell Robb and
  Katharine Robb Meehan, with David Tabatsky.
Description: Lanham : Rowman & Littlefield, [2022] | Includes bibliographical
  references and index.
Identifiers: LCCN 2021032027 (print) | LCCN 2021032028 (ebook) | ISBN
  9781538149485 (cloth) | ISBN 9781538149492 (epub)
Subjects: LCSH: Finance, Personal. | Generation Y.
Classification: LCC HG179 .R54414 2022 (print) | LCC HG179 (ebook) |
  DDC 332.024—dc23
LC record available at https://lccn.loc.gov/2021032027
LC ebook record available at https://lccn.loc.gov/2021032028

To Lee

CONTENTS

ACKNOWLEDGMENTS

I have so much to be thankful for, not only in the creation of the original manuscript, but with the substance of the final text and writing.

The genesis of the book's topic is a result of monthly breakfasts with two of my former schoolmates from the 1950s: Dr. Fred Lovejoy, associate physician-in-chief of Boston Children's Hospital, and Thomas Piper, PhD, former deputy dean of the Harvard Business School. On numerous occasions, we discussed how we could advise our grandchildren, who are millennials, during this challenging period in their life.

A critical element in publishing a book about millennials was to secure a top-notch literary agent who would present the manuscript to a major publisher and have it accepted for publication. I engaged Nancy Rosenfield of AAA Books Unlimited, who in turn secured a contract from Suzanne Staszak-Silva, executive editor of Rowman & Littlefield, a well-known publisher. An important part of the drafting process was my assistant of forty years, Liza Redheart, of Naples, Florida, who has been invaluable to me as a friend and an associate.

As a deadline with the publisher loomed, I was diagnosed with an aggressive form of melanoma, followed by a successful operation. The side effects of toxic medication caused a malaise that seriously threatened my ability to complete the project. Nancy Rosenfield came to the rescue and urged me to engage David Tabatsky, an accomplished writer and editor, as a co-author to complete the book. I cannot say enough about David, as I may have been forced to default on my publishing contract without him.

With reinvigorated energy and insight, David vastly improved the content. He also initiated Katie Meehan's critical participation as a twenty-eight-year-old millennial (and my granddaughter), who has had a very successful career. Her keen perspective on the millennial generation, along with contributing her observations in each chapter through Katie's Korner, have added a great deal to the book.

Thanks, too, to Meghan McEnery and Max Lemper-Tabatsky for their contributions.

I am indebted to many others, including my eldest son, Scott Robb, business development director for CBIZ Company, with 100 offices, and assistant professor at Dudley College, who introduced Emily Sprague, his former student, as a case study on how to find a postgraduate career/job, and my second son, Eric Robb, a partner in an investment firm and father of Katie, for describing his mentorship with David Wendall.

Again, my thanks to Fred Lovejoy, who wrote about his mentor, Dr. Charles Janeway, and Professor Tom Piper, a lifelong friend and advisor, Tom Tremblay, whose case study on finding a business to buy is certainly unique, especially regarding his entrepreneurial approach and willingness to "stay with it" once there is a chance to succeed, and Alan Lightman, a close friend and author of more than a dozen books, including *Einstein's Dreams*, which sold over a million copies, who advised me on my writing endeavors.

Finally, and most important, my partner and wife of more than fifty years, Leslee Robb, who has been an inspiration for me—always—thanks for her unbelievable love and support during my medical problems. She has been a saint and encouraged me to continue this journey.

INTRODUCTION

Millennials have come of age in a complicated world. This generation, also referred to as Generation Y, or Gen Y, includes those born between 1982 and 2000.[1] They face obstacles like no other generation before them as they try to build careers, start families, and plan for the future. Even with an unprecedented amount of information available online, it's up to older generations to help these young people navigate this tricky climate so that they can get ahead.

This is what *Your Money Mentors* strives to accomplish.

This generational group accounts for 72 million folks out of America's 330 million people, which equates to approximately 25 percent of the total population and roughly one-third of the workforce. They are considered the high-tech generation, one which is employed more than any other so far in history.[2]

Millennials have now eclipsed the baby boomers (52 to 70 years old) as the nation's largest living generation, and they now make up 50 percent of the workforce. According to the Bureau of Labor Statistics, that number will climb to 75 percent by 2030.[3]

Millennials are better educated than previous generations and are highly computer literate. However, members of Gen Y need seasoned advice when it comes to facing life's challenges. They need to know what different jobs entail and how to go about selecting the best ones for themselves at various stages of their development. In todays' hyper-competitive world, millennials need a blend of old (networking) and new (internet) job-hunting skills.

This book is targeted to those of you who need and want advice during a difficult and challenging time. Then, again, you may be a parent or grandparent of a millennial, seeking to help a younger family member or friend while gaining a better understanding of their lives.

Many millennials are transitioning from college to the workforce and/or seeking careers and are seeking advice and direction. This book provides what parents might have overlooked or failed to take the time to advise their children on as they were growing up. There is no perfect pathway in raising children, but this book supplements the learning process.

According to Neil Howe, in a January 16, 2017, article in *Forbes* magazine, "Millennials lead other generations in reading, and they read more than older generations."[4]

This observation is confirmed by Amy Rea in *Library Journal*, who said in a January 6, 2020, article that, compared to other generations, "Millennials lead the way in both buying (31 percent) and borrowing books from the library (34 percent)."[5]

"Millennials are also helping to keep bookstores alive, thanks to their preference for traditional print books over digital ones" and because a lot of information they favor in a book is not available on the internet.[6]

Surprise! Surprise! Some things (i.e., life necessities) are not available online!

That was news to me, encouraging I might add, as the elder member of the team, with four children, seven grandchildren, and my first great-grandchild. I must admit I enjoyed pointing this out to my offspring and theirs. I have navigated more than six decades of economic environments, which provided me with a vast understanding of financial matters pertinent to every stage of life. I have been fortunate to work in a wealth of areas, particularly mergers and acquisitions, while holding top positions at highly prestigious firms, including Tully & Holland, Inc. (managing director), Atlantic Management Company,

Inc. (managing director), O'Conor, Wright Wyman Inc. (vice president), and Benchmark Consulting Group (principal).

For the past several decades, beginning with my own children and young professionals coming up in the financial world, I have been mentoring young millennials through their various financial woes. My motivation for becoming a mentor was simple: I was tired of watching my grandchildren struggle aimlessly in the dark, missing good job opportunities, flailing financially, and growing increasingly unhappy.

I began researching the millennial problem extensively. Not only did I rigorously study the rises and falls of our economy; I also interviewed hundreds of millennials to get their perspectives, to ensure their voices, fears, and desires were being heard. I must admit that my favorite subject was my own granddaughter, whom you will meet shortly.

One thing that was echoed in nearly every survey I conducted was that millennials felt that the decks were stacked against them. They couldn't see a way to survive in the current economy, let alone get ahead. Every one of them needed a mentor. And now, with this book, I can help them and extend my mentoring skills to an even broader audience.

As millennials, one of the major and most important considerations concerning future success is anticipating possible vocations. After you read through the first section of the book, which explores personality factors, relationships, and educational options, the second section will help you explore options and weigh the pros and cons of your possible choices. To add to the analysis, we cite a successful entrepreneur who selected numerous vocations, and we explain his rationale for doing so.

Aside from possible vocations, we elaborate further on the types of jobs available after college, using metrics, such as stress factors, average salary, and projected job growth.

Compared to years past, securing meaningful jobs after college is much more challenging now. In fact, some surveys show that only 41 percent of college students earn a degree in four years, while 55 percent accomplish this over a period of six years.[7] Stated differently, only 50 percent of college seniors (1.7 million) land jobs within six months of graduation, and initially these jobs are unrelated to their college major. An important ingredient to their success in this regard depends on their internships during their college years.

Millennials face serious challenges, such as overcoming adversity and handling stress. The book addresses these issues with potential solutions, such as the value of a mentor, the meaning of friendships, how we make decisions, and the process of letting go.

Most important, we explore budget techniques, those that ought to be at our fingertips for use on a daily basis, because most millennials, in spite of whatever business school or program they have studied in, have not properly addressed these fundamental issues of money, which affect nearly every facet of our lives.

Let's look at some hard facts, which reveal much about today's millennials.

On the plus side, according to the Pew Research Center, "Among Millennials, around four-in-ten (39%) of those ages 25 to 37 have a bachelor's degree or higher, compared with just 15% of the Silent Generation, roughly a quarter of Baby Boomers and about three-in-ten Gen Xers (29%) when they were the same age."[8]

On the downside, millennials also carry enormous student loan debt, an astounding $1 trillion. At least two-thirds of millennials owe $10,000 in student loans, while more than a third owe more than $30,000. Approximately 48 percent of millennials cannot afford to accept the lower-paying entry-level jobs in the professions they studied for because of this debt.[9]

Let that sink in for a minute. Instead, they seek out jobs that don't require college degrees—ones that are high paying at the outset but don't have the same promise for growth.

Sound familiar? I wish the system were different, but even if the current administration in Washington manages to provide student debt relief, it will more than likely not be nearly enough to ensure adequate relief. And one more thing: while the new administration favors eliminating tuition costs for community college and even state universities, this well-placed generosity will not cover private institutions, and those tuition costs remain steadily on the rise.

These money worries are current but also future based. Many in this generation currently need to move back home after college because they literally cannot afford to live on their own. At that point, their future seems bleak. They get married and have kids later as they struggle to support themselves. This brings great stress as they begin to think about being able to adequately provide for a family. Planning for retirement is not even on their radar, as they don't believe they ever will be able to retire and they worry that Social Security will be exhausted by that time.

Despite these obstacles, or maybe because of them, millennials want a strong work–life balance. More than others before them, this generation craves a separation between professional and personal pursuits. They work to live; they don't live to work. They want to be able to make a living and maintain a positive quality of life. They do have a strong work ethic, and professional success is important to them. But it's equally important for them to develop and nurture satisfaction outside of their work. When their workday ends, the job is over for them. In fact, while they are considered the most tech-savvy generation, they are also the ones most likely to unplug when on vacation.

In addition, millennials are also strongly socially conscious. Approximately 61 percent of millennials feel personally responsible to at least try to make a difference in the world. Being involved and being able to give something back to the world is a big deal for this group. They want to be able to contribute money and time to causes that are important to them.

For so many reasons, millennials need sound money strategies to help them not only build a firm financial foundation but also flourish so they are able to give something back, whether it's time or money or both. They need help navigating the course of their financial lives, and who better to help them than a seasoned financial professional who has advised four generations in money management—a money mentor—and his well-educated offspring.

I never had the benefit of what we can also call a personal financial advisor. My father died when I was twenty, and neither one of my grandfathers were alive during my upbringing. I feel that the advice in *Your Money Mentors*, both the financial guidance and the personal skills we share, would have benefited me enormously if I could go back in time. That is why I wrote this book. This is the guide I wish I had when I was younger and starting to build my financial future.

Your Money Mentors shares what I have learned over sixty years of being immersed in finance and more than eighty years of being alive. It provides sage advice that extends well beyond the balance sheet. But as I mentioned earlier, it's not just me preaching here; I think you'll thoroughly enjoy and learn from the second voice to come.

The first part of the book, "Foundations for Success," teaches soft skills, those that are not necessarily taught in a classroom. Here, you will receive advice about making the right relationships and understanding how to communicate with others for maximum impact, among other important interpersonal tips. You will be shown why mentors are important and how to filter advice. This is especially important with the abundance of information available online, as too much of it is misguided, inaccurate, and downright ridiculous.

The second part of the book, "Careers," gets right into best practices for finding the right job and negotiating a strong employment deal, navigating the world of the gig economy, and what to look for if you're looking to become an entrepreneur.

The third part of the book, "Making Your Money Work," explores the nuts and bolts of personal and professional finance, covering topics that include budgeting and planning; the ins and outs of banking; assessing and making a plan to get out of debt; when it makes sense to buy or rent/lease a home or car and the various types of loans available; planning for having a family and all the expenses involved; having a plan for emergencies; and valuable information about planning for the distant future, from investing in 529s for kids' college educations and 401Ks for retirement, to setting up financial contingencies in the case of illness or death.

As a trusted parent and grandparent, someone who's been around the financial block more than a few times, and a person who's been able to thrive in periods of economic upturns and downturns, *Your Money Mentors* will equip those of you who are millennials (and others, too) with the information and skills you need to thrive.

Speaking of millennials, rarely has an individual of this generation impressed me so much as Katie Meehan. Of course, I am biased because she is my eldest granddaughter, who was born in 1992 when I was on a bike tour in Germany with my son. We anxiously received a message at a local restaurant in the countryside.

"It's a girl."

Those three beautiful words still ring in my ears. I proceeded to buy a round of drinks plus cigars for all the patrons of the restaurant. Over the succeeding years, as a model millennial, Katie has made me and our entire family proud of her accomplishments, both in her career and within her personal life.

Now, as a twenty-nine-year-old, she has progressed and matured rapidly from her internships during her college years. The experience gained from working for a statewide land conservation organization in Massachusetts and then an international conservation nonprofit allowed her to grow her skillset, credibility, and professional network.

The network she built from her internship experiences led to her first postgraduate job in 2015, working for the Massachusetts state government in the field of conservation and agriculture. She started as a junior program coordinator and then quickly rose to senior program coordinator, managing a statewide program that promoted local companies on a regional platform.

In the fall of 2018, Katie changed jobs and began working as an events coordinator for the Kripalu Center for Yoga & Health, the largest wellness retreat center in the United States, which has received international acclaim and recognition while welcoming more than 40,000 guests annually and employing close to 500 staff.

After making inroads as an events coordinator, she was quickly promoted to executive assistant, serving as the CEO's strategic thought partner, managing the executive office, coordinating organization-wide projects, drafting speeches and communications, supporting the board of trustees, and more.

As a millennial facing numerous challenges not only in the job market but coordinating with her recently married husband, who lived hundreds of miles away in the western part of the state, Katie has shown her attributes as a leader, organizer, and problem solver.

While most millennials cannot expect to be as successful as my granddaughter, or at least as quickly, she certainly can be a model example. In fact, I've invited her (and other members of my family) to participate in this book and feel fortunate that she took the time to jump in and offer her opinions, insights, and suggestions. Truth be told, she did this while nine months pregnant, so by the time you are reading this, she has become the happy mother of her first child, and I have been blessed with my first great-grandchild. Yes, I know I mentioned this before, but it merits repeating.

Let me introduce her to you now, in her own words, as you will be hearing from her throughout the book, in what we call Katie's Korner, where she offers her firsthand experience and perspective as a productive and valuable member of the millennial community.

KATIE'S KORNER

When my grandfather told me he was writing a book about financial guidance for the millennial generation, it came as no surprise. In my memories from early childhood, Russ was not the picture of a warm and fuzzy grandfather; there was no playing on the floor with toys or taking us out for ice cream or weekends at grandma and grandpa's house. Rather, I remember my grandfather at holidays, always gifting us books, asking us about our schoolwork and later our summer jobs. I had six grandparents (as a result of divorce and remarriage), and he was the intimidating one.

"Why does he always interrogate me about my classes and my grades?"

"Why is he asking me if I have a mentor?"

"Doesn't he know I'm only a sophomore in high school? Mentors are for adults!"

As I neared the end of my college years and then transitioned into my early career, I began to realize that the questions he had been asking all along were not meant to interrogate but to challenge me with the really important questions that would help me to think about my career path and my financial health in a way that was strategic and set me up for success.

Every grandparent has *something* that they can authentically offer their grandchildren. For Russ, it was his insight and expertise in this area. So, instead of feeling intimidated by this person, I began to feel lucky to have him in my life.

A few years out of college, I was working in Boston while still formally living on the other side of the state in the bucolic Berkshires of

Western Massachusetts. I would spend a night or two a week staying at my grandfather's house while I was in the city. During this formative time, I had the pleasure of lively and engaging discussions with Russ on everything from whether or not it was a good idea to go back to school for a master's degree and how much should I be investing into my retirement plan to what would be the best approach for negotiating salary when offered a new position, what is the value of a mentor, and so much more.

These were not lectures. They were two-way conversations. My ultra-experienced grandfather imparted traditional wisdom, and I pushed back where it felt like the truths of his generation no longer held up for mine. The give-and-take was terrific, hopefully for both of us.

One conversation I recall vividly occurred when I left my job in Boston for a new line of work back in the Berkshires. This would be the fourth job in five years since I graduated college. My grandfather questioned why I, and the millennial generation in general, were so quick to move from one employer to the next. In his generation, it wouldn't be uncommon to work for the same company for ten years, twenty years, or even your entire career.

"Why should I stay? After two years, I can clearly see that there's no care for the staff, a lack of active career pathing, a poor benefits package, and no contribution to retirement funds, to name a few reasons. If they're not invested in me, why should I be invested in the company?" Employers of the past, who offered employee training, clear upward mobility for motivated individuals, and pensions are few and far between. It behooves millennials to know their worth and be savvy about navigating the job market as it exists today.

That said, our exchange was not a debate between two generations separated by five decades; it was an exchange of two real, lived experiences and how even in those differences there was incredible insight and lessons to be learned.

These discussions became the highlight of my time traveling between Boston and the Berkshires. At an especially formative period in my career, I had the fortune of a grandfather who pushed and prodded and asked the hard questions that shaped how I navigated career and financial decisions, both strategically and intentionally.

I came to realize that not everybody has a grandfather (or grand-mother, parent, sibling, friend, etc.) in their lives who can play this role. Sometimes, I found myself in conversations with colleagues and friends where I was sitting on the other side of the table, playing the role of my grandfather, asking the questions or coaching them through decision-making.

In that respect, I hope this book serves to share that knowledge and insight with anyone who is seeking help. Russ has deep wisdom to offer in this area, and I'm grateful to have had his presence in my life. I know he can help you, and I will do my best to add my two cents.

Part I

FOUNDATIONS FOR SUCCESS

The major aim of this book is to address the challenges millennials face learning to manage their money during and after their years of education and to organize their finances accordingly. This undertaking can be enormous and challenging. Without cultivating helpful relationships and exploiting the advice of mentors during this critical period of maturity (twenty to thirty-eight years old, depending on your source), the probability of managing one's money wisely is less assured.

Our intention is help you achieve success. I wish I had enjoyed access to a book like this when I was that age, as it would have provided me with the support I needed.

With the loss of my father at age twenty, no living grandfather, and two years in hiatus due to military training in the Mediterranean, I could have clearly benefited from the advice you will find here. There were numerous situations during the early stage of my adult life when my parents, God bless them, did not advise me on everything that I have endeavored to cover here in this book. My message throughout (augmented by Katie) is that the advice offered for millennials will be helpful for most aspects of their life, including personal, academic, and vocational issues.

The genesis of this book reflects the void in my earlier life when I was working my way through life at a similar age to today's millennials. Now, as the father and grandfather of those eleven offspring I previously mentioned (including Katie), I have had a chance to review fundamental life skills for financial success and to observe how they have played out and continue to manifest themselves in the lives of my family—past, present, and future.

The challenges speak for themselves, as millennials face uncertain times.

For example, three quarters of all college graduates do not end up working in careers related to their college majors. According to a survey of 817 American adults who have actually earned a bachelor's degree, which was conducted by college planning website Best Colleges, 82 percent of the participants reported that their degree was a "good financial investment."[1] That said, 61 percent of those surveyed said they would change their major.

Millennials look around at their brethren and/or their elders, and, as research from Stanford College shows, they realize that two-thirds of all workers are unhappy with their jobs, and 15 percent of them actually hate their work.

Stanford's research also showed that younger millennials by and large do not have a clear vision of where they want to go, what they want to accomplish in life, and what they are passionate about. Despite these challenges, millennials seek a meaningful life, whether that might come through changing careers and/or changing spouses.[2]

Like the best-selling book and most popular course at Stanford University, *Design Your Life*, by Bill Burnett and Dave Evans,[3] this book offers advice for the millennial generation, primarily from me, as your coach, so to speak, and from Katie, my millennial granddaughter.

Let's begin with the basics, what this section explores as your foundations for success. As millennials, you may like to think you are charming, responsive, engaging, intellectual, humorous, and inquisitive—all positive personality traits, without a doubt. Who wouldn't aspire to exhibit these characteristics?

The truth of the matter for you and other millennials is that when you "improve" your personality (i.e., expand it beyond its natural capacity), you will improve your interaction with people, both socially and business-wise.

For example, while I do not mean to be preachy, I would advise anyone in this age group to pay close attention to their own personal characteristics and to assess them as honestly as possible. Right now, answer the following questions candidly because fooling yourself on the basics will only result in your becoming a fool.

1. Do you listen way more than you speak?
2. Do you ever put down other people?
3. Do you own your mistakes?

Your answers to these fundamental questions will go a long way toward determining how you will focus on your future. They inevitably lead to a central pivot point that each of us reaches in our life, and the direction we take, whether it comes naturally or through great debate, will determine our success in our personal and professional life.

It comes down to this: Are you a "visionary" or an "implementer?"

You may not have a definitive answer right now, but it's surely a question you must consider, and as you do the work to figure it out you will probably reveal quite a bit about yourself that you didn't previously know.

While this book is a financial guide for millennials, covering subjects including budgeting, debt reduction, and investing, a large part of one's financial success depends on one's personal and business relationships. The value of their relationships is dependent on the quality and practicality of the advice given and the millennials' willingness to accept and respond to such communication.

It all begins with personalities!

❶

THE PERSONALITY FACTOR

Success or failure in one's endeavors, such as personal relationships, business, or politics, can hinge on striking a balance between talking and listening. During the early years of life, we are taught how to speak. Experts agree that this is a crucial developmental milestone and a fundamental indicator that a child is developing normally. However, the importance of developing the *skill* of listening is often overlooked by parents, educators, and bosses.[1]

In his book, *The Lost Art of Listening*, renowned therapist Michael P. Nichols, states that "Listening is a skill and like any skill it must be developed. Listening is a natural outgrowth of caring and concern for people."[2]

A couple of years ago, my wife and I got together with a longtime schoolmate whom we had not seen for quite some time. We enjoyed our reunion—at least I did—until he abruptly uttered something alarming to me as we said our goodbyes.

"You really need a hearing aid."

I was stunned. After he left, I confided with my wife on this matter.

"The real problem is that you interrupt people when they talk to you," she said, "and you change subjects without transitioning in a timely fashion."

Just when I thought she was done, she proved me wrong.

"And you talk *at* them, not with them."

Ouch! That criticism was an eye-opener, and fortunately I was advised not to get defensive but to accept the observation, learn from it, and move on. Sound advice, especially for someone who makes a habit of dispensing it.

I was later reminded that I have a tendency to state my definitive position on a matter without first exploring the other person's position or by suggesting that they expand on what they are saying *before* I expound on my thoughts.

As Michael Nichols writes: "To listen well, you have to restrain yourself from disagreeing or giving or sharing your own experience. To listen well, you must hold back what you have to say and control the urge to interrupt or argue. Most people aren't really interested in your point of view until they become convinced that you've heard and appreciated theirs."[3]

COMMUNICATION TECHNIQUES

The most effective communicators are usually those people who are the best listeners. A good listener is someone you look forward to being around. They pay attention to the speaker and encourage that person to expand on their ideas and feelings.

One key to effective listening is to pause slightly before responding to someone in order to really understand what the other person is saying while also paying attention to their nonverbal cues. This subtle pause also signals that you are listening carefully.

Success in personal and professional relationships often relies on your ability to communicate well, but it's not always the words that come out of your mouth that determine the effectiveness of your communication. Your nonverbal cues, typically referred to as your "body language," are the ones that speak louder. Body language is all about your physical behavior, including your expressions and mannerisms, which you use to communicate nonverbally. These often manifest themselves instinctively as opposed to consciously.[4]

In many cases, the listener may ask a question or two before giving his opinion or may ask the speaker to repeat his statement to draw out his thoughts. Of course, the context of where a discussion takes place and with whom you are having it is important and will determine how you approach it and what particular listening skills you might employ.

For example, the speaker says, "I am depressed." The listener could pause and then say, "Oh, you're feeling depressed?" Without being intruded upon, the speaker will voluntarily commiserate with the listener.

There are several techniques for responding when a talkative person gets bogged down on a particular topic, which is of little interest to the listener. The latter may jump in and say something like, "I have a question for you, and then we can return to the topic. I need your advice (people love to be flattered) on another subject before we get completely sidetracked." This is often a highly effective way to steer a conversation to a more useful outcome.

Timing is clearly a communication issue as to when and how a particular subject is introduced into a conversation. From my experience, women tend to do better when it comes to knowing when it is best to do this, while men seem more inclined to ramrod a subject into the mix without taking the temperature of the room. This is only my personal observation; I wish it weren't the case, but we can all do better trying to change this too.

Some believe that women make more productive CEOs than men because they are considered to be better listeners. Men are known to seek power as CEOs, while women seek consensus through relationships.

Corine Jansen, director and chair of Global Listening Board, states the following:

> According to Larry Barker and Kittie Watson, authors of the book "Listen Up," men and women usually employ different listening styles. Men are more likely to be action-oriented listeners, which means they focus on listening to information pertinent to the task at hand. Action-oriented listeners have little patience for speakers who ramble off topic or include unnecessary details. Women are more likely to be people-oriented listeners. They connect with the emotional message and undertones of a conversation and are more concerned with the

occurrence of the conversation than with the pertinent information discussed.[5]

A team from Cambridge University found key differences between the brains of men and women. In women, the parts of the brain that are linked to emotions, calculating risks, and the ability to listen were more prominent. In men, the areas of the brain tied to motor skills and coordination were denser and larger.[6]

While there is no doubt that legendary figures such as Albert Einstein or Thomas Edison would have little trouble being hired by a relevant company, a recent *Bloomberg Businessweek* survey of 1,320 MBA recruiters concluded that 68 percent of employment recruiters value communication skills above all else, followed by analytical thinking (60 percent) and the ability to work collaboratively (55 percent).[7]

Another survey, conducted by the World Economic Forum, disclosed a number of reasons some employees are successful, including personality (78 percent) and cultural fit (53 percent), while employees' skills (39 percent) were found to be considerably lower.[8]

These characteristics regarding personality factors and why soft skills matter are just as relevant for millennials as other folks. For those millennials seeking jobs after college graduation, it is estimated that only 50 percent of the 1.7 million seniors land jobs within six months of receiving their degrees. A 2019 Gallup report on the millennial generation revealed that 21 percent of millennials report that they have changed jobs within the past year, which is more than three times the number of nonmillennials who have done something similar.[9] The key ingredient we have seen to obtaining a job relevant to one's level of education is often through friends, mentors, and relatives.

That was true in my case when I was in my twenties, then working for the American Express Credit Card Division and the Colonial Management Mutual Funds. I had an older mentor in college who helped me gain my acceptance to the University of Pennsylvania, and it was a great loss for me when he passed away a few years later. Two of my sons had influential mentors, which will be discussed later in the book.

According to Anjuli Sastry, the cofounder of NPR's *Women of Color* mentorship program, which has paired up more than 100 NPR employees for mentoring, "The right mentoring relationship can be a powerful tool for professional growth—it can lead to a new job, a promotion or even a better work-life balance."[10]

For millennials seeking improvements in their personal and business relationships, the following qualities define a good mentor:

1. Relevant expertise or knowledge
2. Enthusiasm for advising the mentee
3. The ability to give direct feedback
4. Empathy
5. A willingness to be a sponsor

Considering all these qualities, the mentor should be in a position to support the mentee with their professional development and career growth.

Sastry suggests that, if you are looking for a good mentor, you will improve your chances of finding the right person by following these five suggestions.

1. Know your short-term and long-term goals.
2. Whom do you look up to?
3. Do the research.
4. Be cognizant of your existing network.
5. Recognize the difference between a mentor and a sponsor.[11]

THE IMPORTANCE OF SOFT SKILLS

You may be wondering what soft skills can do to improve your financial acumen. Simply stated, you need both soft *and* hard skills to advance financially in life. Some pundits say that soft skills are more important in a job than hard skills, so let's define soft skills and then examine their attributes, such as leadership, teamwork, and adaptability.

Soft skills we see most in demand in today's business world include the following:

Integrity
Dependability
Effective communication
Open-mindedness
Teamwork
Creativity
Problem solving
Critical thinking
Adaptability
Organization
Willingness to learn
Empathy[12]

As you can see, these soft skills define character traits, such as developing positive relationships with others. They are known too as emotional intelligence, which complements hard skills of knowledge and occupational know-how. If you are resilient and have a willingness to learn yet can work under pressure while exhibiting self-management, then you probably have superior soft skills.

Let's not overlook the importance of hard skills, though, whether they exist in the field of engineering, medical education, or computer literacy. Of course, they are important skills to have in your toolkit, but, while hard skills frequently get you an interview, soft skills get you the job. So there you go, as far as how soft skills have a direct impact on your finances. Hard skills open the door, while soft skills enable you to open a bank account.

That's because technical skills are basically taught, while soft skills are learned. Recruiters seek those who demonstrate teamwork, a strong work ethic, a positive attitude, and the ability to problem solve to communicate clearly.

When it comes to representing yourself through a résumé and job interviews, you will be showcasing your hard and soft skills. You will share specific stories from your past experience that relate directly to the requirements of the job you are seeking. We will delve into this more in chapter 4, "Making the Most of Starter Jobs and Internships."

While it may be somewhat surprising for some of you, nearly three-quarters of job recruiters value communication skills above all else.[13]

Millennials should be aware that, in a study conducted over the course of a dozen years, of the CEOs who were fired, one-third were let go for bad decisions, while two-thirds were let go for poor communication and being indecisive.

Although nearly all CEOs make mistakes at one time or another, they are often specific and a one-time incident. Indecision, on the other hand, is a trait and a characteristic, which can be repeated over and over. It's not knowledge based. It's a personality flaw, but it's certainly not the only one. We can see plenty of other examples of these shortcomings among those in leadership roles, including failing to delegate responsibility, an inability to say no, a lack of curiosity to explore different opportunities, and an unwillingness to face conflict and pressure by staying calm and resolute.[14]

In this day and age, some pundits believe that the internet has changed everything. With the advent of the ubiquitous use of computers, such as millennials texting a hundred times a day for connectivity and emailing to sustain relationships and conduct business, one can easily reinforce this argument.

In fact, this relatively recent world of multitasking redefines what that word even means. On top of the device explosion, the internet has changed the way business is conducted, from Uber, the largest taxi company, which owns no vehicles, to Facebook, the largest media company, which creates no content, to Airbnb, the largest real estate company, which owns no buildings, to Alibaba, one of the largest retailers, which owns no inventory. For a quick moment, we might equate these enormous companies to an empty house sitting on a plot of land, up for sale, a shell of a residence with no one living inside it, waiting to be bought and occupied by living, breathing human beings. However, that would be a fundamental misunderstanding of these companies, which, while skeletal in nature, possess an enormous amount of substance, at least for those who subscribe to their mission and feel comfortable with their practices.

Based on the above analogy, one might conclude that a person's soft skills are of less importance than previously described. On the contrary, developing life skills, which is the ability to relate well to people, is more important now than ever.

In a 2016 report released by the Harvard Graduate School of Education, called "Turning the Tide," the authors suggest that the college admission process is becoming less about the numbers and more about the whole student. They say that "Many parents fail to focus on what really matters in the college admissions process. In an effort to give their kids everything, these parents often end up robbing them of what really counts."[15]

It's important to note here that what "really matters" is a fluid thing and may be interpreted differently by each set of parents.

In a *New York Times* interview on October 3, 2015, Gary B. Smith, CEO of Ciena, the broadband and telecommunications company, said that "Early on in my career, I was told, 'It's all about people.' I got it intellectually, but it took me quite a while to really get it. It really is all about people, and if you get that right, the other stuff will get addressed. But you have to work at it all the time."[16]

The Harvard study goes on to say that "Much of today's life, both politically and businesswise, is full of ambiguity, which explains why many millennials are unemployed or underemployed, and this situation places a premium on exploiting business relationships and networking."[17]

CEO Smith had some great advice for new college grads:

I tell them about the most important lesson I learned: It's all about the people you work with. Relationships really matter, and you need to get that right, both for your career as an individual and as a future leader. I think a lot of people pay attention to the technical stuff and the hard stuff about whatever discipline they're in. But it's the softer side that will get you every time if you're not paying attention to it. It's probably the biggest determinant of whether you're going to be successful.[18]

FIRST IMPRESSIONS

Is what you see what you get? Perhaps. First impressions are very important. In fact, some people will draw an opinion of another person within minutes of an introduction. Several key ingredients play a part in how this initial meeting goes: how one dresses for the occasion, how one acknowledges the other party, and whether there are any feelings of enthusiasm and the expression of sincerity.

If you come upon a situation where you appear bored with the other person and fail to engage in a relevant, if not compelling remark, chances are, as trivial as it may seem, the interviewer will consciously or unconsciously form an immediate negative opinion. And, if that person does not feel overtly negative, they may simply become uninterested quite quickly, which is just as damaging.

In an article, titled "The Weird Science Behind First Impressions," Jory MacKay writes that "Not all choices can be made rationally, whether we find someone attractive or trustworthy, because it happens in a matter of seconds. Studies have shown that people who communicate in an expressive, animated fashion tend to be better liked than difficult-to-read people. We are also more inclined to like people with whom we have something in common. Additionally, being a good listener can also help put you into someone's good graces when you first meet them."[19]

When meeting someone for the first time, nonverbal language, which we identified earlier as body language, is important and influential. Many body language experts seem to agree that more than 50 percent of all human communications are nonverbal.

In an article by Michelle Trudeau, Phil McAleer, a psychologist at the University of Glasgow, Scotland, who led a study there on the science of first impressions, is quoted as saying, "From the first word you hear a person speak, you start to form this impression of the person's personality."[20]

Also in the same article, Jody Kreiman, a UCLA researcher who studies how we perceive voices, is quoted as saying, "In less than a second, the time it takes to say 'hello,' we make a snap judgment about someone's personality. On hearing just a brief utterance, we decide whether to approach the person or to avoid them. Such rapid appraisals have a long evolutionary history. It's a brain process found in all mammals. Things that are important for behavior and for survival tend to happen pretty fast. You don't have a huge amount of time. It has to be a simple system of communication."[21]

The study of body language has produced dozens of books and articles, along with clinical research and academic assessments. I was surprised to learn how one expert analyzed that a tightlipped smile stretched across the face in a straight line, with teeth concealed, implies that the interviewee has a secret they are not going to share, possibly due to the dislike, distrust, or a rejection signal of the other person.[22]

Body language experts use all sorts of analysis, depending on whether the person's arms are crossed when sitting or whether someone is constantly shifting their weight or fiddling with their feet or hands.

We can find detailed analysis about the hidden meaning of how we interpret other people's facial expressions, handshakes, or the tone and pace of how we speak. To think that body language innuendos have become so meaningful is rather frightening; in essence, if body language is negative, the longer (if ever) it will take two people to mentally connect with each other, which can often result in creating a bigger gap of mutual respect.[23]

PERSONALITY TRAITS

People skills are the foundation for professional success, which in turn leads to financial benefits.

Much of this depends on an individual's personality. A number of traits are worth noting, such as modesty, flattery, appreciation, and one's ability to encourage another person to talk about themselves. One of the unsung skills in the conversational arena is the ability to ask revealing questions to accurately understand the situation at hand and/or the other person's interests, motivations, and frustrations. How this is carried out can be crucial in developing meaningful relationships, both in the personal and professional realm.

It's even better if one can find something in common with the other person. Outwardly, valuing the other person's ideas is a high compliment, and restraining oneself from vocally disagreeing with the other person, at least initially, is a positive step to take in that direction. Perhaps one of the most difficult actions a person can endure is to admit that they have made a mistake because it is a humbling experience. Ironically, when President Kennedy went before national television and took full personal blame for the failed Bay of Pigs invasion in Cuba, his popularity rating went up, not down. How useful and inspiring it would be today if our leaders exhibited the same honesty, humility, and sense of purpose.

Perhaps my favorite example of tactful communication is a creation straight out of Hollywood, in the form of the great actor Peter Falk and his portrayal of Columbo, an urban police detective. He had a reputation for being "dumb as a fox," meaning he often pretended that he did not understand another person, and so he would ask them to repeat their last remark or to elaborate further on the meaning of what they had just said. His charming and often disarming style of questioning usually revealed critical information in his quest to solve difficult cases.

Managing disagreements and/or conflicts between people is yet another challenging communication skill. It requires patience, knowledge of the matter at hand, and confidence.

For example, let us assume that you want to rent an apartment for approximately $1,000 per month, but the landlord is asking for $2,000 per month. First, it is best if you become knowledgeable of the surrounding apartments in the area with facts regarding rentals per square foot; various amenities available, such as parking; and the terms of the lease, including deposits or surcharges. Then, with that information at hand, you ask the landlord to explain their rationale for setting the price at $2,000 when other apartments in the area are charging considerably less. Assuming the landlord is still willing to talk with you regarding your interest in renting the apartment, you should then launch into your sales pitch, pointing out your high credit rating, personal references, and the ability to rent immediately. If you and the landlord can split the difference for $1,500 per month, then you would save $6,000 per year.

This scenario, complete with a relatively successful outcome, may be easier said than done. But the basic premise and dialogue are based on real experience, and it demonstrates the usefulness of positive communication. It's easy to imagine that the renter could have read the body language and vocal tone of the landlord and adjusted their negotiating strategy accordingly. This type of behavioral observation can go a long way in any type of friendly negotiation.

Although for many millennials, renting a living space may be a sore subject, it is a reality of life today and should be accepted at face value. Of course, everyone may want to own their own home, at least at some point, but, for many millennials, especially those living in large urban areas, this is quite a difficult thing to take on in today's unsteady economy, which has only been exacerbated by the pandemic.

No matter what type of communication it is, your personality does make a difference. Even if you have an enormously high IQ and a brilliant mind, on average you still have to communicate effectively to persuade others to endorse your propositions. As a tip, there is a belief that one has to be a good listener, in fact an earnest listener, such that, if you talk more than half the time, for example, you will be less likely to achieve your objective. Additionally, if one perpetually interrupts in their discussions with others, as I apparently have a tendency to do, it is considered not only rude but gives off the appearance of being disinterested in the other party. Take my word for it: this is not something you want to hear about yourself, not from an old friend, not from your spouse, and certainly not from a boss as they are escorting you out of the building where you used to work.

Looking at how toxic politics have become in this day and age between the two major political parties, we should reflect on how successful presidents Eisenhower, Reagan, and George H. W. Bush were in bygone years because they were not only somewhat conciliatory; they were also willing to fraternize with their adversaries to achieve a semblance of compromise, adaptability, and teamwork.

For those millennials who have become so dependent on our world of email, Twitter, Instagram, Facebook, and LinkedIn, let's realize that these great intentions cannot replace the positive affect of face-to-face meetings, where your personality traits can really shine.

Hard skills, of course, are absolutely important in getting a solid job; no doubt about it! These skills include data analytics, programming, coding, digital literacy, search engine optimization, data visualization, and web development.

But, if you search for "why one does not get a job," many reasons pop up, including the following ones that seem most relevant to our discussion:

A lack of enthusiasm and passion
Not properly researching the company with whom you are
   interviewing
Being less than fully prepared
Not effectively stating why you should be hired
Conveying a sense of entitlement at the interview
Lacking a positive connection or desire to connect
Not exhibiting sufficient confidence or selling yourself in a good
   way
A lack of follow-up communication
Not being proactive and creating the right impression
Just being not that likable[24]

According to this collective analysis, all these reasons involve soft skills. Perhaps the reasons included here are not universal nor totally conclusive, as so much depends on each type of job you are seeking, but the point of the matter is clear: soft skills are critical.

SPECIFIC SOFT SKILLS

Throughout high school and college, most millennials were judged and assessed by the hard skills that influenced what they achieved, such as their grades, scholastic test scores, the degree of difficulty of their courses, their awards, outside activities, and their internships.

After academic school, one's soft skills, known as "people skills," become much more important in a person's vocation, their community life, and in the friendships they develop. Soft skills are personal attributes that enable someone to interact effectively and harmoniously with other people. They usually reveal basic emotional intelligence.

General Dwight D. Eisenhower, affectionately known as Ike, was outranked in the early period of World War II, but it was his superior ability to successfully deal with people that enabled him to ascend to the top of the military ranks and subsequently win election as president of the United States and commander in chief for the proceedings of D-Day. It was also Ike's charisma that led him to win reelection and become a two-term president.

If millennials want to acquire soft skills, not to mention becoming a two-term president, they should heed some or all of the following traits:

Communication Skills

These reflect an ability, willingness, and transparency to speak, present, and write clearly and effectively as a result of listening carefully and actively.

The advent of the internet has, of course, been one of the great inventions of our times, but it is not without its shortcomings, which have adversely affected our soft skills. Communicating one's bereavement, for example, should be done in person, face-to-face, or on the telephone or with a handwritten letter, but not with an email or text, no matter how much you think it might be acceptable.

I know of an office incident, when the owner of a small consulting firm had the corner office in a palatial business setting, while his "right-hand" managing director was situated in the adjoining office. Even though the two offices were separated only by an adjacent wall, the owner would send out demanding emails regarding business matters. Granted, the managing director reciprocated with a return email, although physically the two men were literary a few feet away, separated only by an office partition.

One day, the boss expressed an ultimatum, and the managing director snapped.

"I'm out of here!" he said.

In retrospect, the managing director should have risen from his desk and walked a few steps into the owner's office to address the matter face-to-face. As a result of the above incident and the miscommunication, the five-year relationship exploded, and the managing director resigned on the spot. Clearly, a lack of people skills ruptured the relationship permanently. As this demonstrates, communicating effectively is a critical soft skill.

Adaptability

This means being diplomatic and respectful even when in disagreement. Furthermore, to be able to adapt to change and handle multiple tasks is an important soft skill.

In an article, Warren Buffet is quoted as once saying, "Exercise humility and restraint. Learn to change your behavior as you mature by emulating those you admire and adopting those qualities they possess."[25]

Another quote attributed to the iconic scientist Charles Darwin is noteworthy: "It is not the smart nor the strong that survive, but those who have the ability to adapt."[26] While hard skills are apt to include technical abilities and knowledge, soft skills allow us the ability to adjust, and to do it quickly. Since these are infinite examples of adaptability, I'll select one example from my personal life in the hope that it will convey the message.

When I was in my mid thirties, I owned a manufacturing company that produced 3,000 canoes annually. The company still exists today, now located in Newburyport, Massachusetts. The company was marginally profitable at the time I ran it. Along came the oil embargo in 1973. As one of the original fiberglass canoes, the major ingredient was resin, an oil derivative. Paranoid about not being able to obtain the necessary resin, I sold the company to an outfit in Maine, which had numerous cost advantages to the Massachusetts corporation.

Fast-forward: I adapted quickly by becoming a distributor for six other canoe and kayak companies, thereby reducing my risks and investment. In this situation, my soft skill was recognizing a threatening situation and adapting accordingly. While it stung in the short term, in the long term, it proved to be the correct decision.

Teamwork

This is a key attribute, which employees seek when hiring millennials, often reflective in how well millennials collaborate with others in their critically important internships. Teamwork is a fundamental attribute in the armed services, in successful athletic teams, and in working with others in business. Even families refer to themselves as having good teamwork.

The ability to work well with others in a company, in education, in nonprofits, or in other institutions is paramount and a very important soft skill. It is believed that nearly half of the new hires fail in the first eighteen months and nearly 90 percent of millennials think of changing jobs in three years. Assessing one's teamwork capabilities can be critical. This is also true of group effort under the umbrella of entrepreneurship, which we will discuss in a subsequent chapter.

All in all, your personality has as much to do with your career success as the degrees you have earned and the résumé you have assembled. Treat it like a plant. It needs water and sunshine and a bit of TLC to grow and prosper.

KATIE'S KORNER

In my experience, both as an employee and a hiring manager, if you don't have a solid foundation of soft skills, it practically doesn't matter what kind of hard skills you bring to the job. These are the skills that help to first get you hired, and, later on, they can lead to promotional opportunities, especially to leadership positions.

For example, managers accept that new employees will have to be taught how to use the company software or file a quarterly report in accordance with the organization's format and expectations, but managers do not want to teach a new hire how to manage their time, communicate professionally, collaborate with teams, or act appropriately in a variety of work-related situations.

These soft skills are the ones that can set you apart in the interview process. At a time when a college degree is less of a distinguishing factor than it used to be, bringing a set of well-developed soft skills to any job is invaluable to the manager and ultimately the company.

In other words, you become an asset and not a liability.

Many of these soft skills have been detailed and discussed at length in this chapter. However, I would be remiss not to emphasize the two that have served me the most. The first being social–emotional intelligence skills, defined as the ability to be aware of our own and others' emotions, and the wherewithal to use that information to lead yourself and others.

So much is communicated outside of an exchange of words—body language, attitude, intonation, what's left unsaid, and many other examples, depending on your specific situation, the culture of the workplace, and the people you interact with on a daily basis.

These additional layers of information add richness and depth to an understanding of a situation, whether it's an interview, a team meeting, or a presentation to the board.

I am always analyzing what is being said, what is not being said, how it's being said, why it's being said like it is. . . . Sound familiar?

The additional context you gain from the full range of an interaction with an individual or group allows you to better navigate that interaction and make decisions. The best leaders I have worked with have honed their social–emotional skills and it shows—consistently. Not only are they more effective leaders; they are more respected. They have mastered four components of emotional intelligence, which can serve all of us well:

Self-awareness
Self-management
Social awareness
Relationship management

These are the tools necessary for anyone in management positions and will also go a long way toward helping those communicate with those managers.

The second soft skill I regard highly is communication.

I am referring here to writing, speaking, and listening. The power of good communication skills cannot be underestimated. Writing and speaking are fairly straightforward. Word choice and grammar matter. They are a reflection of you and how people perceive you, whether that's a hiring manager, a colleague, or a client.

Like an artist whose art is on display in a museum for critics and fans alike to interpret, once an email is sent or a statement is made verbally, your words are now up for interpretation by the other party. So be ever careful about the words you use, and try your best to construct a sentence in a way that has the highest chance of expressing what you intend it to.

The wisest people I've worked with, from entry level all the way up to CEO, believe in the value of asking for a second set of eyes to review any important communications. Find those people in your circle whom you can rely on to give you honest and helpful feedback before you hit send on an email or launch into a presentation. You might also try reading it aloud and making sure it sounds like you and how you want to come across.

Less obvious is the skill of being a good listener.

Listening is at the core of optimal communication. The thing about listening is, we tend to think we're listening when the other person is speaking while, during this entire time, our brain is working on preparing a response. To truly listen, we must give ourselves permission to listen by opening our ears and eyes (so as not to miss both the spoken and unspoken pieces of information) and to not feel pressure to respond instantaneously.

If you are someone who tends to speak up often, you might try sitting back and observing the flow of the conversation. Who is speaking? Who is not speaking? What is the tone of the conversation? Is it a productive conversation?

Breathing in slowly and quietly might help you do this.

Analyzing the room in a group meeting is a skill any successful leader must master. This goes hand in hand with the social–emotional intelligence skills discussed here. It also applies to observing and analyzing others, as well as yourself.

I'm sure you've heard the expression, "Read the room." It's a cliché for a reason!

The practice of self-observing from a place of inquiry will only improve your ability to understand how your emotions impact others, and as a result you can better manage your emotions in any given situation to serve your end goals.

To do this most effectively, I recommend that you be compassionate to yourself and not overly judgmental. This can go a long way to creating positive communication.

Armed with developed social–emotional intelligence and well-honed communication skills, you go from being an adequately skilled employee, based on the hard skills you possess, to being an exceptional team member, who not only can accomplish the finite tasks but can also navigate the ins and outs of the workplace to your advantage.

CHAPTER I REVIEW

Let's review our study of soft skills as they relate to personality factors. This will help you remember that these personality factors will enable millennials to better focus on what truly matters in gaining financial success.

1. Communication skills provide the ability to articulate clearly and concisely. One is able to exude integrity through body language, tone of voice, eye contact, head nodding, uninterrupted listening, and an attentive response.
2. Take verbal personal responsibility for your mistakes and move on. This will build trust with others, and they will gain confidence in you.
3. Be tactful and calm with others in a face-to-face private setting where one person is criticizing someone else.
4. Be curious, explore opportunities, obtain feedback, and compliment others.
5. Build strong relationships with your peers.
6. "What goes around, comes around."

2

FRIENDS AND MENTORS

If there is something more important than establishing *meaningful* relationships with family, friends, and business associates, then I am not aware of it. Throughout our life, from our first day in nursery school to the day we register for social security, we are constantly connecting with others, and these interactions often provide substance and purpose for our existence on this planet. The camaraderie we create with our teammates in Little League, recreational soccer, or variety basketball, along with the relationships we cultivate in after-school art programs, alumni associations, and parent groups, go a long way toward aiding our mental and physical health. For many of us, these connections remain a part of us as we age. Consider what happens to professional athletes when they retire and are frequently asked if they miss playing the game. Their answers are often the same and seem to be inevitable.

"Do I miss the game? No, not so much, but I miss being with my teammates."

Friendships do not happen all by themselves, even though the best ones can feel as if they do, as if they require no real care or work. However, when we look just a little closer, we can see that this is rarely the case. For example, family friendships are often built on trust. Business friendships are built on respect and for mutual benefit, such as quid pro quo and networking. The friendships we develop with local merchants and service providers are established on a basis of trust and only over many years.

This book is targeted for millennials who need and want advice during a difficult and challenging time in their life. Parents might have overlooked or failed to take the time to advise their children growing up. They may simply not know what to do or say. There is no perfect pathway to take while raising children, so that is where friends and mentors come into the picture and can often be most helpful.

Millennials are better educated than previous generations and highly computer literate, but they need mature advice in facing life's challenges. In the aggregate, millennials, those twenty-three to thirty-eight years old, number in the range of 72 million (and growing with immigration) and represent one-third of the total workforce.[1]

When it comes to job-hunting skills, millennials need a blend of old (person-to-person networking) and new (online) talents. They need to know what different jobs entail and how to go about selecting the best jobs for their personalities and skillsets. Most of the vital attributes of human capital are not taught in the classroom, but by friends and mentors, such as the best way to communicate, team building, conflict resolution, negotiating, and leadership.

Clark Crouch, a prize-winning American poet who was born in a rustic farmhouse in rural Nebraska, once said, "Leadership is getting the right people to do the right thing for the right reason in the right way at the right time with the right use of resources."[2]

I couldn't have said it any better myself!

Crouch wasn't spouting off with idle talk, however. He was left on his own at the age of twelve and worked his way through school as a cowboy during the summer and later as a telephone operator, messenger, store clerk, school janitor, printer's devil, and truck driver. He served in the US Army Air Corps during World War II and with the US Air Force during the Korean Conflict, and later became an administrator for the Atomic Energy Commission and an independent strategic planning consultant, assisting national and international organizations for twenty-five years, before retiring to become what he calls a poet lariat. So when Mr. Crouch opines about leadership, he is speaking from great experience.

As a group, a large part of millennials' success depends on their personal and business relationships, including their ability to seek out mentors. As your professional goals evolve, success is often contributed to constructive networking, which is the art of building relationships over time. I have often been told by Harvard Business School graduates that it is not so much the classroom or book knowledge they learned there that has the most influence on their future; it is the classmates they befriended and still enjoy.

I consider myself lucky that I have about fifteen close friends, maybe 100 personal and business acquaintances, and possibly 1,000 people I know from past interactions.

We all define friendship a bit differently, but I think we can agree on this: a friend is someone with whom you maintain some form of regular communication, while an acquaintance is someone you don't have much contact with but would be willing to do a favor, such as an introduction to a potential employer.

Let's not forget that, in solidifying strong relationships, the importance of one's spouse or partner can be paramount. In a *New York Times* article, "The Four Secrets of Success," Nicholas Kristof writes: "The most important decision you will make is not the university you attend, nor your major, not even your first job. It's who you marry or settle down with. The right partner provides crucial emotional support, is likely to parent your children, and comforts you when life inevitably goes wrong. A key to a successful career is a great partner. Learning to manage a relationship may take practice, so get started and cuddle!"[3]

While Kristof is right about the value of a great partner (legally married or not), it's not ideal for everyone, especially before they are ready, and, for some, it does not have to be the determining factor on your road to success in life.

In fact, for some people, millennials included, a genuine and meaningful partnership can be created well outside the realm of marriage. That said, I am eternally grateful for my marriage.

We should not underestimate the value of friendship.

According to data from YouGov, approximately 30 percent of millennials report that they are always or often feeling lonely, and 22 percent of them say that they have no friends.[4]

The study does not specify why, but it's not a big leap to surmise that social media use and wavering mental health play a role in these alarming numbers.

Millennial journalist Arwa Mahdawi writes in *The Guardian*, "Our culture is based around celebrating romantic and familial milestones: engagements, weddings, christenings. We are not taught to venerate or celebrate friendship in the same way we are romantic relationships. We are not taught that friendships can be just as complex, if not more so, than romantic couplings; that losing a friend can be as heartbreaking as losing a lover. So, when we get to a point in our lives when our friendships start to change, there is no wonder it can feel so lonely."[5]

I surely hope you are not one of the 22 or 30 percent, and, if you do consider yourself to be in one of those groups, I encourage you to reach out and make an effort to improve your situation.

THE YIN AND YANG OF MENTORING

Mentoring refers to a relationship between two people, the mentor and the mentee, sometimes called the protégé, a French word for a person being tutored. Since the word *protégé* is more apt to be used to describe someone being taken under the wing and mentored by a famous person, we will not use it here, as we are not terribly concerned with a mentee who may be destined to follow in the footsteps of greatness and even excel beyond the achievements of their mentor. While there is nothing wrong with that, I'd prefer to focus on the needs of millennials and not the mentoring history of France. Still, a mentor passes along valuable skills, knowledge, and insight to help a mentee develop their career, and that is a relationship I recommend.

In its purist sense, mentoring is about supporting and developing the all-around growth of the mentee, not just making them better at their job or famous.

A mentor is a person of experience, prominence, and influence who will provide you with something for which you do not have access, such as advice or personal connections. Mentors are people who possess wisdom, resources, or skills that can help you, but the most successful and meaningful mentor/mentee relationships are those that become mutually beneficial and are based on intergenerational connections.

This reminds me of an old saying, "You will receive only that which you are first willing to give," meaning there should be a yin and a yang in the relationship of giving and receiving.

Back in our school days, we read how Socrates mentored Plato and how Plato mentored Aristotle. While there was certainly a teacher/ student relationship in these two cases, we are led to believe that the mentees in these situations contributed by indulging in research and discovery and sometimes serving as the devil's advocate to provoke deeper dives into various subjects and to challenge the status quo of the day.

Socrates was one of the Greek's greatest philosophers, and Plato was deemed to be his greatest pupil. The quid pro quo in this relationship was Plato's eagerness to carry forth the philosophies of Socrates to subsequent generations, an achievement that was definitely realized.

When I think of the most valuable characteristics of a mentor, I picture a person who is older, admired, and respected, someone who engenders good chemistry, offers encouragement and career guidance, and fosters a simpatico relationship with the mentee.

Later in this chapter, you will read several examples of mentor/ mentee relationships. In my case, after my father died when I was twenty years old, my uncle became my mentor. I had recently been honorably discharged from the Marine Corps before going to college. My uncle was an attorney, so there was no obvious business connection he had for me. But I hugely admired his outstanding character and personal ethics. For him, I may have represented the son he never had. Unfortunately, he too died prematurely, so I lost the chance to continue this promising and supportive relationship. This was a severe loss at the time.

It seems most mentor/mentee relationships are business oriented. For example, former New York City Mayor Michael Bloomberg's mentor was William R. Solomon, an investment banker who led his mentees with a sterling example of hard work, intelligence, and empathy. One could argue that Benjamin Graham's philosophy of investing was more of a mentorship for Warren Buffett than that of his role as a professor in Columbia University's M&A program.

The list goes on and on of influential people we know and admire who often rose to their level of prominence with the cagey and pragmatic help of a mentor.

DIFFERENT TYPES OF MENTORING

According to David S. Rose, author of *The Start-Up Checklist*, "A true mentorship relationship takes years to develop, is between two people who have worked closely together for a long time and can last a lifetime."[6]

Let's examine two basic types of mentoring.

Sponsorship Mentoring

Usually, the mentor takes a personal interest in the mentee's career and hopes to guide the mentee in their career path and open doors to possible employers and/or customers.

For example, after Bill Hewitt and David Packard invented the audio oscillator, the first product made by what would become the iconic company, Hewlett-Packard (which by the way was made in David Packard's garage in Palo Alto, California[7]), their former Stanford professor, Fred Terman, introduced them to twenty-five potential customers. Obviously, that certainly helped!

It is possible to have several mentors in each segment of one's career to provide much-needed advice, such as during the following stages:

Assessment of the job market during your junior year of college
Once employed, getting advice on potential upward career movement
Oops, need help changing careers and/or companies?
Are you now "stuck" in your current job?
What now? Are you currently laid off?

While some of these situations are somewhat draconian, they demonstrate an obvious need for a mentor, which still applies for many millennials. A mentor can help assess your strengths and weaknesses, facilitate the decision-making process, and provide a resource for bouncing ideas around and determining a best course of action.

Development Mentoring

The mentor is apt to be someone within the same company, university, hospital, etc., with a formal relationship between the mentee, where the mentor helps the mentee achieve clearly defined goals, such as grooming the mentee to run divisions, departments, or companies. In the tech world, information technology departments of companies have frequently used formal mentoring programs to develop technical staff and bridge competency gaps.

If one thinks of a mentor as a "great" teacher, then one can resonate with the motivational speaker and author William Arthur Ward's quote: "The mediocre teacher tells. The good teacher explains. The superior teacher demonstrates. The great teacher inspires."[8]

Mentors are important in advancing one's careers.

In the book *Pivot*, Adam Markel states: "You will need and want the assistance of others. You're going to need other people."[9]

Even the iconic Steve Jobs's forceful personality was substantially influenced by his college mentor at Stanford University, Robert Friedland.

According to Walter Isaacson, in his authorized biography of Jobs, Friedland was a powerful influence on the young Steve Jobs. They met at Reed College in Portland, Oregon, where Friedland was student body president. A charismatic and forceful personality, Friedland persuaded Jobs to make a pilgrimage to India, which he did, and Jobs later joined his mentor at the All One commune, which Friedland ran on a property owned by an eccentric uncle. Jobs helped look after the commune's apple orchard.

Daniel Kottke, an early Apple engineer (employee no. 12), said that "Friedland was charismatic and a bit of a con man and could bend situations to his very strong will. He was mercurial, sure of himself, a little dictatorial. Steve admired that, and he became more like that after spending time with Robert."[10]

CASE STUDIES

The following case studies of mentor/mentee relationships demonstrate how their development progressed through a series of unique circumstances. While each relationship between the two parties is different, we can see that some dynamics are consistent.

Case Study I

Eric Robb was a research analyst for a wealth management firm, Loring Wolcott & Coolidge (LWC), which managed several billion dollars for individuals, families, and small institutions. As part of its business model, LWC retained an outside firm run by David Wendall to make investment recommendations and to review client portfolios once a month.

As a research analyst, Eric attended these monthly meetings and observed David Wendall's analysis, thinking, and investment approach. Eric learned a great deal from Wendall as they compared research notes, investment ideas, and economic analyses.

Over time, Wendall saw promise in Eric and sponsored him for membership in a local investment group of twenty seasoned portfolio managers. At each meeting, members presented investment ideas, along with their analysis and valuation rationale. Wendall observed the young analyst's analytical skills, and, as time went on, his confidence in Eric's ability grew.

Eric eventually left LWC to pursue an MBA, but he and Wendall kept in contact. When Wendall's firm started to expand, he realized he needed to add research analysts, so he hired Eric several years after he had completed his MBA. Eric became a steward under the tutelage of Wendall. For example, he learned the importance of obtaining as much information as possible, but he also realized that one cannot gather all the information on the industry and/or the company so an experienced analyst had to rely on making an investment decision with most of the available relevant information.

Eric was being groomed to become the senior management director when Wendall announced his upcoming retirement. Sadly, a succession plan was not fully in place when tragedy struck. On a regular day at the office, Wendall had a heart attack and died at his desk. While a succession plan for Eric to eventually lead the firm was in the works, it had not been firmly put into place.

This story did not have a happy ending, but it clearly shows how a mentor and mentee relationship developed, allowing both parties to benefit from each other.

Case Study 2

The following case study of Charles A. Janeway, as a mentor to Dr. Frederick Lovejoy, former associate physician in chief and deputy chairman of Children's Hospital, was written by the latter, especially for this publication.

My mentor, Dr. Charles A. Janeway, was entering the last four years of his chairmanship of the Department of Pediatrics at the Harvard Medical School and the respective leadership as the physician in chief of the Children's Hospital in Boston.

It was at this time in 1970 that he appointed me as his chief resident. A chief resident in medicine is like clerking for a Supreme Court justice. It is a truly unique opportunity that gives one an important jump start in one's career. Its responsibilities include the leadership of the residents in a training program, specifically in the Children's Hospital, with over sixty interns and residents. It also affords the opportunity of an extremely close working relationship at a young age with the department chair.

In this case, it afforded me the opportunity of working with one of the most revered figures in academic pediatric medicine in the United States, and in fact the world. I had come to know Dr. Janeway well, having grown up next door to him in Annisquam during the summers. For better or worse, that allowed him to take stock of a developing young man and was probably influential in my selection as his chief resident.

How was Dr. Janeway a mentor to me? Here are five ways that come to mind.

1. Everything I learned from him I learned by example. As a result of daily contact with him over four years, I witnessed his skills, knowledge, and attitudes in a very impactful way. I saw how he taught. I saw how he handled problems. I saw how he led a large pediatric department. Every day was a learning experience for me that was carefully saved, analyzed, and inculcated into my very being for the future.

2. I witnessed his teaching students, residents, fellows, and faculty in teaching conferences as frequently as one to two hours every day of the week. I witnessed his leading weekly meetings with his faculty, setting policy and defining expectations and standards. I witnessed his leading internship selection and expectations and standards. I witnessed his leading during internship selection and faculty recruitment, working through dilemmas involving the house staff, and finally coming to terms with successes and failures with the sickest of patients.

3. Through daily exposure and by example, I learned what makes up the substrate of a great pediatric department. Acting as his stand-in for the care of very sick patients, I learned the limitations of medicine. Through working on academic papers with him, I learned how to write a scientifically sound paper for publication.

4. Through meetings at the end of the day, I learned the history of academic medicine and pediatrics and of his remarkable career at Johns Hopkins, Yale, and Harvard. I learned of his prestigious father and grandfather and their immense contributions to academic medicine, and perhaps, most importantly, I learned the history of our department at the Children's Hospital and the faculty from the past who were responsible for its immense success.

5. Finally, once again, he taught me by example, not by directive. To illustrate this, I offer an example: I came to him at the end of my chief residency with my dilemma as to whether I would pursue a career in infectious disease or pharmacology, toxicology, and poison center work. He laid out the pluses and minuses of both careers. I asked him what I should do. He replied, "That

decision is yours to make. You will have to live with your decision, not me."

In short, Dr. Janeway was an immense mentor who served as a role model of a revered academic physician, scientist, teacher, medical educator, researcher, and preeminent leader of a superior pediatric department.

REVERSE MENTORING

As beneficial as the case studies demonstrate, mentoring doesn't always have to be someone older mentoring someone younger—not at all!

Reverse mentoring, or peer mentoring, is not a totally new concept. Former General Electric CEO Jack Welch famously had junior workers at the company train 500 of his top managers in how to use the internet in the nineties.

"We tipped the organization upside down," he said at the time. "We now have the youngest and brightest teaching the oldest."[11]

Reverse mentorships can help build a more inclusive workforce. Listening to younger workers and exchanging ideas with them can alter a company culture and make it more open and representative of a diverse workforce.

Dr. Sanghamitra Chaudhuri, a University of Minnesota professor who has researched reverse mentoring, reports in *MarketWatch*, "At Procter & Gamble, they noticed a lot of turnover of women employees, so they partnered young women employees with senior level executives, to learn what would keep these women in the organizations. As a result, they saw a decrease in turnover."[12]

Reverse mentoring also helps retain millennials, who data shows have become the majority generation in America's workforce. At the same time, however, they are also the most likely people to leave their jobs. A 2018 Deloitte Millennial Survey found that 43 percent of millennials planned to leave their job over the next two years. Dr. Chaudhuri's research found that millennials in reverse mentor programs feel more loyalty to the company and are more actively engaged.[13]

Congresswoman Alexandria Ocasio-Cortez (D-N.Y.), who has a following of more than 2.4 million people on her campaign Twitter account, makes national headlines on a consistent basis with her tweets. Two years ago, she gave her fellow House Democrats a series of social media trainings, along with Rep. Jim Himes (D-Conn.). Her session focused on "the most effective ways to engage constituents on Twitter and the importance of digital storytelling," as *USA Today* reported.[14]

Ocasio-Cortez, one of thirty-one millennial representatives in Congress,[15] uses Twitter and Instagram on a regular basis to communicate with her constituents, her colleagues, and the nation as a whole—all in effortless millennial-speak. She is the youngest woman ever to serve in the US Congress and one member of the youngest freshman class since 2011.[16]

Ocasio-Cortez's training illustrates a larger trend. While traditional mentorships have featured senior-level executives and managers taking younger, less experienced employees under their wings, many professionals are learning that there is also much to gain when the junior worker becomes the teacher.[17]

KATIE'S KORNER

While it is highly desirable to find a long-term mentor, someone who will be with you through many stages of your career, it's not something you can manufacture overnight, and it shouldn't be forced. As my grandfather mentioned, these relationships take time to build.

I did not find my first serious mentor until I was five years out of college. Until then, I found that I could tap into the knowledge and experience held collectively within my wider professional network and this allowed me to achieve similar results with an ad hoc approach.

Especially at a time in my early career when I did not have a clear sense of my career path, turning to individuals in my network to provide guidance on specific topics, such as evaluating potential job opportunities or navigating a tricky situation at work, filled the gap.

As my path shifted, so did my network. The value with this approach is that you can begin to benefit from seeking out perspective and advice without having found the "perfect mentor." This is something that takes a bit of proactive effort and a large dose of luck—you'll meet the right person at the right time. Sounds like something out of a fairy tale, but it's not.

Be open-minded about who in your network could serve as an ad hoc mentor. It does not necessarily need to be someone older or vastly more experienced than you. Finding peer mentors is an easy place to start.

Who in your cohort do you respect and admire?

Odds are these colleagues and/or friends have the time to spare and may be navigating through a similar phase in their career. It's likely that they can provide insight that is relevant based on their own similar experiences. You might find they are also seeking someone to act as a "sounding board" and it could turn into a two-way peer mentoring relationship.

It pays to keep a circle of trusted advisors around even after finding a true mentor. Mentors do not come in only one shape or size, and no one person knows everything, especially as your needs and goals change.

It is most beneficial to maintain a circle of advisors to provide a variety of perspectives and opinions. When it comes to friends and mentors, you can't have too many.

CHAPTER 2 REVIEW

Relationships are important elements, essential really, not only when it comes to personal development but also in the world of vocational development.

Advice and guidance in the classroom are one part of it, but close friends and mentors usually are the most beneficial, except in some cases, your marriage partner.

I have shown two examples of successful mentor relationships. One was a millennial in the investment business who was being groomed to take over the business from his mentor, and the other was a chief resident for a major hospital who received a jump start in his career by the chairmanship of the department and the physician in chief of the Children's Hospital in Boston.

Regarding mentors, the best relationships resemble the yin and yang of meaningful friendships and should be mutually beneficial.

One should be aware that there are different types of mentoring, including "sponsorships" or "developmental," and there is also "reverse mentoring," when younger workers, for example, may guide senior workers in how to use the internet effectively.

Even if you have a true mentor, keep any previously trusted advisors you may have in your circle.

When it comes to friends or mentors, learning to cultivate and manage a relationship may take practice, so get started early.

3

CONTINUING ONE'S EDUCATION

Almost everyone agrees that higher education is important, but there is a difference of opinion as to how necessary it is when it comes to the likelihood of achieving success. In that regard, should millennials continue their education beyond high school, beyond college, and beyond master's programs?

For starters, it is estimated that there are 20 million students enrolled in higher learning and that workers earning a bachelor's degree will, on average, earn at least a million dollars more over their lifetime than those graduating with high school degrees only.

Millennials are the most educated generation. According to the Pew Research Center, some 63 percent of millennials value a college education and plan to get one. Of that number, 19 percent have already graduated from college, and the remaining 44 percent plan to graduate from college. Some 27 percent of millennial females and 21 percent of millennial males have college degrees. This is in stark contrast to only 20 percent of Gen X females and 18 percent of Gen X males, and, when it comes to baby boomers (53–71), only 14 percent of females and 17 percent of males have degrees. Not only are millennials the most educated; they are continuing the Gen X trend of more women earning degrees than men.[1]

With their increased levels of education, in quantity and often in quality too, beginning in preschool all the way through earning PhDs, millennials may be the best educated generation, but they are now shouldering a collective amount of student loan debt in the range of $1 *trillion*. Because the price tag of getting such a good education is already so high (and continuing to climb each year), millennials have become quite clever about their education choices.

Unlike previous generations, who viewed education as a birth rite and a smart investment in their future, millennials see their education as an expense, as a cost of a certain type of living, if you will. At the same time, they consider higher education to be an expense that may be quite unnecessary unless it will lead them to a result they intentionally want to pursue. Many millennials may opt to forgo school—undergrad or grad—until they find a program that is a good fit—academically, culturally, and financially.

So does any of this explain a 2019 Gallup poll, which said that 51 percent of American adults consider a college education to be "very important," a number twenty points less than a similar survey taken in 2013. This drop was even more pronounced in the eighteen to twenty-nine age group.[2]

In fact, from the 2014–2015 to the 2018–2019 academic year, annual undergraduate enrollment across all American institutions of higher education (public and private) fell by 1.25 million students, a decline of five percentage points.[3]

The reasons for this vary and must be viewed through a prism of race, student debt, and family economics. A study conducted by the Center for American Progress, using data from the Integrated Postsecondary Education Data System (IPEDS), which is run by the National Center for Educational Statistics, recommends that the federal government, states, and institutions take the following actions:

1. Invest big in debt-free college.
2. Increase the maximum level of Pell Grants.
3. Conduct equity audits to identify policies and procedures that colleges need to adjust.
4. Conduct similar work to better understand the Black enrollment decline.

5. Adapt programs to meet the need of Latinx students.[4]

When considering how any of this may affect millennials, we must also acknowledge the unusual and unprecedented cause and effect of the pandemic and how it has upended the normal trends, especially when it comes to the relationship between the economy and higher education. Normally, postsecondary enrollment increases when the economy stumbles, particularly at community colleges and institutions offering short-term training. But the ongoing pandemic, even with the rollout of vaccines, and the ongoing challenges it represents will inevitably continue to influence how institutions operate in the coming years.

Public colleges and universities are already facing enormous cuts to their operating budgets as states and municipalities cope with monumental declines in revenue. These budget shortfalls will probably cause tuition and fees to rise, along with a greater load of student debt.

With all of this in mind, policymakers should be especially concerned, along with the business world, which is always looking for new graduates (on all levels) to hire. These trends raise significant questions, which millennials are being forced to face as they consider higher education and/or specialized opportunities to earn advanced degrees.

Should millennials continue their education to accelerate their career? Should they pursue what is available to them beyond high school or college and even beyond a master's degree to attaining a PhD?

We know that young adults today are much better educated than their grandparents, especially those considered millennials. We can see this by the share of young adults with a bachelor's degree or higher, which has steadily climbed since 1968. Among millennials, 39 percent of those ages twenty-five to thirty-seven currently have a bachelor's degree or higher, compared with just 15 percent of the silent generation, roughly a quarter of baby boomers, and nearly a third of Gen Xers when they were the same age.[5]

For now, let's focus on the pros and cons of receiving a master's degree.

A typical college graduate is between twenty-two and twenty-three years old. If you are an academic guru, graduate school will teach you much more about a preferred subject you love, which is balanced by professional requirements for a degree in subjects such as medicine, law, engineering, and architecture. With a graduate degree in hand, there are more job opportunities in courses of acute interest, which require such advancement, or perhaps an opportunity to change careers while gaining intellectual growth and public respect.

In 2017, the Urban Institute reported that one in every four Americans with bachelor's degrees is overqualified for their job. According to a survey by *Business Insider*, that number is even higher (about 35 percent) for college-educated millennials. For example, compared to baby boomers, 4 percent more male millennials and 13 percent more female millennials have completed a bachelor's degree.[6]

How does this information account for students pursuing advanced degrees? What is it they are hoping to achieve? Of course, the answers vary with each person. And we can see roadblocks along the way, almost at every turn, so how can a millennial figure out the right path?

RISK AND REWARD

Considering the financial burden for most graduate students, is a graduate MBA program worth approximately $100,000 for two years (and rising), plus the loss of income for that period? This sounds like an overwhelming, somewhat existential question, so let's break it down into a reasonable process we can explore without developing too much stress, either as a student contemplating a mountain of debt or a family debating whether to make the investment.

There are several ways to pay for one's continued education:

1. Personal savings
2. Contributions from parents, through gifts, loans, or other means
3. Scholarship programs (Federal Student Aid, FAFSA)
4. Service commitments through fellowships
5. Tuition waivers

6. Employer reimbursement
7. Student loans

Notwithstanding the above possibilities, continued education should be taken quite seriously because it is much more difficult than undergraduate-level college courses, and it occupies, if not monopolizes, valuable time during arguably the best years of your life.

For some millennials inclined to follow the example of their parents, this may include the possibility of postponing one's marriage and starting a family. This exact consideration may not apply to most millennials these days (Katie happens to be an "outlier" regarding her marriage and starting a family), but the possible conflict of interest is not necessarily all about marriage and children. For some, choosing to leave a girlfriend or boyfriend behind as they opt to attend graduate school thousands of miles away may be enough to give them pause. Or it may come down to choosing between living near your family or coming home once a year as you pursue a higher education somewhere far away. These scenarios differ with each person, and of course there are many more factors that come into play when making such a big decision.

However, no matter how we slice it, finances play a pivotal role, and loans are usually the major hurdle and/or obstacle to overcome, first at the undergraduate level and then continuing for those pursuing a master's degree or higher.

Keep in mind, the educational level of American adults has been on the rise as more college graduates go on to earn master's, professional, and doctoral degrees. Since 2000, the number of people age twenty-five and over whose highest degree was a master's has doubled to 21 million. The number of doctoral degree holders has more than doubled to 4.5 million. Now, about 13.1 percent of US adults have an advanced degree, up from 8.6 percent in 2000.[7]

In 2019, according to new data from the Board of Governors of the Federal Reserve System, households with graduate degrees owed 56 percent of the outstanding education debt, an increase from 49 percent in 2016. To put that in context, only 14 percent of adults age twenty-five or older hold graduate degrees. The 3 percent of adults with professional and doctorate degrees hold 20 percent of the education debt.[8]

Among adults ages eighteen to twenty-nine, 34 percent say they have outstanding student loans for their own education. This includes those with loans currently in deferment or forbearance but excludes credit card debt and other loans taken out for education. Looking only at young adults with a bachelor's degree or more, the share with outstanding student debt rises to 49 percent.

Student debt is less common among older age groups. Roughly one in five adults, ages thirty to forty-four have student loan debt, as do 4 percent of those forty-five and older.[9]

Nationally, 21 percent of the US population earns a master's degree, with an average payout of ten years on higher education loans. Nationally, student loan debt in the aggregate is $1.3 trillion, surpassing auto and credit card debt, and is second only to home mortgages.

The risk-and-reward equation may have a lot of latitude, depending on your circumstances and goals.

Harvard Business School graduates tell me that their success is not dependent on attaining an undergraduate degree, not by a long shot. It's the MBA and developing life skills that really count and that doing business is about developing a network of relationships, many of which begin at the graduate level.

Joel Peterson, a graduate of Harvard Business School, who is currently the chairman of JetBlue, a Stanford business professor, and author of *The 10 Laws of Trust*, says that graduate school provides an opportunity to make lifelong relationships. "Take this time to learn from your extraordinary hand-selected peer group," he says, "and drink in the atmosphere, because you'll never experience something so extraordinary again."[10]

Manas Sampat, who received his MBA from Northwestern University Kellogg School of Management and is now vice president of business development and strategy at ijura, a cloud-based cybersecurity platform for mobile devices, concurs and offers his own experience as proof that these people have the potential to play a vital role in your future success.

> "In my 12 years of entrepreneurship and corporate experience," he says, "I have learned that it's your professional network that will be pivotal to help propel you further in your career, especially when moving to a new country, switching careers or looking for new opportunities."

As you climb higher in your career, Sampat says your opportunities will come from internal referrals.

"Companies want to fill their VP or senior director seats with someone they can trust, and often the seat goes to someone recommended by an existing management-level employee or an executive recruiter. Your graduate school alumni could help you land that interview call for your next dream job."[11]

We can see here that pursuing a graduate degree is a matter of risk and reward, not any different really than the essential equations one may face as they venture into the business world, especially in the arena of entrepreneurship, which we will cover in chapter 7.

FROM THE CLASSROOM TO THE BOARDROOM

The fallacy of the American school system comes into clear focus when we examine the crushing bureaucracy at the high school level, which millions of students are subjected to on an ongoing basis. This could be corrected by making education more interesting, which was one of the central subjects in an inspiring book by Jay Mathews, *The Best Teacher in America*, which tells the story of James Escalante, the most famous and influential American teacher of his generation, who pioneered the use of Advanced Placement (AP) courses in calculus at Garfield High School in East Los Angeles, a school that had been historically riddled with gang violence.

What transpired in this high school became the impetus for the popular film *Stand and Deliver*, which won the Independent Spirit Award for Best Feature in 1988.[12]

As we have seen in that story and through similar accounts of innovative and progressive schools, there are much better ways to educate America's children that not only provide them with the fundamentals but also push them in positive ways to become free thinkers and innovators in their own right.

In my own family, I have seen considerable variance in the path from high school to professional success, which my children have taken. They demonstrate how continuing education requires passion, persistence, positivity, and purpose. When our four children were of the equivalent age of millennials, they graduated from college and went on to matriculate from graduate school.

Our eldest son attended Lake Forest College outside of Chicago. While he received the second highest award at graduation for citizenship and leadership, his grade average was just that—average. He began his postgraduate job history by selling office copiers, mainly to law firms in Boston, as he thought it would give him a jump start in finding a more prestigious job.

Our second son went to Occidental College in California, where he focused on business courses. His chosen career was investment management, so the necessary credentials included graduating with an MBA, which he subsequently achieved at Babson College in Wellesley, Massachusetts, a highly regarded business school.

Our third child, a daughter, was elected as a state representative from Claremont, New Hampshire, then moved to Vermont, where she started and later owned a successful retail store. She went to a small liberal arts graduate school on a part-time basis and paid for it with student loans and personal funds. She was driven by a desire to increase her knowledge of worldly affairs.

Our youngest son, after graduating from San Diego State, became a tennis teaching professional for twenty years, which yielded him ample earning and a healthy lifestyle, and during that time he never found it necessary to attend graduate school.

I mention my children here not only because I am proud of them but because they provide examples of the variety of options that many millennials have enjoyed. Of course, it bears repeating that some groups in our society, in our case White middle-class Americans, often benefit from more opportunities than their fellow citizens who must overcome obstacles, such as racial bias, economic hardship, and a lack of appropriate and much-needed support.

CAREER CENTERS AND POSTCOLLEGE RESOURCES

For those fortunate enough to attend brand named colleges, know that they do not guarantee future success. In fact, utilizing college career centers after graduation can be most helpful by accessing the center's alumni databases, such as LinkedIn, to connect personally with alumni in similar jobs or with desirable companies, where previous networking can make the difference between getting an interview or languishing on the pile, along with hundreds of other anonymous applicants.

Networking is the name of the game.

I encourage everyone to research the alumni from your school, reach out and speak with them and learn their stories. Today, with so much contact information easily available online, there is no excuse to let these opportunities slip away.

For example, you can research hiring trends from the school and take note of which sectors of business they tend to dominate, what levels of compensation are possible, and which companies prefer to hire from your school.

From my lifetime of experience, I have seen evidence repeatedly that your professional network will play a pivotal role in propelling you further in your career, even more so when you move to a new area, switch careers, or seek new opportunities.

As you ascend the ladder of your respective career, more and more doors may open from internal referrals. That's because companies usually want to fill their executive positions with a known commodity, someone they can trust, and these people often come from recommendations from someone already inside the company or from a recruiter who personally knows the person they are pushing for the job. In many cases, one of those key players could be someone you were in contact with during your student days.

Once again, it's not only what you know; it's *who*, and it's making connections with those folks and cultivating them after graduation. That makes it even more important for colleges to make sure that every student has a plan for entering the job market and identifying career pathways and the specific skills they need to navigate them.

Unfortunately, it's not enough just to make this type of assistance available because, according to a Gallup Poll survey, 78 percent of graduates report that they rarely, if ever, used their college's career services office.[13]

But 49 percent of graduates reported that the career-related information received from faculty and staff members outside of the career services office was very helpful for them.[14]

These statistics could be explained by the fact that not everyone is sure about what they want to do once they have completed their studies and have a degree in hand.

For example, how many times have we heard undergrads ask a question like, "What should I do with my life based on my college major?" Even when a student feels pretty sure about their desired major, by the time they finish four years of school and graduate, they may not feel the same way as they did when they began their course of study.

Thinking ahead, recent college graduates should be aware that the longer they are out of a job, the longer the runway will be in finding meaningful employment.

For this reason and many others, that is where career centers can serve such valuable functions. Some universities have former students and current professors set aside time to advise soon-to-be graduates, using their previous work study experience and/or advising their former students on what direction would be best for them, considering their course of study and ultimate goals.

A career path is a lifelong process with a series of experiences. Getting a meaningful job postgradation rests largely on obtaining the right internships in college, as it is estimated that companies hire 50 percent of their employees based on what they achieved through internships.

Keep in mind that internships either lead to jobs with the same company or act as a foundation for professional networking, which can lead to postgraduate job opportunities in the field but not necessarily with the company where the internship took place.

When it comes to college career services, they not only are incredibly valuable; they give you a chance to take advantage of the available resources offered on campus and later to you as an alumnus, and you should make the most of the money you spend on your degree!

That means being proactive and leveraging your relationships. This is essential and can be done by accessing the connections through networking with alumni, seeking advice about certain careers or introductions, or getting recommendations with relevant companies. Your chances of success will surely increase if the relationship is enhanced by some form of legitimate quid pro quo, or a situation where both parties will mutually benefit.

Millennials have come of age through a blend of traditional networking and the more recent methodology of job hunting through the internet. The challenge is to whittle down one's job opportunities and/ or career paths, as the various career fields from 1950 to 2010 have tripled from 270 to 840.[15]

Millennials should not be overly discouraged if college career centers are not totally successful at fulfilling one's needs by providing databases for alumni profiles or introductions to possible mentors. As I mentioned, there are numerous online platforms, which can provide similar chances to accomplish the same opportunities.

THE NEW REALITIES OF COVID

Even with COVID-19 vaccines becoming available more and more over the next months, will colleges and universities be able to consider a return to normal and the possibility of safe reopening and staying open?

While pandemic relief will be remarkably welcome, another crisis is facing the world's higher education. Millions of students in undergraduate and graduate programs are getting their degrees and heading off into the most uncertain job market in decades. Many students are unemployed, underemployed, or inappropriately employed for several reasons. That said, some fields are welcoming graduates now more than ever.

For example, entry-level openings for college graduates as logistics analysts, distribution managers, and loan officers have risen, up nearly 30 percent since 2019, and each of these jobs pays close to $50,000 a year. Even in fields where there are far fewer openings today than before, entry-level opportunities for recent graduates remain, especially for jobs such as business and financial analysts and software and web developers, both of which pay over $50,000. These jobs may be outside a student's field of study, but that doesn't mean they are out of reach.[16]

It's becoming more evident that finding a place in the postcollege job market is more about acquiring skills than it is about where someone went to school or their specific degree. Students with problem-solving, communication, and technical skills are still attractive to employers and may also garner a higher salary. Possessing a toolkit like this could make the difference between watching Netflix all day and having a good job that you like.

All institutions of higher learning should be providing their students, whatever their major might be, with the basic skills employers need. For example, psychology, a perennially popular major with more than 100,000 graduates a year, is a field with limited prospects for those who don't pursue advanced studies. But a psychology major who acquires data analysis skills through research or internships can unlock more than 100,000 additional entry-level jobs paying on average $60,000, versus $39,000 for psychology majors overall.[17]

That said, I am not suggesting the end of liberal arts educations or abolishing the social sciences. Far from it. But these schools can also provide their students with the necessary technical skills to thrive in this new and ever-changing digital world we live in.

Helping graduates forge a backup path means colleges will have to adjust their education models and expand their course offerings. That will enable graduates to find work in an otherwise depressed economy and teach them the value of adaptability. Universities often enjoy bragging about their commitment to lifelong learning. Considering our present challenges, now is a great time to prove it.

SETBACKS AND ASPIRATIONS

There is an expression I've heard countless times that speaks to the challenges all students face after graduating school and entering a life full of adult responsibilities.

"Life is defined by setbacks; success is determined by the ability to rebound."

This is especially relevant today, as we are a country in crisis on multiple fronts.

We could also view this ongoing process through the approach taken by Angela Duckworth, a MacArthur "genius" grant winner, a renowned psychology professor at the University of Pennsylvania, and the author the *New York Times* best-seller, *Grit: The Power of Passion and Perseverance*.[18]

In an interview, she said, "I think the questions on the grit scale about not letting setbacks disappoint you, finishing what you begin and doing things with focus are things I would aspire to, or hope for, for all of our children."[19]

When it comes to forging a path ahead into a career and life in general, I share Ms. Duckworth's aspirations for all millennials.

KATIE'S KORNER

I have spent a lot of time thinking about the value of my bachelor's degree. Over the four years I spent earning that undergraduate degree in environmental science and policy, I took classes from a small liberal arts college, Smith College; a large Ivy League university, Columbia University; and the University of Massachusetts's flagship campus in Amherst, Massachusetts.

The realization I came to at the end of four years was that the difference in quality of education and caliber of both students and professors was barely noticeable if it existed at all.

It's worth recognizing the privilege I had in being able to study at these three fine institutions, and that realization has not escaped me in the ensuing years since I graduated. I am also aware that many students will not have the luxury of even contemplating these questions because they are simply trying to stitch together enough money to meet the application fees.

That said, it could be even more important for those facing a deep financial commitment to make sure that every dollar they spend is right for them, for who they are and who they aspire to become.

From my experience, which is all I can honestly speak for, I would pose a question that I think is worth asking for anyone about to begin or continue their higher education.

What is the value proposition for going to one institution over another?

In doing this exercise, may I encourage you to think beyond liberal arts colleges and universities because it's worth considering even more diverse options, such as a community college or a nontraditional degree program. In fact, you might even ask yourself if you need a degree at all.

I would extend the same thinking to another question.

"Should I spend more time and money to pursue a master's degree after earning my bachelor's?"

This exercise will help you to determine where it is you want to go with your career, what it takes to get there, and what you need as an individual to achieve that.

Let's address these three issues right here.

Where do you want to go with your career?

This is a question that is harder to answer at eighteen years old, heading to college directly after high school, than it might be later, when you are considering grad school. It challenges you to think in a broader sense about what kind of person you are and therefore what kind of work you think you would find fulfilling.

Some people love the idea of dressing up in slacks every day and riding a subway to work in a big city. For others, it's about working with your hands in a studio or workshop. Do you think you'd like working in a large company at a cubicle or for a small start-up, working remotely, which so many of us have begun to do over the past year or so? Maybe you envision being a small-business owner and working for yourself, or you already aspire to make it to the C-suite.

Once you have a rough idea of the field you want to enter, you can begin to better understand the potential future earnings of those types of jobs. If you are in a position where you will need to borrow a large amount in student loans, you'll especially want to understand how well positioned you will be upon entering the workforce to pay off those loans. While the federal government may soon pass legislation with some partial debt forgiveness, for many people it will not even come close to covering the brunt of their debt.

What does it take to get there?

As you start to formulate an idea of where you want to go with your career, you can then better assess what it takes to get there from an academic and/or experience standpoint. There are obvious career paths that undoubtedly require a specific set of educational credentials, such as becoming a lawyer or a doctor. There are others that expect some level of specific training, such as engineering, accounting, or social work. And then there are career paths that are more flexible regarding the required specific educational background and focus more on a set of skills and competencies. All this information is easily accessible, either by asking your teachers or advisors or by surfing the net for reputable sources.

In the early years of my career, I most definitely fell into the latter category, as I coordinated and managed events. I was hired not because of a specific degree I'd earned but rather due to my skills in project management and high level of organization, communication, and relationship building. It's also important not to forget that, in some cases, your real-life experience is just as valuable as your academic education.

There are some career paths that place more importance on the experience you bring to the job over an educational degree. These positions often include computer programming, product management, and other tech-related positions. Jobs that are not tech related, which do not require a degree, can include administrative assistants, pharmacy technicians, online advertising and social media roles, customer service representatives, payroll clerks, and many more.

Figuring out what kind of education you would most benefit from to get where you're planning on going is a huge piece of the puzzle and will go a long way toward determining what kind of institution is best for you and how much money it is worth to spend on your education.

Finally, what do you need as an individual to achieve your desired career?

Here's the piece that I rarely hear people talking about—what *you* need to get where *you* want to go.

Some students thrive in larger student bodies, while others benefit greatly from the tighter-knit system of a small liberal arts college.

Some can do just as well with online courses, while others need an in-person format to stay focused and on target with their studies.

I knew fellow students who struggled when they were so far away from home and others who chose to study nearer to their family because it served as a critical support system during that time in their life.

Some institutions allow students to design their own major and take the initiative on pulling together coursework that allows them to pursue the degree of their dreams, while others would be better suited to select a college that already has an existing program and a prescribed set of courses.

One thing I've noticed is that a smaller college, one with a few thousand people, tends to offer more student support and services in a way that is both easily accessible and at times forced upon the student so that even if they don't take the initiative, they still end up receiving the benefit of the service.

This might be, for example, in the form of a requirement for all undergraduate seniors to make one appointment with their career development office to graduate, and this is part of the value you get from paying tuition.

A larger university, with tens of thousands of students, tends to offer similar support and services, at least on paper, but these institutions leave it up to the students' discretion to take advantage of the opportunities.

If you are the type who is unlikely to use and enjoy these benefits, it's less likely you'll get the full value of your tuition. In a few words, I would summarize this as follows: Are you a self-starter, a motivated type of person, or are you someone who needs some shepherding and guidance to reach your full potential?

Knowing who you are and what you need to find success will undoubtedly help you determine what kind of academic institution you'll get the most value from attending.

Answering all three of these questions will help you build a better understanding of what kind of education will serve you and your wallet best. It won't hurt at all to write down all the pluses and minuses and to ask people who know you best where they see you fitting in best and making the most of your investment.

Comparing one academic institution to another is like comparing apples to oranges. The same goes for one student to another. The cost of an education these days is exorbitant, so the decision should not be made lightly. Even if you land on the realization that you'd be better off taking out large sums in student loans or digging deeply into your savings to cover the cost of a pricier tuition, you'll know it's for the right reasons.

Finally, with a realization that not everyone will have the same options and opportunities, so regardless of what institutions and degrees you are considering, I would still pose this challenge: to do everything you can in your power to look in the mirror and be true to yourself because this experience is yours and belongs to no one else but you. Your education is yours, so choose wisely and make the most of it!

CHAPTER 3 REVIEW

Some professions require postgraduate degrees (e.g., legal, medicine, and architecture), and some vocations strongly recommend it, such as those within the educational field. Other students take postgraduate courses because they are truly interested in the subject or they are marking time until they decide on a definite career path to pursue.

In a recent *Wall Street Journal* article by Jeffrey Selingo and Matt Seligman, "The Crisis of Unemployed College Graduates," they state, "Millions of students are set to graduate this spring into the worst job market in decades. This is especially troubling because the first job after graduation is critical to launching a career. Those who start behind tend to stay behind."[20]

Without scholarships for grad school or underwriting costs from parents, the cost for two years can be $100,000 or more, plus the loss of two years of salary amounting to possibly another $100,000.

At this point, one must weigh comparing the grad school with gaining valuable "experience" pursuing a job or career. If one is stuck in progressing in a chosen vocational life, then continuing one's education can be worthwhile.

Part II

CAREERS

In his best-selling book, *The Art of Work*, Jeff Goins says, "Work was never meant to be something we do just to make a living. It was meant to be a means of making a difference—in our lives and in the lives of others."[1]

If you are a millennial just completing college, an MBA program, or graduating with another type of advanced degree, you are probably contemplating your ultimate career path. However, no matter where you might be in this process, your biggest concern must be securing a job, and part 2 is devoted to the various choices you may have, including internships, starter or entry-level jobs, and positions in the gig economy as well as advice for entrepreneurs.

For many millennials, this challenge means finding a self-supporting job that pays decently, complements your talent and passion, and creates a solid career path. More than likely, all these characteristics will not be met, or even available, with your first position.

Over the past half century, there has been a paradigm shift in the types of jobs and/or careers available. After World War II, average workers were often rewarded with lifetime employment with a solid, reputable American company. They were enticed by generous pensions and other benefits, especially once the labor union movement took hold. New neighborhoods popped up in the suburbs, which created a new lifestyle for many of these workers.

However, over time, the security of this stable workforce changed because of the advent of global competition, breakthrough technology, and employees' seeking short-term advancement with other companies in lieu of maintaining long-term relationships with their current employer. Those positions of lifetime opportunity slowly became overtaken by a constantly relocating workforce, and this was only exacerbated when large corporations moved their factories and businesses out of the country and the American economy became much less insular.

What were previously considered to be pristine jobs became overlooked by large chunks of the middle class. With each succeeding generation, people started searching for other ways to find meaningful and satisfying lives, while still aiming to hold on to at least a semblance of traditional job security.

Millennials have their own version of this evolution. They come to the workplace with record levels of education, but, many of them, in pursuit of their own brand of excellence, have been crippled by mounting student loan debt. They entered the workforce during the Great Recession when many markets became saturated. Despite a decade of economic growth, many of them will probably earn less money than their parents for the duration of their working lives.

According to the Deloitte Global Millennial Survey 2019, based on the feedback of more than 13,000 millennials from forty-two countries, "Economists think this is simply bad luck, but as a result, millennials have less wealth, less property, lower marriage rates and fewer children than each generation born since the Great Depression. Dissatisfaction with pay and absence of opportunities for advancement are the top reasons for millennials' seeming lack of loyalty to employers. Forty-nine percent say they would quit their current job in the next two years if they had a choice."[2]

The American Bar Association observes, "This has created a generation of lawyers who look closely at: (1) commitment to work/life balance, (2) compensation and (3) training and professional development, when evaluating potential employers."[3]

Millennial lawyers today prefer collaborative environments and nonhierarchical management, whereas their predecessors did not. This means that the legal profession needs to adapt and adjust, which they it is in certain ways while still maintaining the old guard in others.

This example demonstrates how millennials are still in great flux as they navigate a rapidly changing landscape, now made even more complex by the short- and long-term effects of the pandemic.

As the Deloitte survey pointed out in the context of the current global economic expansion and the opportunities it presents, "Millennials are expressing uneasiness and pessimism about their careers, their lives in general, and the world around them."[4]

These trends are certainly not unique to the world of law practitioners. Millennials are reconsidering all kinds of careers and how they even approach entering, much less remaining, in them. But contrary to public perception, this generation is not ready to blow up the status quo.

According to a survey provided to CNBC by Qualtrics, a survey software firm based in Provo, Utah, and Accel Partners (a Qualtrics investor), a venture capital firm, "Almost 90 percent of millennials surveyed said that they would choose to stay in a job for the next 10 years if they knew they'd get annual raises and upward career mobility. Most millennials are planning to stay in their jobs for at least six years, and 77 percent would be willing to take a salary cut in exchange for long-term job security."[5]

James Goodnow, a thirty-five-year-old attorney and coauthor of *Motivating Millennials*, says, "Millennials want stability—yes, that may shock you, but it's true. Many baby boomer executives think millennials are just cashing in on a short-term gig so they can scrape together enough money to go hike Mount Kilimanjaro or buy an unlimited annual skydiving pass."[6]

Years ago, both employer and employee would make long-term commitments to each other, but nowadays both make frequent corporate changes and move to different vocations. In their State of the American Workplace in 2017, Gallup reported that millennials will change jobs for the following reasons at the following rates:

Paid vacation, 64%
Flextime, 63%
Other insurance coverage, 60%
Flexible location (off-site part-time), 50%
Flexible location (off-site full-time), 47%
Student loan reimbursement, 45%
Tuition reimbursement, 45%
Paid maternity leave, 44%
Paid to work on independent project, 42%
Professional development programs, 41%
Paid paternity leave, 37%
Childcare reimbursement, 30%[7]

When it comes to job applications, millennials submit their résumés on average to twenty-six companies. Despite their individual efforts, friends and family are credited with much of the job originations. While internships at an early stage are critical for millennials to be successful in producing job offers (discussed in chapter 4), their cumulative collection of skills, connections, and credentials, along with interviews and recommendations, play a significant role in how an employer decides whether they are fully qualified and a good fit.

PHASE ONE: ASSESS YOURSELF

The millennial challenge, as defined here and throughout the book, is to be self-supporting and engaged in a career. The key ingredient is a job that offers something more than just a paycheck, and most agree that this means avoiding a job that takes you nowhere. Additionally, for a career you may have chosen that requires special knowledge and skills to be able to rise to a certain level of expertise, you may need to acquire further education.

Instead of assessing someone else to suggest a career choice, I have decided to analyze myself regarding my core competencies as a model for you to follow. Let's face it, I am not a detail-oriented person, so, if I were to choose a career right now for myself, I would have to rule out being an accountant, an engineer, or an architect, just to name a few situations where I would not succeed. Furthermore, I am not an exceptional student, so grad school would not be my strong suit, which essentially rules out the medical profession.

It probably behooves us to ask why Thomas Edison was so successful. In his case, it was two major characteristics: a natural and intense curiosity about why things are the way they are (or not) and his sheer determination and perseverance to succeed and overcome all obstacles. For example, Edison took six years to develop the light bulb. He produced more than 1,000 patents.

We could also ask the same question about Benjamin Franklin, who was quite successful, in his time. His two primary characteristics for success were curiosity and positive psychology and communication.

Obviously, we can all learn a lot from Edison and Franklin, and, at the risk of sounding like a doddering professor, I suggest you read about both. You may be pleasantly surprised by how relevant their experiences remain today.

Returning to the analysis of myself, I was self-taught in the mergers and acquisitions (M&A) business, having read the most relevant books on the subject, plus having written several books on the subject myself, one of which evolved into a second edition. I also became the president of a trade organization with 5,000 members, which later grew to have 12,000 members.

Not to extol my positive attributes, as if I did this all on my own, I selected responsible team players and was well organized. Luckily, my deficiencies were overcome by my attributes. However, I established my career in a rather nontraditional way.

Most important, I had a healthy sense of confidence (but not too much), and I was not afraid to put myself out there and take my chances in the real world.

PHASE TWO: POSSIBLE JOBS

Searching for a job out of college is a lot more difficult today than it was in the 1950s. Embarrassingly, back in those days, I used what was called "the old boys' network."

My father, who served in World War II, had previously befriended the CEO of American Express. Since my father had died by the time I was job eligible, I called the CEO of AmexCo and asked him for a job. I was hired as a newly launched "trouble shooter" for a new financial product: the recently introduced credit card. For some of you not familiar with them, it's a small plastic card, the size of a business card, which can be used to purchase essentials and other things and can also lead people into unmerciful debt if they are not careful.

In due time, I left the company in New York City and worked in sales for a mutual fund. I then made a radical career choice by buying into a small private manufacturer that made fiberglass products, including canoes and kayaks. It was called Lincoln Fiberglass back then and is now referred to as Lincoln Canoes and Kayaks. My move into this work was a case of genuine serendipity, which is often the case when it comes to finding a career.

Based on the information that I have provided here, I will fast-forward to the current year and superimpose myself as to how I would approach the job market now.

First, I would contact those companies in which I had internships to determine whether I could interview with them. Second, I would contact the sales departments and/or the personnel department, seeking an entry-level sales position for a consumer products company, such as Proctor & Gamble. Third, I would contact recent alumni of my university who work for consumer product companies.

PHASE THREE: A ROAD MAP

A logical way to establish a career is to assess yourself, make a list of possible jobs, and then create a road map to guide you to your destination. A designated career cannot necessarily be determined early on, but it often occurs through serendipity after other choices are rejected.

Let's look at the careers of certain professions to appreciate the effort one must exert.

To Become a Doctor

1. Explore your undergraduate options.
2. Take premed classes and earn good grades.
3. Participate in meaningful extracurricular activities.
4. Prep for the MCAT (Medical College Admissions Test) and ace it.
5. Prepare applications to multiple medical schools.
6. Impress med school interviewers and get at least one acceptance letter.
7. Enroll in the right type of medical school for you.
8. Pass the first portions of the allopathic or osteopathic national medical licensing exam.
9. Apply for and match with a residency program.
10. Graduate from medical school.
11. Start your residency and get a general medical license.[8]
12. Achieve board certification within your medical specialty or subspecialty.

From the time one begins undergraduate college to attending medical school and finally through a residency, the average student will spend eleven years in their quest to become a licensed medical doctor. The initial compensation for an average student who has completed all these steps will be in the range of $223,000 to $329,000.[9]

To Become an Engineer

1. Earn a bachelor's degree in engineering from a school accredited by the Accreditation Board for Engineering and Technology (ABET).
2. Pass the Fundamentals of Engineering (FE) examination.
3. Complete at least four years of engineering experience.
4. Pass the Principles and Practice of Engineering (PE) examination.

Master's programs are designed to expand and deepen the knowledge and skills acquired as an undergraduate. Master's degree programs in engineering require two years of full-time graduate study.

Doctoral programs require five to seven years of graduate study, while PhD programs are usually designed for people interested in research and education in the engineering field.[10]

According to the US Bureau of Labor Statistics, engineers have a median annual wage of $91,010, and the engineering field projects to have employment growth of nearly 140,000 new jobs over the next decade.[11]

To Become an Officer in the US Army

To pursue a vocation of this type, there are four paths:

1. *Army ROTC*: Students enroll in elective leadership and military courses at colleges and universities. At graduation, ROTC cadets are commissioned as second lieutenants.
2. *Direct Commission*: Direct commission provides individuals who possess leadership, skills, and experience the opportunity to become an Army officer. In addition to individuals from professional fields, such as law, medicine, and religion, the Army has expanded direct commission to look for skilled individuals in a multitude of other fields. Upon completion of an officer training program, they are commissioned at a rank determined by their experience and career branch.
3. *Officer Candidate School*: This path allows college graduates to gain the knowledge and skills necessary to be commissioned as Army officers. Through classroom instruction and training exercises, candidates learn to become leaders.
4. *The United States Military Academy*: West Point is one of the country's oldest colleges. Cadets are immersed in military customs and traditions while working toward a college degree. At graduation, cadets are commissioned as Army second lieutenants.[12]

Individuals with a four-year college degree earn an officer rank immediately upon enlistment. Otherwise, the time requirements depend on which path you choose.

If you decide to become an officer through the Army Reserve Officers' Training Corps (ROTC) or the US Military Academy at West Point, you will become an officer after completing four years of college. Through Officer Candidate School (OCS), you are commissioned as an Army second lieutenant upon completion of the twelve-week course, but you still must have earned a four-year degree from an accredited university. If you join through direct commission, you are automatically an officer when you enter the Army, but your commission may still hinge upon other requirements.

Army officer salaries are generally comparable with mid- to senior-level corporate executives. When you factor in the savings from some of the other benefits of joining the military, such as Army housing and health care, you come out ahead.[13]

SELECTING A CAREER

While these examples illustrate just three possible paths, selecting a single career is not necessarily essential. One can certainly be successful in business, for example, by moving from position to position, such as within the manufacturing sector, which encompasses production, sales, administration, etc. One's skills should be eclectic, but it's perhaps more difficult to secure a job right out of college if one is lacking focused experience.

For millennials, especially those just graduating from college, there is a tendency to postpone a career decision until later or select one that immediately pays the most. At this stage in life, one should select a career, subject to change, based on one's interests, skills, values, relationships, and former internships.

Bearing in mind that criteria, if one seeks a "traditional" career, yet is undecided on the specifics, then achieving an MBA might be recommended, as it can provide a strong fundamental base for whichever direction you might wish to take in the future. As we mentioned in chapter 3, the relationships you make during this phase of your education can pay valuable dividends in your future.

To qualify for an MBA program, the following requirements are in order:

A strong academic record from your undergraduate college.
Undergraduate transcripts and any job records you may have.

Pass the GMAT exam or GRE, depending on the school you are
   applying to.
Submit the entrance forms.
Include recommendation letters from one's supervisor/professor.
Personal letter to the admissions office.

Most students who earn an MBA have work experience. For example, the University of North Carolina at Chapel Hill reports its online
MBA students have already been employed in the workforce for an
average of ten years. While not all programs require work experience
to begin an MBA, employers may want to see a combination of education and practical experience.[14]

CHANGING CAREERS

A friend of mine previously worked for a mutual fund as a security
portfolio manager. He felt the need to give back to society as a high
school teacher, so he attained his credentials by attending graduate
school in education. After a year or two, he realized that as a teacher
he spent a significant time disciplining inattentive students. This left
him in a bind; he didn't want to continue teaching. But he had a
mountain of student loans to pay off, so he stayed on in his job while
looking for a better situation.

Another friend of mine retired as a successful CEO of a manufacturing firm with revenue of $200 million. He then became a professor
at Harvard Business School but left teaching after one year because it
lacked a sense of teamwork with his peers. This left him a bit adrift for
a while, but at the same time, he experienced a strong feeling of freedom, knowing he could use his skillsets in multiple ways going forward.

As these examples show, changing careers can produce positive
as well as negative results. For example, changing jobs from one
law firm to another is arguably an easy transition, but changing an
essential career means changing vocations. That could include further
education (and high tuition costs), a change of location, and a new
culture to adapt to and learn. Depending on your age, personality,

and upbringing, this may be viewed as an unreasonable hardship or a golden opportunity. Which one do you think it might be for you?

When it comes to changing direction in your working life, a job is not necessarily a career. It is usually a short-term direction with a paycheck as the primary motivation. On the other hand, a career is an occupation developed over time based on lifelong ambition.

The rationale for changing careers may be receiving more money, career progression, bigger challenges, and reducing daily stress. In some cases, careers offer more substantial training than what some may perceive to be transient jobs.

It is estimated that one-third of millennials do not stay with their original careers. In a survey by CareerBuilder, employers expect 45 percent of newly hired college grads to remain under two years at their company, and by age thirty-five about 25 percent of young employees will have worked five different jobs.[15]

For those millennials who need to decide whether a career change is necessary, it will behoove you to learn the specific requirements for a new career and explore the list of possible companies you should approach.

Leaving one's career can be stressful. At certain companies, depending on your age, it could be mandatory, which of course is not an immediate concern for millennials, but it could be wise to investigate the culture of a company before accepting employment there to ensure its values are consistent with yours when it comes to whom they hire (e.g., diversity) and how it treats its employees, no matter what their age and experience.

FAMILY BUSINESS

Family businesses are the backbone of the American economy. Studies have shown about 35 percent of Fortune 500 companies are family controlled, while a larger percentage of private companies are family controlled or owned.[16]

Working for one's family business is an obvious career choice because the favorability of being hired is greatly enhanced due to your perceived honesty, inherent commitment, and potential loyalty to the company, despite your lack of specific skills and experience.

While this scenario may work nicely when it's your own family grooming you to climb the ladder from the bottom up, there could be a downside to working for another family's business because in that case you may never breach a certain level of seniority, as it is most likely reserved for family members only.

On a macro scale, family businesses last for twenty-four years on average before they are sold or go out of business, and 30 percent continue to the second generation, while 12 percent continue until the third generation, and 3 percent remain until the fourth generation. Family businesses are run more conservatively, with 30 percent debt versus 40 percent for their peers.[17]

Succession planning and planned governance are positive characteristics for long-term employees, which should appeal to those seeking stable careers. There are approximately 5.5 million (and counting) family businesses in the United States, which contribute 57 percent of the gross national product and 63 percent of the workforce and are responsible for 78 percent of all new job creation.[18]

People who grow up in the realm of a family business may have a difficult choice to make when it comes to following in their predecessor's footsteps or going out on their own to explore a totally unrelated field. Many factors can determine this decision.

Dr. Frederick Lovejoy of Boston, Massachusetts, was born into a family whose business centered around steel distribution and manufacturing gunpowder. By the time he was ready to go to college, he decided to pursue medicine as a profession because he felt he could do more for society as a pediatrician. Dr. Lovejoy was willing to deal with the reaction of his family and was ready to make the necessary commitment to his preferred vocation.

It's interesting to note that the word *vocation* comes from the Latin root *vocare*, which means "to call," a term originally used in a religious sense, as in a call to the priesthood. In a larger sense, far beyond the realm of religion, some people still view a career as a calling. For each of you, this is something to consider as you probe the world of employment and find your own sense of balance between work and other aspects of your life.

CAREERING

Wouldn't it be wonderful if all of us reached our mid-teenage years knowing what career we were going to pursue for the rest of our life? For some of you, the answer might be yes, while for others, having so much certainty might feel unsettling and even stifling.

Some of us can narrow down the various fields of endeavor that we consider to be worthy of our consideration, and we do our best to assess whether we have the talent, personality, and financial where-withal to successfully achieve a desired career. Some of us are not so fortunate and need more time to figure out what we are best suited to do and how to get there.

On the other hand, the best laid plans . . .

You see, life doesn't usually work out the way we imagine it might.

My wife and I have three sons. One of them enjoyed a successful twenty years as a teaching tennis pro until he had two hip replacements. Another son has spent his entire career pursuing that profession. Our oldest son was unable to nail down a career before he was forty years old, but since then he has achieved a successful career of twenty years as an executive in financial services, working for CBIZ Company, PricewaterhouseCoopers, Ernst & Young, and Grant Thornton. He found his career, but later in life!

Perhaps it is worthy to describe our oldest son's business trajectory before he solidified himself as a marketing and sales manager for large accounting firms. At the beginning, when he was still a student in college, he became a bank teller. He applied for a training position at the bank's commercial loan department. Because he did not have an accounting background or experience in commercial sales, he was turned down by the bank. To fill the void, he spent several years going back to school, graduating with his MBA from Tulane University.

Realizing he needed commercial sales experience, he made the short list as a copier salesman with Xerox and IBM. He turned down a sales position with Merck but accepted a sales and teaching position with ADP, selling payroll services. Then, he sold consulting services for various accounting firms. Bingo! He was hired as director of risk assurance by PwC, a multibillion-dollar international consulting practice.

Finding a successful career can be difficult, but, as this example shows, it is doable.

I have four recommendations:

1. If hired, write down the specific jobs and expectations that will be expected from you and determine whether they are not only acceptable but whether you can excel at them.
2. Write down what concerns you might have with the specific job, whether you have the right talents, and whether you fit in with the group.
3. Do your external research on the company to be sure it has the necessary resources to be competitive.
4. Determine whether the company is culturally and financially capable of meeting your expectations, both in the short and long term.

As you will soon discover, part 2 also addresses the new gig economy, which arose out of the 2007 to 2009 recession, followed by the enormous explosion of tech start-ups. A chapter on entrepreneurship describes various case studies with employee concerns, such as a lack of benefits and ability to form unions. All these concerns, plus the effects of the COVID-19 epidemic, are now placing unusual challenges on millennials.

It's up to you to rise to the occasion!

4

MAKING THE MOST OF STARTER JOBS AND INTERNSHIPS

Let's focus for now on various elements of corporate-type careers. Some of you may be looking elsewhere for your initial steps into the full-time working world, which is fine, but I would encourage you to read through this chapter anyway, as you may find some new ideas and perspectives you hadn't previously considered.

The objective of a starter job is to identify an enjoyable and remunerative career that will be challenging and rewarding. Addressing this issue during the teenage years is apt to be achievable if someone that age has a variety of part-time jobs during the school year or in the summer, including internships. Of course, this process may not reveal what's best for you until much later, once you have tried a series of starter jobs, but as the saying goes, "You've got to start somewhere!"

While not critical in choosing a career, a future employer will be receptive to your job application if it is relevant to the knowledge you have obtained from your major in college or the courses you have taken in trade school. The same applies to internships.

So what kind of starter job should I do?

That's a good question, and, for that matter, it's an exceedingly smart one to ask. My simple answer is this: it doesn't matter! It's a starter job, and it's not intended to last a lifetime if even a year. What's important at this stage of your life is to try different things, meaning all kinds of jobs to see what fits you, but that said, you can and *should* bring to the table a sense of what you prefer and how you wish to spend your working time. This applies to the environment, culture, and of course a salary appropriate to these circumstances.

PRIORITIES AND PREFERENCES

Let's begin with a basic set of premises. According to 2019 data from the US Bureau of Labor Statistics, the median weekly earnings for a worker in the United States with a bachelor's degree is $1,248, compared with $746 for someone who has earned only a high school diploma.[1]

Research from the Georgetown University Center on Education and the Workforce shows that a worker with a bachelor's degree is likely to earn 84 percent more over the course of their lifetime than someone without this level of education.[2]

For the sake of this discussion, I will assume that you have graduated from college or are planning to soon. As a college graduate, you probably chose your major for several reasons, which only you really know. When it comes time to pursue a starter job, you ought to revisit what initially interested you in the major and whether you want to keep going in that direction. If so, in what way? If not, what else are you interested in?

There are many considerations to contemplate. For example, if you are determined to earn $100,000 or more annually, right from the start, have you done your due diligence to research the types of work that will offer you that type of salary fresh out of college?

The top-paying college majors yield $3.4 million more than the lowest-paying majors over the course of a graduate's lifetime. Two of them, STEM and business, are also the most popular majors, as they account for 46 percent of college graduates.

STEM (science, technology, engineering, and mathematics), health, and business majors are the highest paying, and they lead to average annual wages of $37,000 or more at the entry level and an average of $65,000 or more annually over the course of a recipient's career.

The ten majors with the lowest median earnings are as follows: early childhood education ($39,000); human services and community organization ($41,000); studio arts, social work, teacher education, and visual and performing arts ($42,000); theology and religious vocations, and elementary education ($43,000); and drama and theater arts, and family and community service ($45,000).[3]

U.S. News & World Report reports the following ten college majors with the best median starting salaries, according to 2020 data from the US Department of Education:

Aerospace, aeronautical, and astronautical engineering ($62,350)
Mechanical engineering ($62,400)
Nuclear engineering ($62,550)
Materials engineering ($63,300)
Computer science ($64,450)
Chemical engineering ($64,750)
Industrial engineering ($65,250)
Electrical, electronics, and communications engineering ($67,000)
Petroleum engineering ($67,150)
Computer engineering ($69,300)[4]

Does this mean that you should not pursue certain careers, such as a teacher or social worker? Not at all. After all, who am I to challenge your passion and desired career? That said, while these are admirable professions, to say the least, starting salaries are nowhere near the $100,000 level that many graduates seem obsessed with pursuing.

For the school year 2019–2020, starting salaries for teachers ranged from $57,845 for those with a bachelor's degree and no prior teaching experience to $87,510 for those with a master's degree and eight years teaching experience, plus additional coursework. New teachers with a master's degree but no prior teaching experience earned an average of $65,026.[5]

But if your major was education or sociology, I'm sure you already knew that and considered this financial situation.

On the other hand, if you are intent on making the big bucks right away and have chosen to pursue the field of corporate finance, are you aware of the extremely high demand on your time, meaning you'll be doing tons of unpaid required overtime, and are you okay with working in what can often be a culture that stresses profit over people?

Just asking . . . as you should too.

Obviously, your starting salary is only one criterion to consider when it comes to choosing a starter job to pursue. Aside from the type of employment, the compensation, and whether the job's characteristics fit your strengths, it would be helpful to identify your priorities and preferences, which some people might call your dealbreakers.

In other words, when it comes to your employment, what are your values?

Table 4.1.

Priorities/Preferences	Deal Breakers
Big salary	Constant dislocation
Fortune 500 company	60+ hour workweek
Stated career path	Boring-type job
Growing company	Struggling company
Compatible culture	Dead-end job

There are certain companies that are great résumé builders even though you may not intend to stay there indefinitely. For example, let's say you have an interest in consumer products marketing and have the good fortune to be hired by Proctor & Gamble in that capacity. If everything goes well, this accomplishment will enhance your marketability for years to come.

In many cases, however, one must ask themselves whether a particular job is worth taking. Here is a list of relevant questions in that area, according to Elaine Varelas, managing partner of Keystone Partners in Boston, who serves on the board of Career Partners International and has more than twenty years of experience in career consulting, executive development, and coaching. She contributes weekly to Boston.com Jobs and *The Boston Sunday Globe* Money and Careers section. These are the questions she suggests one ask when it comes to determining whether your career path is the right one for you.

1. Is there a promise of a better future?
2. Are you doing meaningful work, something you can talk about in a future interview?
3. Are you meeting people? The people you meet could be worth more than the paycheck because they might be able to help you land a better job.
4. Why has there been so much turnover?
5. Does anyone get promoted to full-time with benefits?
6. Do you have other leads? If you do not see the job benefiting you professionally, then your time is better spent searching for a different job.[6]

In an interesting article in the *New York Times*, "Which Company Is Right for You?" Adam Grant, professor of management and psychology at the Wharton School, University of Pennsylvania, discusses one of his students who "suddenly realized that her biggest concern wasn't what she did but where she worked."[7]

In other words, the company's culture, such as its values, norms, and practices, often is more important than the salary level.

This leads to another essential question: Is corporate culture more critical than title or salary?

Adam Grant cites several examples of different cultures in companies he researched, along with questions you may want to ask regarding each of them, including the following:

Apple: Would you be willing to work for someone like Steve Jobs, the cofounder and former head of Apple, who was known to be extremely exacting and critical, but as a leader sought to bring out excellence in all his employees?

Southwest Airlines: Would you be willing to start with a company at the bottom, knowing that Colleen Barrett began her career as a secretary but rose to become Southwest's president?

Walmart: Would you be willing to work for a CEO like Michael Duke, who slashed more than 13,000 jobs while raking in $19.2 million for his personal fortune?

As Adam Grant states: "It's probably wiser to first rule out the worst cultures."[8]

THE PROCESS

Finding a good job after college is a process, which some students might elect to start during high school by beefing up their résumé with extracurricular activities, striving for awards, and pursuing and accepting meaningful summer jobs and internships.

Since 2013, each year's graduating class has had at least 60 percent of its students take on an internship or co-op during their college years. Among those who did an internship, just over half have done more than one. Of those making the most of their internships, 27 percent do two of them and 13 percent do three. Almost unbelievably, 2 percent of them did up to six internships (and reported little to no sleep, constant hunger, and no social life). While most people start internships while they are in college, 31 percent of internships begin after graduation.[9]

It is advisable to start your LinkedIn profile while you are in college and to thoroughly read the book *What Color Is Your Parachute?* by Richard Bolles. This practical manual on job hunting and career changes was updated in 2015 and is considered the most popular job search book, with a 74 percent five-star rating on Google. For many undergraduates and graduates, this is the first step in building a network outside the confines of your college or university and will become a useful building block for years to come. In some cases, LinkedIn serves as your entry point into the field you are interested in entering, and it may even lead to in-person meetings and real personal connections.

Some students near graduation spend hours and hours online look-ing for "job openings." That method should be a last resort strategy, as one should focus on a friend or a colleague to connect you on a personal basis with the key people or the Human Resources Depart-ment of your target company. If possible, search for a personal con-nection you may have, directly or indirectly, with someone at your desired company.

It's important to note here that not everyone, in fact not many peo-ple at all, have specific personal connections that may lead to a desired job. In that respect, not everyone has a parent with the right connec-tions either. I was lucky that my father knew the CEO of American

Express. This certainly opened a door for me, and fortunately I had the qualities they were looking for to get an offer of employment.

When this is not a lucky option, I suggest you use the alumni list of your college. Start with the career center, even though not all your peers may be doing so. In fact, in 2018 Gallup and Strada conducted polls of college students enrolled across forty-three randomly selected colleges and universities, both public and private. The survey found that, after creating or updating a résumé, fewer than 20 percent of undergraduate students reached out to their school's career centers for advice on finding jobs or finding and applying to graduate programs, both of which the recent report identifies as some of a center's most valuable services.[10]

I would encourage you to be stubborn and push your university or college career center to go the extra mile for you. After all, you're paying for their services!

Career service centers are staffed by professionals specifically trained to assist college students with career-related concerns. They work closely with employers who may someday hire you. It's the best place on campus to help you figure out what you want to do with your life and how you can approach the process. They offer career-related resources, in print or online. The more you become known to the career services staff, the better chance you will have that one of the staff will refer you to an employer looking to fill a specific position. It's a good place to meet other students who share your concerns. Exchanging ideas with your peers is always helpful. And finally, and this bears repeating, you're paying for it![11]

Beyond the options on campus, you need to utilize LinkedIn effectively and network like crazy. Sending résumés out in abundance will not work unless you proceed or follow-up with an actual face-to-face meeting with the decision-makers of your target companies. This is not so easy to do, however, not in this age of impersonal digital communication. Securing telephone numbers is almost impossible in certain arenas. Candidates are nearly always directed to a website, which unfortunately equals the playing field a little bit too much and renders personalization and individual flair a thing of the past.

One method for a student's search for employment can be found in the following example. Let's assume a student has a background, interest, skills, experience, and education that suggests a job working for a consumer products company. Let's also assume that this student must be able to live in New England. Using online resources, he can do a search for consumer product companies in New England with sales of over $50 million. After compiling a preliminary list, he may have 50 to 100 companies to consider, and half of them might end up appearing to be worthwhile to pursue.

Now, the trick is to show this list of companies to all those who can conceivably help this student with an introduction to a specific person. This method sounds like a real stretch, but it can work. You never know until you try. That's a cliché for a reason. You never *do* know until you try! Why not call the director of Human Resources at those forty companies and try to pursue a next step based on your interest in applying for a job? What do you have to lose, other than the time it takes to make a call, including the long moments of being kept on hold, when you can be doing more job searching?

EMILY'S JOB SEARCH

The following success story was shared by my son, Scott, a part-time professor at Nichols College and former director of risk assurance at PricewaterhouseCoopers (PwC).

Emily is a second-year associate for PwC's risk assurance and IT audit practice. She grew up in central Massachusetts and had a modest upbringing. During her senior year in high school, Emily was applying to many colleges that had business and accounting programs in the metropolitan Boston area. She received acceptances to several schools but elected to attend Nichols College, located outside the Boston area. Emily wasn't seduced by attending a college with a more prestigious name and reputation with considerably higher tuition. Instead, Nichols offered her a competitive accounting degree, and the lower tuition expenses were well within her budget. This was extremely important since Emily was responsible financially for a significant portion of her college education. Emily's rationale was this: regardless of where she went to school, she confidently felt that she could secure a job based on her merits.

Because Emily was paying for a significant portion of her school, she planned on graduating in three years instead of four. She accomplished this by taking an extra course during the normal fall and spring semesters, while attending summer schools. Throughout college, Emily worked several paid on-campus jobs due to the school's work study program as well as working during school breaks and summer vacations.

After her freshman year, Emily moved back home and commuted to school, which allowed her to reduce her room and board expenses approximately $15,000 per year or $30,000 over the next two years. Emily had secured summer internships in accounting, and, during her second and third years, she landed an internship with PwC's risk assurance practice. Emily worked hard and performed well in her assignments and was awarded a full-time position at PwC upon graduation with the required GPA of 3.5.

In Emily's first year at PwC, she elected to live at home rather than renting a cramped apartment with other young professionals of similar age closer to the Boston office. Emily's commute to PwC's Boston included a train ride and bus rides, which totaled approximately 2.5 hours one way.

Despite the major inconvenience of her daily commute in and out of Boston from central Massachusetts, Emily was able to save most of her salary and max out on her 401(k) contribution. After her first year, she was able to pay the initial costs of renting an apartment in Boston's desirable North End district with her boyfriend.

Emily's second year at PwC ran directly into the COVID-19 pandemic. She and her boyfriend decided to move out of the city and back into one of their parents' homes in central Massachusetts. Emily and her boyfriend were able to save 85 percent of their respective salaries. Today, Emily and her boyfriend are starting a new chapter in their lives by moving together to the West Coast to pursue their career interests with their combined financial foundation in secure shape.

What are the lessons learned from Emily?

First, Emily wasn't seduced by her peers and perceived society stigma by overstretching herself financially in attending the most prestigious school possible. This would have required her to take out college loans, placing her in significant debt. Instead, she lived within her means. More important, Emily developed and executed a plan that enabled her to graduate a year early. After living on campus her freshman year, it gave her the college experience as she developed a network of friends and relationships from her dormitory, classroom, and playing on the varsity tennis team.

She felt confident in moving back home to save another $15,000 per year in college expenses because she has a network of friends and relationships for support when they are needed for school projects and group study for exams.

Early on, Emily realized the value of internships, especially in the accounting field, by parlaying her summer internship into a full-time job. More important, she leveraged the Nichols alumni network and faculty to help provide introductions to various accounting firms and was offered full-time employment at PwC, D&T, and a regional accounting firm.

Emily became an aggressive saver after graduation. Despite major inconveniences of commuting daily into the city in her first year, she saved a significant portion of her salary and contributed the limit into her 401(k). This provided her financial flexibility without relying on her parent's involvement while also getting a head start on her retirement savings.

FINDING WHAT WORKS FOR YOU

Working for a Fortune 500 company may not be in the cards for you. Working for a smaller company may have more upside and could be more interesting. Today, in this country, the average company is only fifteen years old, compared to 1975, when the average company was fifty-eight years old. Nearly all companies in the US have less than 100 employees, so interview with smaller companies as well.

Another possibility is working for the US government (www.usajobs .gov), which appeals to some as a sense of service as well as providing job security.

One of the most sought-after companies for job opportunities is Disney, with approximately 223,000 employees spread throughout forty countries. Disney has numerous internship programs and job opportunities in sales, marketing, and technology.[12]

According to Glassdoor, the best places to work in 2021, according to employees, include companies such as Bain and Co., NVIDIA, In-N-Out Burger, HubSpot, McKinsey & Company, Google, Delta Air Lines, lululemon, Microsoft, and HEB, which form the top ten on their list.[13]

There are also an infinite number of vocational possibilities, but there should be something in your background that allows you to make a compelling case for yourself.

Perhaps a nongovernmental organization is in your future. The nonprofit world is full of fascinating opportunities, and, while these companies may not pay top dollar, certainly not like those in the financial sector, they do provide you with the chance to make a tangible difference in the world.

YOUR RÉSUMÉ

Your résumé must be triple checked by others for grammar and spelling mistakes. Some of the common elements to consider in writing résumés include the following:

1. Provide professional contact information.
2. Use a résumé summary.
3. Use keywords to highlight education, experience, and skills, including Education, Experience, and Skills.
4. Emphasize hobbies, interests, publications, and associations.
5. Mention your GPA and any honors.
6. Include business networking profiles and online résumé links.
7. Avoid mentioning high school.
8. Emphasize soft skills and education.
9. Avoid using fluffy language and use action verbs.
10. Emphasize important highlights.[14]

When the time comes to update or create your résumé, consider including a *Skills* section, which highlights your special abilities, especially those that are most relevant to the position. This is especially important for positions with specific technical skills requirements. To find out what you should include, review the job posting you're applying for and do it carefully.

Look for hard and soft skills mentioned in the job posting, under the headings of *requirements*, *education*, or *desired skills*.[15]

NOW, THE INTERVIEW

In the interview process, you will undoubtedly be asked one key question:

"Tell me about yourself?"

Your response should be a two- or three-minute "elevator speech" and no more. It is advisable to practice this speech and make sure you sound like you! No one wants to hear you try to tell them what you think they want to hear. Share a genuine piece of yourself. Offer some insight into who you are. That shows confidence and affability, two key characteristics any wise interviewer likes to see.

Stick with a short presentation and be aware of three red flags:

1. You're being too formal.
2. Your story is rambling.
3. You sound too rehearsed.

You can feature your best soft skills by doing the following (soft skills in parentheses):

1. Show up on time or early to the interview (punctuality/ dependability).
2. Maintain eye contact (active listening).
3. Speak clearly when prompted (effective communication).
4. Answer questions about your résumé and experience honestly (integrity).
5. Ask follow-up questions (active listening).[16]

You can demonstrate your hard skills by elaborating on your experience and training, providing a portfolio, answering technical questions related to the work, asking relevant follow-up questions, and working through skills tests if they are required at the interview.

It may seem counterintuitive to rehearse not coming off as too rehearsed, but this is a challenge worth exploring. Enlist some of your peers who are facing the same challenge and observe each other and offer feedback. You can even record your speeches a few times on your phones and study any odd or "bad" habits that may distract from an interviewer listening to you.

Anticipate the interview by preparing for obvious questions. Interviewers really like anecdotal examples of your experiences, so think long and hard about how you can weave these occurrences into your answers. This is also your chance to smile, to say something funny or even self-effacing, and lighten up the moment.

YOUR FIRST JOB

Starter jobs begin with traditional childhood and youth jobs, such as delivering newspapers or cutting a neighbor's lawn or walking their dog. Parents should encourage their children to try these jobs and hopefully keep at them until they become habitual and more and more rewarding. They will give these kids a good foundation for what's to come later.

Moving up to the high school level should expand the options to include babysitting, house painting, and all kinds of endeavors, depending on one's creativity and sense of entrepreneurship, which we will discuss in chapter 7.

Opportunities and connections can lead to permanent summer jobs, such as camp counselor, landscaping, construction work, or a waiter or general kitchen worker.

By the time millennials reach college, networking and seeking mentoring relationships will play a significant role in determining what type of part-time job they will seek.

Once you reach the level of postcollege education, the job hunt becomes much more serious. By that point, a graduate either seeks employment based on their previous internships or a college major. Serendipity can play a major part in the decision, such as when an unusual opportunity that is unrelated pops up, triggering an entirely new way of looking at the job market.

FOLLOWING A CAREER PATH

The concept of following a career path is certainly more different today than ever. Benjamin Franklin started working at age twelve and served for many years as an apprentice to his brother, who owned a printing company. Can you imagine anyone doing something like that today?

The average tenure for millennials with their first job out of college is two years, and then they change jobs four times during their first decade out of college. That's nearly twice the rate of the previous generation. College grads today don't just change jobs; they often jump into entirely different industries.

The biggest job changers work in the fields of media, entertainment, government, and nonprofits. Millennials who remain in their position the longest are usually employed in industries such as manufacturing and oil.

According to Guy Berger, the LinkedIn economist who analyzed the career trajectories of 3 million college graduates, "a college degree used to slot you into a 40-year career. Now it's just an entry-level point to your first job."[17]

If that remains the norm, which is debatable, considering the upheaval we've experienced over the past year or two, courtesy of COVID-19, then it might be advisable to work for a large reputable company, which will add credibility to your résumé. Hopefully, by the time you are age twenty-five to twenty-seven years old, you will have a clearer direction for the next phase of your life.

Of course, everyone must follow their own career path. I learned this while watching two of my children navigate their way through decades in the job market. As two young men with MBAs they earned in their early twenties, both of my sons took different routes. One was president of a $200,000 investment club in college, who later worked for four different investment firms before becoming a partner in a fifth investment firm. While he changed companies several times over three decades, he stayed in the same profession. My other son started his postgraduate working life selling office copiers, mostly to law firms in Boston. He moved on to selling payroll services for ADP, before settling in as a sales executive for three large accounting firms, the most recent as director of risk assurance at PwC, the largest accounting firm in the world. Individually, they took different routes in their working lives, but they were equally successful.

THE WORLD OF INTERNSHIPS

Starting in high school, progressing into college, and tapering off after college, internships can set the tone for your future career choice and subsequent job offers. In some cases, internships will turn into job offers. Even when they don't, they are worthwhile because they help you gain exposure to different careers and offer a real behind-the-scenes look at what those careers really involve. Committing to a part-time situation or an intensive summer position can be very instructive on many levels. This exploration can be invaluable, as it may lead to a job or perhaps it will show you exactly why you do not want to pursue a certain career. In either case, internships are excellent résumé builders and will help you develop relevant skills for a job you may later be seeking.

To take full advantage of the internships a company offers, especially one you are drawn to, write a letter to the appropriate person in that company, stating how you heard about the job opening. Mention your relevant qualifications and why you would be a good fit. Additionally, include your résumé, showing similar hard skills for the job at hand, including your familiarity with the various relevant software programs.

Internships provide valuable work experience and enable you to research the company, providing important knowledge for the subsequent interview process, which inevitably will prove your ability to transition into a specific job opportunity. Although there is greater corporate demand for internships, companies are willing to accommodate interns to benefit them so it aligns with their coursework.

As a potential intern, one should focus on desirable companies, but beware of how they usually operate. Large companies funnel everything through their online job postings and Human Resources department. It would be wise to consider the realities of today's job-seeking process, which includes working one's network and trying to make personal connections. This is the most realistic and accessible approach I can recommend.

Mobile devices have now become an integral part of the job-seeking process. A recent report in Glassdoor showed that 45 percent of millennial job seekers prefer to use their cell phones to search for jobs and they are willing to conduct that process at least once a day. It's no secret then that, if a company fails to create an easy, mobile application process, they can expect millennial job seekers to search elsewhere.[18]

Your options are good in this respect, as there are new apps popping up all the time. That said, I suggest you search for the newest apps that are being used. Be careful with this because apps are always changing.

I see millennials making several mistakes when it comes to applying for internships, especially waiting too long to apply. I suggest you apply six months in advance of your desired start date.

Customize your request.

While it's much easier to use a generic application, what's the point? No one wants to be anonymous or feel as if they are being taken for granted, including those in charge of hiring at a company. Target your approach to a specific person whenever possible and focus on a specific position. Mention any previous internships you have held as well as extracurricular activities.

In the important cover letter if applicable, you should mention that you possess skills and requirements that the employer is seeking, especially those aspects that pique your interest because they align with your coursework. Some colleges offer full course credit with a corresponding three-month internship.

Nonpaying internships yield serious work experience, which enhances your résumé and establishes a network of professional contacts who can be helpful after graduation. Most internships are nonpaying, but many of them will pay off later.

Unpaid internships are in decline across the United States. The National Association of Colleges and Employers (NACE) reports that the percentage of students working unpaid internships fell from 50 percent in 2012 to 43 percent in 2017. Overall, however, internships have grown. NACE did another survey that year, which showed that nearly two-thirds of the graduates they asked said they had an internship at some point while they were in school, a number 10 percent lower than ten years earlier. Internships, including unpaid ones, have long been considered valuable opportunities to gain relevant work experience, network with professionals in your field, and build your résumé while working toward a degree.[19]

Unpaid internships have been criticized for exploiting young people and putting students from less wealthy families at a disadvantage, as they are less likely to be able to afford to work without pay. The criticism has prompted more companies to offer paid internships, but companies in popular areas, such as the media, publishing, and the arts, can often still get away without paying, leading to a less diverse workforce.[20]

THE ULTIMATE GOAL FOR INTERNSHIPS

Obtaining a worthy, self-supporting job of your choice soon after graduation is certainly a top goal for an internship program. A survey study on internships conducted by recruitment software specialist iCIMS showed that two-thirds of 2019 college grads completed at least one internship before graduating.[21]

From my point of view, which you may take with a grain of salt, an ambitious millennial seeking an expectant starter job out of college should have multiple internships throughout their education life span. If a millennial repeats their internship with a large company, they will undoubtedly help rookie interns and can designate themselves as a "staffer" on their résumé or designate their position as an "assistant" instead of as an "intern." Let's point out here that embellishing a résumé is *never* a good idea, and it *will* catch up with you sooner than later.

In *The Ultimate Guide to Internships,* Eric Woodward says, "most young people leaping into today's job market have two things: a niche and career capital."[22]

The definition of career capital is to know everything about something and that you can offer greater value in a particular area. Career capital offers rare and valuable skills, connections, and credentials.

For those seeking an internship, one method is to call the Human Resources person and ask, "Do you have an internship program?" If you are an undergraduate in college, inquire whether the institution has a career center.

As starter jobs out of college become more and more competitive, internships for millennials become increasingly important because in most cases relevant experience trumps one's GPA. What have you done in the real world? Achievement in the classroom is all fine and good, but potential employers are often more swayed by your track record in the workforce, even as an intern.

The challenge in this regard is getting the word out to likely employers, which is often accomplished by effective networking.

According to Google, 60 percent of interns nationwide are unpaid. Those interns who are paid average $12.88 per hour. An intern attending MBA school is paid more to gain valuable experience, plus they will occasionally receive university credit.

An intern plays a supporting role by assisting, earning, and growing in knowledge and performing clerical duties, such as writing memorandums, filing, drafting reports, and creating PowerPoint presentations. Additionally, experienced interns will talk to clients, email, and organize events and, depending on how experienced the intern is, shadow.

During the academic year, the intern will work ten to twenty hours per week and forty hours during the vacation period. Internships will last from ten to twelve weeks. The Fair Labor Standard Act specifies that employment must be temporary to be an intern, but an intern is not considered an employee. The government rationale is that an intern would displace a paid employee. For the employee, however, past relevant internships are a plus.

In applying for an internship, the résumé summary should show that the internship position is relevant to one's background and/or college major. Internships are a way to create a vocational plan during the postundergraduate period or to leverage potential job opportunities. Many college graduates attend graduate schools, unless they are mandatory for a certain profession, to decide what type of job they should seek or to avoid the stigma of being unemployed. Graduate school can be expensive at around $50,000 a year and a loss of two years of productive employment at $50,000 per year, totaling $200,000.

KNOW YOUR SWOT!

While you are in college, especially before you begin your last two years, it is important to do a thorough self-analysis so that you can determine your strengths and weaknesses. This process, originally designed for companies to look within, is commonly known as SWOT, which stands for strengths, weaknesses, opportunities, and threats. Through a series of questions and situational problem solving, you can determine your best tendencies and the areas where you probably need work.

For example, if you are not detail oriented, then a career as an accountant, attorney, or engineer would not be recommended. If you are gregarious, well spoken, and a solid organizer, then a vocation in sales or as a teacher would be a possibility.

I recommend that younger millennials start the thinking process early when it comes to determining what type of career and/or job they should pursue in preparation for the journey to find their "calling," or vocation.

Start by gathering a team of peers to help you with the process, and you may even schedule a time to do this for each other, one or two hours at a time. That's all you need to get started, and it should be fun. Make sure you choose your peers wisely and try to have people who know you but are not your best friends.

Experiment. Brainstorm ideas and encourage everyone to share their ideas. Once you do that, create a ranking system, using some form of a voting process.

Then, it's time to begin asking the questions to determine your strengths and weaknesses. Keep it light. After all, this is not meant to be a therapy session, and you certainly don't want to get into a situation that creates conflict. That said, be honest with each other and, ultimately, about yourself. The whole point of this exercise is to help each other determine a reasonable path to follow in your early stages of searching for a career.[23]

By the way, the word *vocation* is derived from the Latin word *vocar*, which means "to call," as in the religious sense, as there often is a calling to priesthood.

As a young person, ask your elders about their work, motivations, and ambitions to determine whether any of these explanations lights a spark of interest for you to personally pursue. Read biographies of businesspeople and newspapers for current events. Try new endeavors by getting out of your comfort zone. Even iconoclastic leaders, such as Lincoln, Edison, Ford, and Truman, experienced initial failures.

Today, there is no set way that one finds a lifelong career or job. In fact, the concept of lifelong employment is probably a relic of the past for many people. We could say that the process to secure an ultimate career is really what's important, as each of you will need to carve out your own individual journey.

When it comes to this journey, "Know thyself" is my best advice.

KATIE'S KORNER

In the spring of your senior year in undergraduate school, when you're applying for your first postgraduate job, it can feel like an impossibly steep hill to climb. For many, your job résumé may read something like summertime ice cream scooper, weekend babysitter, and occasional odd jobs and . . . oh yeah . . . with a newly earned but untested bachelor's degree.

How does a résumé like that convince a potential employer that they should hire you? Even if *you* know that you've got potential and are worthy of a job, if there's little substance on your résumé or in your cover letter, it's a daunting process applying for a first job out of college. At a time when having a bachelor's does less to distinguish you from the crowd than it used to, every little boost to your job search counts. This is where a summer internship comes into play. Internships, whether they're paid or unpaid, allow you to begin to put what you're learning in the classroom into practice; gain some realistic job skills (the kind they don't teach in the classroom); and, most important, build your professional network.

What I am not trying to argue is that you must know someone inside a company or organization to be hired. I have found that, by having a wider network of professional connections, you are more likely to learn of potential job opportunities. In a world of online job postings, endless digital applications, and a lack of transparency regarding hiring processes, efficiency and efficacy is key.

While going to school for my bachelor's in environmental science and policy, I interned one summer with a statewide land trust that hired a couple of interns to help their team of conservation stewards and horticulturalists during the summer months. We did everything from weeding gardens to maintaining hiking trails.

This was far from what I aspired to do with my career, but it was in the right field and in the right geographic location. The internship program allowed us to meet professionals who worked for similar organizations in the local area. I always made sure to follow up after meeting these other professionals either by getting their contact info or finding them on Facebook or LinkedIn. When I found out that there was a local group of conservation professionals who got together once a month for drinks, I made sure to start showing up and reinforcing those connections.

Sure enough, in the spring of my senior year, one of the contacts I'd made during that summer internship passed along an email about a job opening with her company, the largest worldwide conservation organization. She did not "get me the job," as she had no direct connection with the hiring manager, but she proactively passed along information that led to my first job out of college.

This pattern, of knowing someone who passes along information about a job within their own organization, is how I went on to find the next three out of four jobs. In turn, I've also played the opposite role by passing along information about job opportunities to people I know who are a good fit for a particular role.

This is a big part of the professional culture, from the first job out of college all the way to the C-suite. The sooner you get a jump start on building your professional network, the easier it will be to get that first job out of college.

CHAPTER 4 REVIEW

When it comes to starter jobs postcollege, unlike a period during the 1950s or later in the 1970s, summer vacation was a time of sunbathing and swimming. Not anymore! Getting a starter job is serious business, beginning with summer jobs in high school and graduating to internships in college and after college.

Let it be said that experience trumps scholastic grades, especially if the internships focus on your college major or concentrates on STEM and/or business courses. Students nowadays are taking 46 percent of their college courses in the latter two disciplines. Ideally, if one is interested in working for consumer product companies, one would benefit with an internship with a company like Procter & Gamble, aka the iconic brand producer.

Finding a starter job is not easy by any means. Searching online for an internship is too impersonal, so utilizing a college career center for referrals can be a good option and establishing personal connections with recommendations is even better still.

Emily's case study is one to emulate, as she worked her way through college in a near record time of three years to save money. She landed a job at PwC and rented a place with her boyfriend, but then they moved in with their parents together to solidify their savings and get a leg up on their future.

This chapter explained the *process* of obtaining a worthy starter job, which is so important when it comes to setting a benchmark for future employment and a strong message of one's work ethic. Interestingly, many companies end up hiring their interns for permanent jobs.

5

LANDING THE RIGHT JOB FOR ANY STAGE IN YOUR CAREER

Since the job market for millennials continues to be challenging, let's explore several solutions, which may alleviate certain obstacles you could be facing. Whether you are an applicant or an employer, we have your point of view in mind.

When it comes to landing the right job, how do you define what's "right" for you? As we explored in chapter 4, there are numerous considerations for everyone, depending on your age, experience, strengths, and weaknesses. You can find advice from family, friends, teachers, advisors, and career counselors, but the final arbiter is you.

What's right for *you*?

When you project the various stages of your working life, whether it's in one career or a combination of different ones, how do you see yourself? Your answer will probably depend on several factors and may easily change as you move from one phase of your life into another.

Some data may help you find an initial perspective.

The *Harvard Business Review* examined what graduates might expect after securing a semipermanent job, which they believed to be their initial career choice. According to the feedback they received during their research, they estimate that 44 percent of their graduates will move up the career ladder of their choice; 25 percent will move to a different company within a relatively short time; 22 percent will start their own company, and the other 9 percent will do something else entirely unrelated to their degree.[1]

Of course, this all depends on what your initial career move may be after you complete an undergraduate degree. For some, that single piece of paper may be their ticket to the job of their choice. For others, it's just a launching pad for graduate school.

In *U.S. News & World Report*, reporter Ilana Kowarski wrote in March 2020, "Although in rare instances it is possible to get into an MBA program immediately after college, that is not the typical route. Most MBA hopefuls need to gain work experience in order to become competitive candidates for business school, some admissions experts say."[2]

Stacy Blackman, president of Stacy Blackman Consulting, has found that highly selective MBA programs are looking to accept individuals who are already quite accomplished in some facet of the working world. She told Kowarski that the most impressive MBA candidates are those who already qualify as "top performers" and have received "fast promotions."[3]

This might suggest a clear path for graduates with bachelor's degrees who wish to attend business school. Get a job first! Get your feet wet for a few years. Learn the ropes, make some mistakes, develop a network, and build your résumé before you get back in the classroom.

On the other hand, why not go straight into an MBA program?

It's no secret that MBAs can be pricey, but graduates command much higher salaries than they would with an undergrad degree alone.

So what should you do if you want to pursue an MBA? You can start by answering these questions to the best of your ability. How you respond should be a good indicator of where you stand now and what your next move should be. Remember, there are no right or wrong answers. There's only one determining factor—what's right for *you*.

1. Do I mind postponing my full-time career (if I'm even sure what I want it to be)?

2. Does my MBA offer hands-on learning?
3. Do I have firm career plans?
4. Will I get a good return on my investment?
5. Do I need to boost my network right now?[4]

Some college graduates work in "the real world" for several years and then move on to an MBA program. Students who focus on a business future often consider two possibilities, whether they will start a professional career right away or enroll in an MBA program. Of course, the answer to this conundrum is that there is no one-size-fits-all solution because each situation varies and MBA programs do too, which means that certain MBA opportunities may be a better fit coming right out of college than others. Prospective applicants must research what's possible for them to be sure about which program suits their needs and goals.[5]

We see certain tendencies that indicate that MBAs are the right training ground for consultancy and investment banking jobs but they are not necessarily important for start-up companies looking to attract "techy" guys and gals, not financial modeling experts.

When it comes to management consulting versus investment banking, for example, how do you know which one may be the right fit for you? When I say investment banking, I am referring to front-office advisory positions where you work on large transactions, such as mergers and acquisitions, debt issuances, equity issuances, and restructuring. As for management consulting, I mean advising management teams of large companies on strategic decision-making, such as choosing to enter a new market or how to respond to a new competitor. Naturally, there can be some overlap, depending on the position. Each path, whether it's investment banking or consulting, has a different hierarchy. Both often begin with analyst positions and move to associate titles before branching out into different ladders of promotion. It's best to survey your realistic options and create a list of arguments for pursuing either field.[6]

It all comes down to knowing yourself, a process that should begin at the undergraduate level, accelerating each year until you are able to research graduate school options that fit your personal preferences.

The Princeton Review offers good advice when it comes to considering graduate schools, whether it's an MBA or any other field of academic endeavor.

1. Know your goals and set realistic expectations of what you can expect to achieve.
2. Do specific research on job placement for the programs you're considering.
3. Identify several target organizations (i.e., places you'd be happy to work one day).
4. Understand how graduate school differs from college.
5. Know what makes a successful graduate student and assess whether you are mature enough to proceed with the immense responsibility of executing reliable productivity.
6. Determine whether an MBA will be enough or you will also need a terminal graduate degree, such as a doctorate (e.g., PhD) or terminal master's (e.g., MFA), or a nonterminal graduate degree (e.g., MA or MS).
7. Plan far ahead; the further ahead, the better. That begins with getting all your application deadlines in order and meeting them.
8. Know that there are benefits and drawbacks for both choices and weigh the pros and cons.[7]

What is the right time to go to graduate school? It is when you know you can be a successful student and make the most of your investment of time and money. This will require effective planning and taking real initiative. You'll also need to be mature enough to bounce back from disappointments and the resilience and stamina to complete a long project on your own, without much interaction or direction from faculty advisors. More than anything, you will need to be mentally ready for what often feels like the never-ending grind of graduate studies. You may not be ready yet, as you are reading this, but you can be in the future. It takes practice and commitment, of course, but you can learn to be great at anything if you devote your mind and resources to what's needed. In the meantime, you can do a good job of preparing for your future by keeping an eye on top programs. Think about where you want to go and how you're going to get there. You'll never be too old—or too young—to pursue graduate studies, and this process my turn out to be the best path toward finding your ideal career.

There is a plethora of advice for new college graduates, which can be found pretty much wherever you look. Some say to go where one can be a big fish in a small pond and have a real impact. Others advise going with a large company to build a more credible résumé.

I look at it like this: you've gotten to this place in your life through your own hard work and dedication, along with the help of many others who know you and care about you. Why not seek out their advice? Of course, I'm referring to family, friends, teachers, advisors, and career counselors, as I first mentioned. They helped to get you this far, so why not consider their advice one more time? The final choice is still yours.

I think of the legendary basketball coach John Wooden, who guided young men at UCLA for many years. His words of wisdom still ring true, and they are more than apropos for this moment.

"If you want to go fast, go alone. If you want to go far, you need a team."[8]

ASSORTED CHALLENGES

Let's go back to the pivot point that all college graduates face once they have their diploma in hand. For that matter, this moment should arrive weeks, if not several months, before that big day comes. If you wait until May, when you're standing in a cap and gown, that might be too late for most job opportunities, especially in the hyper-competitive world we live in today.

The desire of an applicant applying for a job in the short term is to live paycheck to paycheck, just to keep money anxieties at bay, with an annual vacation and maybe an occasional splurge, like buying a relatively new car or, probably to be realistic, a plain old used one. The applicant with long-term goals desires to be ultimately debt free *and*, at the same time, build up significant savings, with retirement funds too and something more like two vacations per year and a stress-free education account for the children's future college tuition.

Many millennials work at jobs unrelated to their college major and are unable to land a fulfilling job six months after graduation. According to *Business Journal*, a report from Gallup shows that 21 percent of millennials say that they've changed jobs within the past year. Millennials are also less willing to remain in their current jobs. Half of them agree that they plan to be working at their company in a year, which means that, for businesses employing millennials, half of them do not see a future with those companies.

Since many millennials do not plan on staying in their jobs, it seems reasonable that they are pursuing new options. Gallup found that 60 percent of millennials say they are open to a different job opportunity and 36 percent report that they will hunt for a job with a different organization in the next twelve months if the job market improves.

We look at these numbers and wonder why millennials are so likely to move around. Of course, there are many factors at play here, but a central reason could be their low engagement in the workplace. Gallup has found that only 29 percent of millennials feel truly engaged at work, meaning only about three in ten are emotionally and behaviorally connected to their job and company. Another 16 percent of millennials are actively disengaged, which means they are not going to behave in a way that is beneficial for their company.[9]

This does not bode well for employers and employees and suggests that millennials may no longer have a clear career path partly because of the lack of relevant work experience because so many of them experience prolonged periods of having trouble finding relevant careers or jobs. This creates a conundrum when companies demand highly knowledgeable and flexible workers.

Recruiters placing millennials for jobs put more emphasis on the degree of difficulty of college courses than high grades as a predictor of career excellence. This is an important point to consider when choosing what courses to take beyond the requirements of your major.

College and postcollege internships can lead to full-time jobs for millennials, as we can see by the 2019 Internship & Co-Op Report released by the National Association of Colleges and Employers (NACE), which said, "70 percent of employers make a full-time job offer to interns, and 80 percent of students accept said offer; in other words, more than 56 percent of interns land a full-time job from their internship."[10]

TO GAP OR NOT TO GAP

Might this suggest taking a year or two off after graduation to pursue meaningful work before possibly going to graduate school? To gap or not to gap—is that the question? If so, consider information put out by the Gap Year Association (GYA), a nonprofit dedicated to making quality gap years more accessible to more young Americans. According to their executive director, Ethan Knight, the search-programs function on the GYA website has gone from 500 searches per month to 2,300 in the time of COVID-19.[11]

We don't know how this trend may continue, but there is still much to consider regarding the concept of taking a gap year, especially when it comes between completing your undergraduate studies and going on to a graduate program. For the record, GYA defines a gap year as "A semester or year of experiential learning, typically taken after high school and prior to career or post-secondary education, in order to deepen one's practical, professional and personal awareness."[12]

Katherine Stievater, founder of Gap Year Solutions says, "In normal times, gap years have been growing in popularity because they offer students a chance to take a break from the traditional academic cycle. Sometimes students are burned out after 12 straight years in a classroom, and the stress of balancing academics, extracurriculars, college applications and social pressures. Other students need some more time to mature before the relative independence of college life. And sometimes students have known about gap years through friends or family members and have long had a plan to take the time off to travel or experience new things."[13]

Tiffany Waddell Tate, CEO of Career Maven Consulting, has found that identifying one's core values is a major reason to take a gap year. This includes gaining clarity on academic and social areas of interest prior to beginning college or making a career pivot.[14]

Dr. Corinne Guidi, an educational consultant at Bennett International, says, "Gapping is an opportunity to go against the grain for a bit while keeping their future educational plans in sight. Deciding what to do during one's gap year should not be stressful or overwhelming. Instead, I always encourage students to reflect on things they enjoy and notice what excites them as they are researching possible jobs, internships or even virtual experiences."[15]

Of course, there are pros and cons to taking a gap year, and what could be a positive for one person may prove to be a negative for someone else. Once again, you must figure out, as best as you can, what's best for you at this point in your life.

Pros
It will make your résumé stand out.
You will meet new people and gain a broader perspective.
You will gain stories through new experiences.
You will avoid burnout after years of schooling or work.
It's a great way to learn.
It's a break from traditional education.
You will become more mature.

Cons
You will be pausing your studies or traditional job for a year.
You might get homesick.
There are financial and personal risks.
It can be expensive.
It can be stressful.
There is the potential to waste a lot of time.[16]
You will become more mature. (*joking!*)

When the Gap Year Association published its 2020 Gap Year Alumni Survey, it revealed some potentially helpful information. Here are some of the highlights:

Students who have taken a gap year overwhelmingly report being satisfied with their jobs. The highest rated outcomes of gap years include gaining "a better sense of who I am as a person and what is important to me" followed by "the gap year gave me a better understanding of other countries, people, cultures, and ways of living" and "it provided me with additional skills and knowledge that contributed to my career or academic major."

Eighty-eight percent of gap year graduates report that their gap year added significantly to their employability.

In today's work environment, people who work best with others, those denoted as having emotional intelligence (EQ rather than IQ), tend to be more successful.

Gap years often solve issues of academic burnout with healthy choices and satisfy multiple learning types.

Gap year alumni are provided with practical field experience that is applied and referenced to university learning. They develop cross-cultural understanding and competence through cultural immersion and learn creative problem solving as a form of taking any challenging situation and turning it into an opportunity.

A gap year experience offers the opportunity to create one's own version of success, to explore comfort zones and the self by doing something challenging and to increase ownership for one's own life direction.

Finally, a gap year experience helps people understand what it means to be a global citizen in an increasingly multicultural landscape.[17]

THE WORLD OF JOB HOPPING

When it comes to postgraduate options, we can see a growing list of examples of how students choose to pursue opportunities. My own four children took divergent career paths during their postcollege years, and by looking at their choices we can see how their varied and interesting journeys have all ended up with satisfactory results.

Child #1: After receiving his MBA, he has always been employed in corporate sales, selling commercial copiers with ADP, and has held positions with three major accounting firms, including PwC as director of risk assurance.

Child #2: Since his college days, including earning an MBA, he has worked for high net-worth clients in the investment business and is currently a partner in one of the firms.

Child #3: She has fast tracked from working as a ski instructor in Vermont, to becoming a state representative in New Hampshire, to owning a successful retail store for more than ten years, to working as a medical equipment salesperson.

Child #4: After more than twenty years enjoying a successful career as a teaching tennis pro, earning six figures plus annually, he also became a medical equipment salesperson.

While my children grew up in similar circumstances, they have taken different paths in their careers. I imagine that, if they had grown up in the millennial generation, they may have responded differently to the fast changes in our economy and in business in general. For example, they may have changed jobs more often, as tech-savvy millennials are doing today in a rapidly changing work environment, to embrace change and not work for a stagnant company. Many millennials do not want to wait around in a work environment where the people in charge do not support how this generation sees the world.

In fact, some would say that, while millennials and Gen Z workers are job hopping, perhaps they are not doing it enough.

Tara Sinclair, a senior fellow at Indeed, says, "There has long been this maligning of millennials as being job hoppers. I think that that's the wrong story. Job hopping is something we want to see more of."

According to a new study from IBM's Institute for Business Value, the trend of millennials moving from one job to another, seeking better pay and career mobility during the COVID-19 economy, is expected to continue into the next few years. Gallup identifies millennials as the most likely generation to switch careers and suggests that six in ten millennials are open to new job opportunities.

Gad Levanon, vice president of the Labor Markets Institute at The Conference Board, says that those in their thirties and forties are much more likely to shift jobs and take risks compared to older workers who are more established in their careers.

Sarah Stoddard, a career expert at Glassdoor, says that most millennials cite their reasons for changing jobs as a desire for mobility and higher wages, a need to feel more valued, having a more flexible schedule, having a better work–life balance, receiving more skills development, and being in a better position to negotiate salary.

Switching jobs has become more common and accepted, according to Vicki Salemi, a career expert at Monster. While new job seekers may struggle, employers are becoming more open to candidates they may not have considered in the past.

Data from Monster's Future of Work 2021 Global Outlook found that industries, including health care and hospitality, are becoming more open to graduates without previous experience in the field, while nearly half of large businesses surveyed are reporting higher acceptance of candidates living outside their geographic area.[18]

THE CASE OF JOHN SMITH

When it comes to landing the "right" job, let's look at the example of John Smith, who over a period of thirty years worked for four financial companies before ultimately landing what became the right job for him with a fifth company. He rationalized this long journey by acknowledging that sometimes change is necessary if it is to advance one's career. This is difficult to argue with, so let's see how it played out for John and what lessons you might learn from his experience.

As an undergraduate college student, John majored in economics. While reading a local newspaper, he saw an advertisement for a paid internship at Paine Webber, a well-known brokerage firm. Most internships were not paid at that time, plus it was in the field of his acute interest, investing in the stock market.

John was hired as a telemarketer telephoning potential prospects to arrange interviews with a designated Paine Webber broker. Realizing the value of working as an intern, he spent the next two summers during vacation periods working for Saddlebrook, a software company focusing on the back office of banks handling client problems. Upon graduating from college, John Smith spent two years earning his MBA at Babson College.

For the next two years, John worked at Coopers & Lybrand, a large national accounting firm, engaged with a team of five employees in tax, audit, and employee stock ownership plan assignments. Wanting to focus on being an equity analyst advising portfolio managers, John obtained a position for two years at Sun Life. Thinking he was about to make his final transition to an investment firm, the owner brought John aboard in a mentor/protégé relationship as part of the succession planning. But then the owner suddenly died, leaving the remaining management in question.

With the tragic death of John's future partner and the departure of two other key partners, John decided to work in the financial center of a large city. He joined an investment firm for four years. However, a larger firm acquired that firm and expected John to buy nonvoting stock in an entity, which turned out to be totally unreasonable.

Once again, and for the fifth time in thirty years, John changed jobs by becoming a partner of a highly regarded and experienced investment firm, where he expects to remain for the long term.

This case study is an example of someone who made a career out of a vocational specialty, which happens to be investments, even though change sometimes is necessary if it is to advance one's career.

What changes are you willing to encounter in the pursuit of a satisfying career? If you have exceptional natural talent and the necessary acquired skills, it could result in an unbeatable combination for achieving an ideal outcome for your career choice.

KATIE'S KORNER

"What's right for you?" is a key question in this chapter. Regardless of whether your career path follows a straight path or resembles more of a pinball's trajectory, there will inevitably be decisions for you to make along the way, and they can keep changing, for better or for worse, depending on your circumstances.

It's easy to get caught up in thinking that the "right" job opportunity is based on the title, the salary, and what is perceived as "success" by society. But only you know what is right for *you*, and this will often include a broader set of considerations than just title and salary.

At one point in my career, I chose to take a modest pay cut because the company I had been working for could not offer advancement opportunities that suited my desired lifestyle. The new company offered enough to make up for the pay cut in the way of potential career growth; flexible work hours and location; and on-site benefits, such as free parking, a gym with fitness classes, free coffee in the mornings, and a cafeteria with discounted meals for employees. The employee culture was also much more appealing, as it prioritized work–life balance and educational opportunities, both of which I highly value. And even with the pay cut, the salary was still enough to cover my living expenses.

So, while it may have been a sideways move in terms of title and pay, it did put me in a better position to move forward with my long-term career goals. This was hard to explain to some people (who may simply have trouble listening), and from the outside my choice may have appeared like a backward move.

However, my gut sense, after much deliberation and making a very extensive pros and cons list, was that it was *right for me*. At the end of the day, that's what matters most!

While it's good to seek outside opinions from those you respect before making a big decision, when all is said and done, you are the one who will have to get up and report to work every day. So I will share with you the words I wish someone had spoken to me earlier in my career: make the choice that's *right for you* and ignore what you imagine others may think about your decision.

CHAPTER 5 REVIEW

Times have certainly changed for millennials seeking reputable careers or jobs after college. They now realize that engaging in internships as undergraduates is a recommended pathway to securing a worthy job postgraduation. Once at a company, some will remain, while more and more seem to be moving to different companies where they can enjoy higher wages, flexible scheduling, greater work–life balance, increased vocational skills, and being more valued for their contributions.

The challenges in determining the right job vary, but they usually involve considering factors such as prior work experience, your passion, and whether an MBA program or taking a gap year is the right choice for you.

There is another option to consider: should you take a job after college to gain experience with a small company, where you may have the chance to become a big fish in a small pond, or do you opt for a job with a large company that will bolster your résumé and offer higher financial rewards while possibly sacrificing some of your health?

My advice? Even if you enroll in an MBA program, you should develop certain career plans, whether it be investment banking, analyzing potential mergers and acquisitions, or working for a start-up tech company striving for an initial public offering.

In determining the right job, consider these qualifications:

1. Competence in the field you endeavor to pursue
2. Compensation and security
3. The risk involved associated with venture capital or private equity
4. The affordability of graduate school

Finally, remember that serendipity plays a major role in your choice of career and jobs. Be open to surprises because uncanny circumstances always pop up, and an offer that seems unrelated to your plan may end up working out well. And don't forget—if one door closes, another door usually opens.

THRIVING IN THE GIG ECONOMY

Beyond the age-old definitions of a *gig* as a light ship, rowboat, or one-horse carriage, let's refer to Merriam-Webster's version of the noun *gig*, which it defines as "a job usually for a specified time; especially an entertainer's engagement," or as a verb, "to work as a musician."[1] "Gigs are what they sound like," says Linda Nazareth, an economist and senior fellow for economics and population change at the Macdonald-Laurier Institute, "assignments, contracts or part-time jobs."[2]

For our discussion in this chapter, let's say that a gig represents a single project or task, sometimes repeated in different circumstances or for a different client, where a worker is hired or "booked" or "jobbed out," often through a digital marketplace, to satisfy the growing need for work on demand. Some gigs last a day, some a week, and others may reoccur intermittently over a multiyear span.[3]

The Bureau of Labor Statistics lists the following groups among those commonly seen in the gig economy:

Performing artists, visual artists, craftspeople, graphic designers, editors, producers
Web and software designers and developers, computer programmers

Carpenters, electricians, painters, plumbers
Media creators, communications consultants, writers
Photographers, translators, and interpreters
Drivers, movers, delivery staff.[4]

Of course, the list goes on and on, and it seems to be expanding rapidly.

Merriam-Webster defines a *gig worker* as "a person who works temporary jobs typically in the service sector as an independent contractor or freelancer" and as "a worker in the gig economy," which it describes as "economic activity that involves the use of temporary or freelance workers to perform jobs typically in the service sector."[5]

Although the term "gig economy" is relatively new, these types of nontraditional work arrangements have been in existence for quite some time.

According to the *Wall Street Journal*, "The gig economy came on the heels of the 2007-09 recession, when high unemployment and stagnant wages made short-term workers relatively easy to find."[6]

The American Staffing Association conducted a study and found that 78 percent of Americans view the gig economy as a new way to label a large amorphous group of people who work independently in the workforce.[7]

According to research by economists Lawrence Katz (Harvard University) and Alan Krueger (Princeton University), gig workers enjoy freedoms that most people working in full-time positions can only fantasize about: determining their own working hours, working from home, and being their own bosses. They determined that the gig economy comprised 16 percent of all workers by 2015.[8]

ADP Research Institute reports that gig workers at American businesses have increased 15 percent since 2010. However, even as the industry grows, income seems to be shrinking as competition among the jobless increases. This has been exacerbated by conditions caused by the pandemic, which indicates that, looking forward, the gig economy is on uncertain footing. That said, it's undeniable that it also represents a growing segment of the job market.[9]

Over the past ten years, many millennials are relying more and more on the gig economy. A recent study from Upwork reported that gig workers have contributed more than $1.2 trillion to the United States economy during the pandemic alone, which represents a 22 percent increase from 2019.[10]

Business journalist Marcia Pledger writes that one reason the gig economy has expanded so rapidly is that "people tend to change jobs more frequently and many enjoy the flexibility of choosing when and where they work."[11]

There has been much written about the gig economy as a relatively new phrase to describe independent contractors who work by themselves or contract out, short or long term, in a variety of settings, including for technology companies, such as Airbnb, Uber, Lyft, Task Rabbit, and Etsy, among many others. Gig workers tend to work for one or a variety of employers like these firms. For example, an individual who sells products on Etsy by day and drives for Uber by night is considered part of the gig economy—a busy part indeed.

The foundation of the gig economy relies on flexible, temporary, and/or freelance jobs, and most of them are found online or through apps. This type of economy has advantages for workers, businesses, and consumers because it makes work a more adaptable process, bending to the changing work world and a demand for maintaining flexible lifestyles. However, the gig economy can have disadvantages too, which happens more and more as a result of eroding the economic relationships that have traditionally bound workers, businesses, and clients together.[12]

I think flexibility and freedom are the key factors, which make so many millennials feel open-minded about doing gig work. Many who graduated high school or college during the recession were getting the message that they shouldn't expect to land solid employment right away and that instead they would have to be flexible and creative about finding work and keeping it coming on a regular basis. For many people in the millennial generation, this outlook has remained, and people have learned to use this mindset to their advantage. It's become a "make lemonade out of lemons" sort of thing for many people and a practical solution to a whole new set of conditions.

Carrie Lane, a professor of American studies at California State University Fullerton, follows employment trends. "It's very characteristic of millennials to want jobs that feel meaningful," she says. "Some industry specialists say this longing to create something of their own may help explain why so many millennials want to be entrepreneurs. Traditional jobs are so insecure today, so what was supposed to be secure is changing. Many of the younger people I interviewed saw doing a whole bunch of things separately as security. They have to be this Jack and Jill of all trades."[13]

I agree, as it applies to gig workers and entrepreneurs, whom we will discuss in the next chapter. If your income comes from more than one place, you never have to worry about losing your entire income in case you're laid off from one job. If you have income from multiple sources, you can also walk away from a job that is unhealthy or unfulfilling.

"IT'S THE *NEW* ECONOMY, STUPID"

This quote became famous during the 1992 presidential campaign between then President George H. W. Bush and candidate Bill Clinton, whose chief strategist, James Carville, famously reminded his team in the campaign war room about what their priority needed to be if they wanted to get elected. Well, it worked, and the Clinton time ushered in several years of a thriving economy. Less than three decades later, in May 2020, the US Labor Department announced that the American economy lost 20.5 million jobs during the previous month and that unemployment rates had risen to nearly 15 percent.[14]

"The damage that we're seeing from the great coronavirus recession is traumatic," says Gregory Daco, an American economist at Oxford Economics. "It's going to take a long time before the labor market recovers to its prerecession state."[15]

How will this affect millennials and their participation in the gig economy, as workers and consumers?

In *Thriving in the Gig Economy*, author, mentor, and entrepreneur Marion McGovern points out that millennials are becoming the largest and fastest growing part of the gig economy and, as they enter the workforce, more and more boomers are retiring and exiting.

"Many millennials came of age during the financial crisis," she says, "when finding a traditional full-time position was difficult, so they migrated to independent work as a matter of course. They often worked as an intern or contract worker as an audition for a full-time role, so they developed an early familiarity with the notion of short-term gigs. As the economy has rebounded, many in this age group view the gig economy as a way to explore career alternatives. Not unsurprisingly then, 90 percent of them do not plan to stay at any one job for more than three years."[16]

While some of those jobs are generally on the low-end skill spectrum, millennials are willing to job hop to find worthwhile work, upward mobility, social responsibility, and work–life balance.

In her book *The Gig Economy: The Complete Guide to Getting Better Work, Taking More Time Off, and Financing the Life You Want*, Diane Mulcahy explains this new phenomenon in the workplace as being because of the following factors: MBA students now don't expect job security with their employer, college graduates can expect multiple jobs in their career with changes every three to five years, only one out of three employees are passionate about their jobs, and most of the job creation does not come from the Fortune 500 companies but from young businesses, such as technology start-ups.[17]

Part of the reason the gig economy was born came from workers needing two jobs to survive and take care of their families. In a 2018 personal finance report on CNBC, Annie Nova reported that nearly 70 percent of people who become "side hustlers" do so for financial reasons, including little to no savings for retirement, debt (from college loans mostly), and monthly expenses that one job won't cover. Nova was told by Kate Bronfenbrenner, director of labor education research at Cornell University, "This is not a choice. This is something being forced on people."[18]

According to Nick Holeman, a senior financial planner at Betterment, "A lot of people hit on the freedom or flexibility of it (the gig economy), but for most of the people I speak with, it's a means of income for them."[19]

We see infinite examples of folks who join the gig economy, often through necessity. For example, I know a family of modest means who lived comfortably but rarely discussed financial matters. The patriarch retired at age fifty-nine from a prestigious law firm so he and his wife could sail the Atlantic Coast. The eldest son worked for

Arthur Andersen & Son, but, when it went out of business, he became a part-time chief financial officer for small companies. Every time he went on an extended sailing cruise, he returned to find out that his clients did not need his services anymore, for a variety of reasons that did not reflect on his ability as an executive. As a result, he and his wife became American Sail Association certified instructors and taught novices how to sail yachts. The youngest son had been a college athletic coach and then a high school teacher. Being a nonconformist and full of an entrepreneurial spirit, he became a tutor for high school students, specializing in SAT and ACT examinations. In the summer, he worked as an assistant tennis pro at the local country club. Without any family obligations, he maintained a modest lifestyle, and, like the rest of his family, they maintained independence.

This family shows how gig work, while not in any original plans for some, can turn out to be the best remedy for taking care of finances while also satisfying the needs of one's personality and indulging a passion for out-of-the-box interests.

BREAKING DOWN THE GIGS

Millennials have embraced a changing economy where the workforce is increasingly mobile, often without a permanent office (even more so now after COVID) and where the goal is to achieve a work–life balance in a role that provides a sense of purpose and value. This also means that it has become customary to change jobs frequently.

In a survey by Intuit on self-employment and gig economy trends, the gig breakdown by vocations was as follows:

Healthcare/homecare, 47%
Skilled trades, 16%
Arts, 9%
Driving, 6%
Sales, 6%
Office support, 5%
Agriculture, 3%
Education, 2%

Information technology (web design, etc.), 1%[20]

Another survey, conducted by Deloitte Insights, which examined more than a decade of data and research collected on millennials entering and exiting the gig workforce, found six notable trends:

1. The proportion of women in the millennial alternative workforce is shrinking, possibly because more millennial women than men are going back to school.
2. The proportion of household income millennials receive from alternative work is increasing.
3. Most alternative millennial workers make less than their traditional full-time employed counterparts.
4. Millennial alternative workers are often supported by someone else in their household.
5. Alternative millennial workers are more likely to find jobs in the arts, maintenance, and administrative professions.
6. Alternative millennial workers appear to be more likely to break the rules, have emotional agility, and work hard.[21]

They also found how a variety of millennials with college experience and those who do not have college experience took part in the gig economy and how this differs by gender.

No degree: Men, 61% Women, 45%
Associate degree: Men, 8% Women, 8%
Bachelor's degree: Men, 21% Women, 34%
Graduate degree: Men, 11% Women, 13%[22]

WHY PEOPLE GIG

It was Uber that really brought the "gigster" classification into the forefront. Uber started in May 2010 and benefited immediately from the influx of smartphone usage. According to a 2016 report in *TIME* magazine, at one point Uber was the fastest growing start-up with also the highest valuation for a private, venture-backed company.[23]

In a very short time, Uber disrupted the traditional taxi industry, went public, and now has a presence in more than seventy-five countries and 650 cities worldwide—and counting. It has encountered a lot of pushback everywhere and has come under fire for how it treats its drivers. This reminds us of the downsides of gigging, especially when gigantic companies, such as Uber, take advantage of their independent contractors. In most cases, companies like Uber offer no benefits, such as health care or a retirement plan.

Despite this, for many people working in the gig economy represents participating in a free-market sense of liberalism and an intentional way of life. For others, gigging is a source of supplemental income while they seek a permanent job or recover from being laid off.

It is not uncommon for recent college graduates, maybe as many as half, to take as much as six months to nail down a reasonable paying job. This economic insecurity forces younger millennials into low-paying jobs, such as in the food service industry or working as a landscaper or substitute teacher.

Then, there are those high-end paying gigs, such as an independent consultant for smaller businesses, where one can charge $100 to $250 per hour, or a freelance writer/editor or a web designer. There is obviously no shortage of gig economy companies, as shown by this remarkable statistic: in 2019, Staffing Industry Analysts reported that world spending on gig jobs reached a massive $4.5 trillion![24]

When it comes to companies running on freelance talent, here are the top fifteen currently doing their thing here in America and globally as well.

1. Airbnb (12,000+ employees across the world)
2. Amazon Flex (the e-commerce giant's delivery arm)
3. Cabify (an Uber company)
4. Care.com (for certified caregivers and home service providers)
5. Etsy (for artists and handicraft professionals)
6. Figure Eight (for professionals looking to contribute to artificial intelligence and machine learning projects)
7. Fiverr (for professionals in technology and media sectors)
8. Onefinestay (for luxury homeowners looking to monetize their properties)

9. Shipt (for personal shoppers looking for flexible schedules)
10. Talkspace (for licensed therapists and psychotherapy professionals)
11. TaskRabbit (for a wide variety of home services providers)
12. Tongal (for experts in the media and entertainment sector)
13. Uber (for licensed drivers across the world)
14. Wag! (for people who love dogs and want to turn it into an income source)
15. Share Now (for licensed drivers to benefit from car sharing)[25]

Hourly rates vary widely, from minimum wage to high end. At rates bona fide professionals can charge, $100 per hour translates into $800 per day, or $80,000 per year, assuming a person works 100 days of billable time (and takes a *lot* of time off). At $250 per hour, which more people are charging if they're worth it, that translates into $2,000 per day, or $200,000 per year, based on 100 days of billable time. Since the pool of workers is so fluid and constantly changing, it's difficult to find any records of exactly how many freelancers are consistently making this type of money, but anecdotally, at least, we can see that more and more are doing well in this expanding economy.

These high-paying jobs in the gig economy are more suitable for older millennials who have had relevant experience before they can represent themselves as a virtual accountant or bookkeeper. This is the biggest challenge: marketing or networking to build a positive reputation and client base. These types of workers also need to provide for their own health insurance and retirement savings. On the flip side for consultants, they can expense many items, such as home office deductions, car mileage, and health care premiums on their tax returns.

BIGGEST CONCERNS WITH THE GIG ECONOMY

It is difficult to predict the future of the gig economy, which affects the millennial generation. There are various conflicting views on this workplace phenomenon. On the one hand, 85 percent of college applicants say that getting a "good job" is their primary motive for going to college.[26] And yet, one out of four college grads are underemployed, have jobs that do not require a college degree, and are living with their parents.[27]

Those enamored with the gig economy can seek a multitude of online listings, but most postings include low-paying jobs, such as delivery or Uber drivers. Another factor to consider is that a high-earning gig worker in anything skill specific needs to begin acquiring these skills at an early age and learning those skills may often require working for free or little pay in an internship. This is unfair to those who come from lower-income families and might not be able to dedicate ten to twenty hours a week to working for free.

Gig workers who will thrive in the future with moderate to good pay will have sophisticated computer or mechanical skills and an established clientele and be conversant with the technical advances.

Here's a central question that any gig worker must ask: Is the job a bridge to something better or a job trap with little to no chance of growth?

In general, the number of contingent workers in this country is substantial, maybe close to 30 percent, or 44 million, but the growth is slowing, according to a 2018 J. P. Morgan Chase Institute Report, which showed that over half of the gig workers were in the transportation industry and that incomes in that sector were falling.[28]

For millennials who are married, it is strongly advisable that one spouse be securely employed by a significant employer that provides benefits, such as paying into social security, pensions, medical insurance, and a 401(k) retirement program. This is especially important for those couples who wish to obtain a loan or mortgage from a bank to purchase a home because of the inherent lack of job security that a gig worker may represent to those institutions.

That said, gig work could be an ideal situation for couples with children who can't afford childcare. One spouse can work full-time, while the other could drive for Uber or another similar company, based on their spouse's or children's daily schedule. They might also find work they can do at home, even while looking after their kids. The pandemic has showed that more and more families are making this happen, despite the many obstacles it presents and the traditional corporate benefits, which are lacking, such as worker's compensation, unemployment insurance, vacation pay, and sick days. Likewise, there is no human resources support, no supervisors to give feedback, and no one to ensure that payments are correct and made on time.

According to the Pew Research Center, there are approximately 44 million independent workers and another 26 million "considering" working as independent workers, which translates to roughly 20 percent of the economy, and it is growing at 16 percent annually.[29]

This shows that the gig economy, with all its challenges, is quite popular among millennials and other generations too. Does this mean that eventually most of our economy will compromise gig work?

MORE CONSIDERATIONS

While there are many positive aspects to the gig economy, and we must also recognize its absolute necessity in some situations, young millennials should be particularly aware of the shortcomings that it represents.

More than two-thirds of large US consumer products companies are currently outsourcing some portion of their workforce, according to a 2020 PricewaterhouseCoopers Retail & Consumer Industry Practice report. Overall, consumer products companies expect the size of their workforce will decrease by an average of 3.4 percent over the next year, which can be attributed to deep cutbacks by several large companies and caution stemming from rising energy prices. Only 50 percent are planning to increase their workforce, while 20 percent of those surveyed expect a net reduction.[30]

This seems to suggest that gig workers will remain in demand for the foreseeable future. But is that the best way for you? Besides the unstable earnings facing young millennials as they try to establish their financial worth, working in the gig economy could potentially stall your career advancement—at least on paper, as it relates to your résumé—while still providing lots of valuable job experience. The question is how to present that experience in a way that is beneficial. Maybe our society needs to see more value in the experiences of gig workers, especially those who might be more developed in their skillset than those traditionally employed in one long-term job.

One more consideration for a gig worker is the self-employed tax obligations, which come through this type of work. If a person is employed by a company, the employee and the employer pay into social security and Medicare. When you are self-employed, you must set it up differently, which all depends on whether you are a sole proprietor, "doing business as," running an LLC, or functioning as an S-corporation. I suggest you consult with an accountant who can help you set up the appropriate system for your situation.

The gig economy has triggered a decline in unionization; some people would say this is good, and others would call it the downfall of the middle class. It is no coincidence that the decline of America's middle class coincides with the decline of union membership (35 percent in 1954, 20 percent in 1983, and 10 percent in 2019). This decline will continue until organized labor makes a comeback.[31]

The gig economy fills a void for many in the millennial generation. This is because many are unsettled, either unemployed or *under*employed, or they wish to change jobs frequently for the experience or even take a pay cut to take a socially responsible job.

For some, the gig economy is the only way to satisfy a higher calling.

Charles Duhigg et al. in an article in the *New York Times Magazine*, "What Makes a 'Good Job' Good?" said, "What is important is whether a job provides a sense of autonomy, the ability to control your time and the authority to act on your unique expertise. Workers want to feel that we're making the world better, even if it is a small matter."[32]

Of course, we all want to improve conditions within the gig economy, which would make it more stable and equitable for everyone. We must strive to protect gig workers especially because it seems inevitable that we are shifting more and more toward a comprehensive gig economy. With that in mind, what does our society need to do to catch up with this new model because in the final analysis there is a much-needed place for the gig economy for the millennial generation. What will you do about your potential role in this endeavor?

KATIE'S KORNER

Is the gig economy well suited for those with the right disposition? For some, it may be too unpredictable, with a lack of guaranteed or known annual income, company benefits, etc., but for others, the flexibility may be exactly what they prefer.

I live in a relatively rural area where the sheer volume of available jobs is much less than in an urban area, so I see many people working two or more "gigs" around town that allow them to live where they want and maintain the lifestyle they desire. They are essentially placing a higher priority on geographic location and quality of life over a particular job and salary. Not everyone wants to be sucked into the "rat race" that comes with living in a big city.

With some gig-style jobs, remote work is possible. Given the changes in society and the workplace due to the pandemic, will we see a rise in millennials placing higher value on working from home with flexible hours? Will that impact the gig economy? Only time will tell.

While I can't see myself driving for Uber or managing an Airbnb, I could see the possibility of taking my expertise and applying it to a consulting gig. I believe I could make that work because I am organized, can manage my own work independently, can effectively plan to line up future work, and know the value of my work and am not afraid to charge for it. Many people undervalue their time and expertise, which is a challenge for those I've seen who have tried their luck with consulting.

When it comes to speaking about what it's like to live the daily life in a gig economy, let me introduce Meghan McEnery, who lives and works in Los Angeles, which some may call the birthplace of the gig economy.

Meghan

Some afternoons, while I sit at my kitchen table editing, I can hear my neighbor Steve, across the alley, playing saxophone. His music is sad and soulful and makes our corner of the neighborhood feel like the 1930s. Sometimes, Steve is practicing for a studio session with a band, where he will record his saxophone arrangements and will be paid an hourly rate; sometimes he is scoring an episode of a TV show, which he'll sell for a flat fee. He also writes music just for himself, and he performs those songs at bars and venues around the city.

When I take a break from editing in the afternoons to go outside and water the plants, he steps out onto his patio and updates me on the progress of his projects that day.

I'm always comforted by both the sound of the saxophone and the presence of my neighbor nearby. Although our work is completely different, our careers have something in common: we're both freelance workers and have shaped our lives around a gig economy.

Steve—out of sheer proximity and a similar schedule—is the closest thing I have to a coworker. We both have ever-changing networks of clients and collaborators—some whom we have worked with on and off for years and some with whom we work for only a day or two. But I find the most stability in my workdays when I hear Steve's saxophone and know that he is working too.

I never planned to be a freelance worker. I moved to Los Angeles after grad school and began editing a variety of subjects so that I could support myself during the months I'd have to be unemployed to move across the country. Throughout college and grad school, and the years in between, I took on small copyediting jobs to make extra cash. Plus, I'd done a few internships at magazines in my early twenties, so I had some idea of how freelancing worked.

At first, editing was just a means to an end while I searched for full-time employment. But with each new project, I learned a new skill or met a new client with whom I connected, and this opened my eyes to new opportunities. I shifted to developmental editing, which allowed for more creativity and gave me a chance to apply the knowledge I'd learned in my MFA program. I began to truly love the work, and I slowly realized I already had the full-time job I'd been searching for—right here in my own apartment.

What I love most about my work is how specifically it's shaped around my experiences, skillset, and values. I work with writers in many different capacities: as a dramaturg, a teacher, a tutor, a consultant, an editor, and a fellow writer. I love to find the commonalities between all these roles. Teaching workshops, for example, has a lot of similarities to developmental editing, and working as a dramaturg has helped me understand how to approach a novel deep in development. What I learn from one type of job ends up being applicable to others in ways I never would have guessed. This helps me to keep growing and makes my work feel fulfilling.

There are some major drawbacks to the gig economy. It's unpredictable, full of rejection, and, when a project is confusing or frustrating, there's never a supervisor to turn to for support. You spend a lot of time doing work you don't get paid for—like teaching yourself new skills or looking for clients. There are dry spells, higher taxes, and no benefits. But ironically, freelance work has provided my life with more stability than I would be able to find in a traditional desk job. I'm able to shape my work around my life, and I know that, even if I move to a new city in the future, I won't have to start over again in a new job.

Los Angeles is a city of gig workers. The actors, musicians, writers, comedians, production assistants, photographers, designers, cinematographers, makeup artists, and choreographers who make up the film industry are mostly gig workers. These freelance workers also tend to have side hustles that are gig jobs as well, like actors who sign up for single-day catering shifts when they need to bring in some extra cash or photographers who drive for Lyft because they can create their own schedule based around their photography shoots. These jobs might not always treat gig workers fairly, and oftentimes the obstacles involved in doing this type of work makes it unsustainable. But many people are willing to make that trade to prioritize the work they are truly passionate about.

Steve is not my only neighbor who is a freelance worker. In my building, the woman living in apartment five is a hairstylist who styles hair for music videos. She's hired for each gig in the same way that a musician is hired for an event, and she also rents a chair in a salon four days a month for added income. The guy in apartment three does voiceover work and auditions for each job before he's hired. He drives for Uber whenever he goes through a dry spell.

Across the street from us is a freelance cinematographer who works on a different project each week and edits his footage from home. Sometimes, when he gets tired of editing his videos and my brain is no longer able to spot typos in a copyediting assignment, we'll meet outside and walk to the donut shop for an afternoon snack. Although I don't have coworkers to share victories and failures or to joke around with during lunchbreaks, I'm still able to find community in my work because I'm surrounded by so many people whose careers are structured similarly. I value this just as much as I value getting to do work that I love.

CHAPTER 6 REVIEW

What is it about someone's personality that makes them an ideal candidate for freelance work? It might be adventurous energy, a willingness to jump into the unknown, or great people skills. If you are considering the gig economy, you would be wise to answer these questions about yourself so you can assess whether you are a good candidate. Or you could just take a risk and try it!

ADVICE FOR ENTREPRENEURS

While many millennials have a strong desire to become entrepreneurs, most successful founders of companies are older and have been working in the business world much longer. Sure, we see flashy profiles of young men and women launching start-ups, and there seems to be a general perception that entrepreneurs are all twenty- or thirty-something college dropouts, but this is largely a fallacy.

Yes, Steve Jobs dropped out of college, and so have several other one-of-a-kind "geniuses." But, for the most part, entrepreneurs complete at least one level of a college education, and there is no easy way to the top, no matter which celebrity biography you choose to read.

For many millennials, being an entrepreneur is the ultimate successful vocation, whether it is a start-up, a company buyout, or a venture-type investment. Obviously, there are risks associated with becoming an entrepreneur of any kind, which can result in possible failure, but, if the venture becomes successful, it can be a highly rewarding endeavor.

Peter Brooke, former founder of the highly successful Advent International, once said, "To me, success is a random event. Sometimes you'll hit it right and sometimes you won't hit it right. If a technology goes wrong, if an industry becomes irrelevant, there's nothing you can do. You've got to diversify your risk, and you've got to pick the right people in the right sectors and let them do it."[1]

RULES FOR SUCCESS

Bill Murphy Jr., a former reporter for the *Washington Post*, wrote a book called *The Intelligent Entrepreneur: How Three Harvard Business School Graduates Learned the 10 Rules of Successful Entrepreneurship*. Here are the ten rules, in a nutshell:

1. Commit first to the ideal of entrepreneurship. Successful founders commit to the ideal of entrepreneurship rather than to a single business model or product. That flexibility helps them react nimbly to market feedback, abandoning products and business models that aren't working.
2. Look for problems to solve before creating business solutions. Most entrepreneurs start by choosing the product they want to make or the service they want to provide and then try to convince the market to buy it. It makes more sense to start a business the other way around: identify what the market needs first, and then develop a solution.
3. Focus on innovation and scale. Despite what we're taught, most entrepreneurs launch businesses in unattractive, static fields and offer no competitive advantage. Clearly, the most successful entrepreneurs combine their deep knowledge of customers' needs with a commitment to achieving outsized scale and innovation.
4. Assemble founding teams with a history of working well together. Teams of two or three cofounders who complement and respect each other generally result in greater success than companies founded by individuals or those with larger teams. This is especially effective when the founders have worked together successfully before.
5. One cofounder is usually "first among equals." Notwithstanding the previous rule, usually one of the cofounders in a successful venture proves to be the outsized, driving personality.

That person's quick decisions and a deep commitment can lead to stronger performance when times inevitably turn difficult.

6. Manage risk and don't spend needlessly. Successful entrepreneurs focus on managing their risks to the point where launching a new company is not much riskier than most other choices they could make and where the risk-adjusted return is higher.

7. Learning to lead requires a lifelong effort. Most entrepreneurs aspire to grow their small start-ups into large ventures, but different team sizes require different kinds of leadership. The most successful entrepreneurs read books, hire executive coaches, and recognize that continually learning to lead is a must.

8. Learning to sell requires a lifelong commitment. Ethical, effective sales technique is one of the most important attributes within new ventures but also one of the least common. The most successful entrepreneurs eventually understand that sales require a balance between making compelling promises and ensuring that they can deliver on them.

9. Persistence means redefining failure. Successful entrepreneurs recognize their legitimate failures and can talk about them reflectively. That said, they also focus on overcoming, learning, and ensuring that failure is never the end of the story.

10. Time, not money, is the scarcest resource. Successful entrepreneurs sometimes get rich, but they are also deeply motivated by the desire to accomplish worthwhile things: to create, to make a difference in people's lives, and to leave a legacy for later generations. The most successful embrace entrepreneurship not just as a way of doing business but as a way of life.[2]

CASE STUDIES

During the latter part of Tom Tremblay's millennial years, after graduating with a Bachelor of Science in Electrical Engineering from Lafayette College and with an MBA from Boston University, he became an entrepreneur. Before that, he was vice president of New England Capital, a venture arm of Bank of New England, where he valued, structured, and negotiated deals. He left his employer and established a buyout company for his own purposes. He raised capital from outside investors, set up an office in the financial district of Boston, and over the next two years reviewed 275 possible acquisitions and made six offers.[3]

While the acquisition of Tom's target company closed after two years, he ran into a string of significant hurdles and delays, as the eighty-nine-year-old owner had a stroke and his son died, the bookkeeper left, and there were serious valuation differences between the owner and Tom. He mollified the owner by explaining his price adjustments for inventory and accounts receivable, the necessary rate of return, and the bank's required debt coverage.

Tom felt that with few companies really for sale the potential buyer should exercise a "full court press" and, if it appears to be a good deal, the financing will follow. This explains some of the risk involved when becoming an entrepreneur, especially in the case of purchasing an existing company. It should remind us of the value of seeking out proper mentorship and seasoned advice from those who have gone this route before and understand the risks and can offer the required expertise. While going it alone is part of becoming an entrepreneur, don't take that literally. It's vital that you assemble an effective team to pursue your business ventures.

Entrepreneurs often originate their product or service to improve an existing idea or concept. For example, let's consider the case of Herb Chambers and the genesis of his more than fifty car dealerships in New England. This began years ago when Mr. Chambers became so dissatisfied with a particular car dealership that he felt he could do significantly better by owning his own dealership. And that's exactly what he did, until he became one of the largest dealership owners in the entire region.[4]

But Mr. Chambers did not accomplish this on his own. A large part of one's financial success depends on personal and business relationships. The real challenge is originating a unique idea, preferably a large national market, building a team of talented and compatible workers, and adequately financing the venture. That said, there is not a singular path when it comes to building these ventures. Each one is unique and should be addressed that way.

When my youngest son was a millennial, living in San Diego, he was determined to open his own business, a wine bar, which would also serve tapas and assorted hors d'oeuvres. He was a wine connoisseur and quite personable. He hired a consultant to draw up a business plan for this venture and started to raise the necessary capital. As his father, I strongly advised against this project because, as a full-time tennis pro, he had no experience running a wine bar. As luck would have it, at least from my point of view, the severe recession hit us all, which coincided with problems raising the necessary capital, so the project was scrapped.

As an entrepreneur, some keys for success are to thoroughly understand the targeted industry; know one's customers, which requires seeking out customer's input; spend wisely; learn from one's mistakes; and deliver more than expected. I suppose this could be the extended version of an entrepreneur's motto, but the short and catchy version would go more like this:

Take a deep breath and jump in!

One of the first American entrepreneurs was Thomas Edison, who, over the course over his long and storied life, developed more than 1,000 patents that carried his name. Aside from his obvious intelligence, Edison was extraordinarily *curious* about almost everything when it came to how something worked or didn't work—and why.[5]

In striving to be a successful entrepreneur, Edward Land, the founder of Polaroid and the inventor of "instamatic" photographs, experienced great failure with having some of his later inventions successfully accepted in the marketplace because he wanted to be sure the projects were nearly perfect, when the ultimate products were continuously refined.[6]

These examples, from Tom Tremblay to Edward Land, show the variety of experiences any entrepreneur might encounter as they embark on whatever their business adventure might be. What impresses me about all of them, and this is a common denominator I see in nearly all entrepreneurs, is a spirit of curiosity and a willingness to take risks and even fail. Some even call this "the art of failure," which Malcolm Gladwell captured so eloquently in a *New Yorker* essay he penned in 2000.[7]

Cartoonist Whit Taylor, a rising start in the comics world, may have said it best in her comment to the National Endowment for the Arts, discussing the challenge of making art. "I think that if you want to grow in any field or improve at anything," she said, "failure is a part of the process. You can't expect to have success without some failure."[8]

I agree, and I think it is pretty much the same when it comes to any form of entrepreneurship in most any field of endeavor.

RECOMMENDATIONS FOR ENTREPRENEURS

One of the reasons there are so many aspiring entrepreneurs is that the internet has drastically changed the way business is done, and the new opportunities are widespread.

Suzy Welch, former editor of the *Harvard Business Review* and widow of Jack Welch, the famed former CEO/chairman of General Electric, feels that entrepreneurs have role models and mentors to inspire them. On her CNBC series, *Fix My Career*, Welch said that that those looking to make it as entrepreneurs need to have three things:

A crazy passion for an idea.
A burning desire to be their own boss.
A product or service that people will pay money for.[9]

Jeff Bezos, founder of Amazon, advises entrepreneurs to build a team to scale a project upward. He stresses that trusted partners must be encouraged to be bold and see every challenge as an opportunity but to disband the initiative if the idea is not working. Bezos goes on to say that entrepreneurs should leverage their strengths, build their network, and never stop networking.

Here is a list of his top advice for aspiring entrepreneurs. Obviously, any one of you reading this who is seriously interested in becoming an entrepreneur will be industrious enough to look up more information about each of these points.

1. Be stubborn and flexible
2. Stick with two pizzas

3. Never stop experimenting
4. Be willing to invent
5. Think long term
6. Tie experimentation, willingness to invent, and innovation all together
7. Present and discuss memoranda, not slide shows
8. Obsess about customers
9. Base your strategy on things that won't change
10. Identify and remove risk

Oh yes, Bezos also reminds us to "Get started now to avoid regret later."[10]

Since we're channeling the founder of one of the world's largest companies, whether you like him or not, let's also include something he said to *Business Insider* about becoming an entrepreneur, because he obviously knows what he's talking about!

> Never chase the hot thing . . . you need to position yourself and wait for the wave. And the way you do that is you pick something you're passionate about. That's the number one piece of advice that I'd give to someone that wants to start a company or start a new endeavor inside of a bigger company. Make sure it's something you're interested in, something you're passionate about. Missionaries build better products. . . . I'd take a missionary over a mercenary any day. Mercenaries want to flip the company and get rich; missionaries want to build a great product or service—and one of those paradoxes is usually the missionaries end up making more money anyway. . . . pick something you're passionate about. Start with the customer and work backwards. Those two things, passion and customer centricity, will take you an awful long way.[11]

The media is full of stories about successful entrepreneurs who have reached celebrity status through their domestic and/or global success. So what skills do these founders of companies have in common that other business leaders lack? And what distinguishes these founders from those who do not create companies?

According to Peter Cohan, who teaches strategy and entrepreneurship to undergraduate and MBA students at Babson University, there are five key skills that enable entrepreneurs to distinguish themselves from business leaders who are not entrepreneurs. These findings were culled from a survey of 1,300 Harvard Business School (HBS) alumni.[12]

1. *Identification of Opportunities*

Founders excel in skills and behaviors associated with the ability to identify and seek out high-potential business opportunities. But what makes for a great business opportunity? Cohan's interviews with hundreds of entrepreneurs revealed four tests to consider:

Does the product relieve deeply felt customer pain that other companies are ignoring?

Does the founder have a passion for doing a market-beating job of solving that problem?

Does the start-up's founding team have the critical skills to build that solution?

Is the market opportunity large enough (e.g., at least $1 billion)?

2. *Vision and Influence*

Founders have strong abilities to influence internal and external stakeholders that must work together to turn a strategy into action and gain results. Harvard researchers found that entrepreneurial leaders have more confidence in their abilities to provide vision and influence than the average leader and that leaders working within established firms rated themselves much lower.

As Cohan wrote in his 2012 book, Hungry Start-Up Strategy, "a successful entrepreneur is able to attract and motivate talent by creating what I call emotional currency, and rather than paying people more money than Google does, they offer a powerful mission which gives work at the startup much more meaning."

3. *Comfort with Uncertainty*

According to Harvard researchers, "Entrepreneurial leaders are better able to move a business agenda forward in the face of uncertain and ambiguous circumstances." You will know if you share this skill if you are willing to start a company even though you have no money, no product, and no customers *but* you do have a clear idea of what problem you are trying to solve and what your solution will look like. That's the point where successful entrepreneurs are far more comfortable living with the uncertainty needed to go from that stage to building a large company.

4. *Building Networks*

One reason for entrepreneurial founders' comfort with uncertainty is that they are good at assembling the resources the start-up needs because they can create professional and business networks that will help them realize their vision.

"Many of the CEOs I've interviewed," says Cohan, "have told me that they often find themselves not knowing how to solve problems, but they are able to get advice from CEOs who have been there before."

5. *Finance and Financial Management*

Being able to raise capital and control cash flow are essential to a successful start-up. The founders HBS surveyed were "much more confident in their skills at managing cash flow, raising capital and board governance than were non-founder alumni."

Cohan's interviews with these CEOs, which became research for a book on scaling start-ups, shows that successful entrepreneurs are great at persuading investors to write them checks. He found that "The most successful sales pitches for money emphasize the size of the market the company is targeting, the value that the company's product provides for customers, and the rapid rate at which the company is winning new customers and retaining old ones who spend more on the company's products."

He also discovered one area where founders are not as good as nonfounders: a preference for established structure. That's because entrepreneurial leaders have a lower preference for operating in more established and structured business environments and would rather, according to HBS researchers, "adapt to an uncertain and rapidly changing business context and strategy."[13]

If you think you are proficient in these five skill areas and passionate about them too, then you may be well equipped to become a successful entrepreneur.

BUYOUT AGREEMENTS

One of the biggest mistakes an entrepreneur can make is not executing an initial buyout agreement with a partner, an investor, or a principal of the business, regardless of the inception details or start-up stage.

Consider this example: Two brothers started an office service business right out of college. Trusting each other, they grew the company over several years to 500 employees with $12 million in profitable revenue. They each owned 50 percent of the company. Then, one brother left the day-to-day work to the other brother and moved out of state. The brother who left expected and received 50 percent of the profits, which were sizeable.

The remaining brother objected to sharing 50 percent of the profits. His brother insisted that he had a legal right to 50 percent of the profits as a shareholder, and he refused to budge.

There was no buyout agreement, so the working brother ended up suing the other brother for the excess monies paid out. Years later, after millions of dollars were spent on legal fees, the two settled.

It's essential to "lawyer up" when it comes to complicated buyouts because it is inevitable that you will run into many thorny issues, such as employee noncompetition agreements, confidentiality agreements, and allocation of future equity to key personnel as well as those prickly buyout agreements. Entrepreneurs should do as much due diligence on potential investors as they will do on any potential business assumptions.

Rachel Flaskey, a senior manager in the valuation services practice at Baker Tilly, a notable accounting and advisory firm, notes six considerations entrepreneurs should know about buy–sell agreements and how they affect their future.

1. They should be developed early.

2. They should include a business valuation clause.
3. They can reduce emotional impact.
4. They should include ground rules.
5. Valuation methods matter.
6. Buy–sell agreements have tax implications.[14]

GENERAL OBSERVATIONS

The popular television series *Shark Tank* often features millennial entrepreneurs, some already successful when they appear and some clearly stuck in the "wannabee" phase of their journey. Most of the show's applicants failed to receive initial financial investments, so they are looking for one or more of the sharks to do the necessary due diligence, which is often a quick math calculation between commercials, to determine whether it is worth their time and sweat equity to invest in a particular venture. This important move is what drives each segment to its climax, when the question is, will a project receive sponsorship to bring it to another level in the marketplace or will it be back to the drawing board for the aspiring entrepreneur? Finding success on that show can be very challenging.[15]

Many entrepreneurs evolve during their millennial stage in life. For example, Albert Einstein came up with $E=mc^2$, his memorable equation on special relativity, and Bill Gates and Mark Zuckerberg left Harvard after their sophomore years to pursue their ideas. However, most entrepreneurs create their ideas *after* working at another company for ten or more years.

Clayton Christensen, a Harvard Business School professor, in his book *Disruptive Innovation* explains that entrepreneurs frequently attach new markets by transforming existing types of products into affordable simplified products that are less expensive but enormously scalable in volume.[16]

The evolution of an entrepreneur's process often begins with self-funding or raising seed capital from friends and family. They will then draft an expanded business plan and raise additional money from financial "angels." After a year or so of surveying potential customers and convincing investors how the business can create value and become scalable, the entrepreneur is ready to approach venture capital funds seeking a partnership. By this time, the entrepreneur's initial ownership investment may be diluted up to an amount equaling even half of the initial funds that kicked off the venture.

David S. Rose, in his book *The Start-Up Checklist*, describes the likelihood of an entrepreneur's outcome, from its initial conception onward.[17]

Outcome	Likelihood
IPO	0.1%
Acquisition	40%
Out of Business	50%
Anything Else	9.9%

Rose goes on to mention the various sources of investments necessary to achieve the needed capital, as described here:

Founders	$25,000
Friends/Family	$25,000–$150K
Angels	$150K–$1.5M
Venture	$1.5M–$10.0M
Later Stage Venture	$10.0M–$20.0M

THREE TAKEAWAYS

An entrepreneur does not have to select a sophisticated product or service but should have a plan for rapid growth even if it is a mundane service, such as yardwork or trash collection. The three major issues included here are meant for the entrepreneur to address: preparation, confirmation, and organization.

Preparation: The entrepreneur should draft a business plan showing the recipients that they are a domain expert in that endeavor. At the top of the plan, they should show there is a growing market for the product or service. Further, the plan should show potential competitors and their profiles. Additionally, the plan should describe their experienced advisors and possible mentors, who will not only advise but add credibility.

Confirmation: In the business plan, there should be a brief survey of potential customers showing a need for the product or service and an explanation of the entrepreneurial products or service's created value and how it will be able to achieve scalability to become a much larger entity. A chain of local dry cleaners is an example of suggesting a huge potential market, but the plan may lack a demonstration of its capability to do so efficiently. In measuring possible success, the plan should include certain achievable milestones.

Organization: For potential customers, investors, and advisors, creating a simple website of the entrepreneur's business is essential for a quick and way easy to present and comprehend all necessary information.[18]

Let's conclude with a quote from Jeff Bezos, which speaks to the creativity and vision necessary to become a successful entrepreneur: "If you double the number of experiments you do per year you're going to double your inventiveness."[19]

KATIE'S KORNER

I very much respect those who choose the path of entrepreneurship. In my youth, I watched my mother start and run her own business. She had identified a gap in the local retail market and, in response, opened her own shop, which became successful enough that she eventually went on to open two additional stores across the state of New Hampshire.

What I saw was someone who had a dream, the motivation, and the commitment to grow and evolve a business to meet the changing landscape, survive the ups and downs, and create a business that thrived over fifteen years.

I also saw that being an entrepreneur is a lifestyle as much as it is a job because you never escape it on holidays and weekends. If you tire from it, you can't just quit. You carry it all—the successes and the failures.

So, from my perspective, it's more than just a job; you must be prepared to adjust your entire life to accommodate your new "baby."

It's not for everyone, and probably not for me, *but* I do know several people who wouldn't have it any other way. One of them is Max Lemper-Tabatsky, cofounder of a new company called Loyal (https://trustloyal.com), who lives and works in Santa Barbara, California. Here he is, speaking about his experience as a millennial entrepreneur.

Max

My first job out of college was much more entrepreneurial than I thought it was going to be. When I joined the consulting firm, the company was only a few years old and had about fifteen employees, with no outside funding. It had been fully bootstrapped since its inception by the cofounders. A few months after I joined, we had our first outside investment, and a year later we grew to fifty employees. Two years later, we were acquired by a public company, and when I left, after nearly four years, the company had almost 100 employees. While I was by no means leading the charge, I became a crucial part of the team.

More important, I essentially experienced a full life cycle of a startup becoming a public company to transitioning to a subsidiary. Witnessing this process unfold has helped in my current entrepreneurial pursuits.

I think that I had an advantage when I began this journey because going to a small high school and liberal arts college helped craft and enhance my social skills in ways that attending a large institution with tens of thousands of people and little to no professor interaction could not have offered. This experience has allowed me to manage teams effectively and in a personalized way, which I have not observed others do who are of my age.

The idea for our business was formed through personal and professional experience. The key driving force to become an entrepreneur, what attracted me to it in the first place, was the independence, mobility, and opportunity to pave my own path. I also was not happy working in a large institution and wanted to be my own boss, *and* I welcomed the challenge.

My cofounder, Miles, and I had no prior direct experience raising capital, so we utilized our networks for advice and connections. Individuals who work at venture capitals love to give advice and discuss what they're looking for in a potential portfolio company. They also love to read pitch decks and give their point of view on your company and story.

Using warm connections is key, as cold outreach can prove very difficult. I'd say don't just reach out to investors because you saw their name in the *Wall Street Journal*. Reach out to them because, for example, they specialize in your industry, understand the problem you're addressing, and have prior experience tackling similar issues. Do your research and utilize it when reaching out to prospective investors.

Of course, building a successful customer base is crucial. Understanding who your customers are and then finding ways to reach them is incredibly challenging. Start with understanding who they are, utilize customer surveys, focus groups, etc., and then you can start to effectively reach your target audiences through marketing.

Finding a balance between paid and unpaid media is what every start-up struggles to figure out. In the beginning, most start-ups pour all their funding into paid media channels, such as Google and Facebook ads, to reach their target audiences. However, for a company to be sustainable and not burn all its cash, you need to eventually acquire customers organically, through press coverage; partnerships; and, most importantly, word of mouth. There really is no substitute for this, and it requires patience.

The biggest risk of going down the entrepreneurial path is financial. You need to be ready to not make any money for at least a year until you get your business off the ground. If you're willing to do this, then the pluses are endless. You can be your own boss. You can build something from scratch. You have infinite learning opportunities. You can control your own schedule. You build resilience as a person, and you can hopefully succeed—all because of your doing, not as a result of others doing anything for you. When it works, this is immensely satisfying. You must learn to accept some failure along the way, but it's all part of the general learning curve. So when things work out, it feels pretty good.

Another relevant plus and minus I should add is that you can work as many or as few hours as *you* want every day. That said, I usually end up working a standard day from 9:00 to 5:00, which is much better than my prior corporate job.

On a typical day, I wake up at 7:30, work out (not always), eat breakfast, and start work at 9:00 by checking emails and going through my calendar of things to do. At 10:00, I have my daily morning meeting with my cofounder, followed by two or three calls with our manufacturers or partners. Then, I walk through sales channels with our team, have a marketing call with our ad agency, post on social media channels, conduct some business-to-business sales outreach, and typically finish up around 5:00 or 6:00.

Maintaining a work–life balance is important and should not be taken lightly.

Success for me is if I wake up every day excited by what I do, who I work with, and who I surround myself with at home. And, like I said, if I'm healthy—in mind, body, and spirit. Beyond that, if I become "successful" monetarily, I won't be upset at all.

For millennials who are considering becoming entrepreneurs, here is what I recommend: Do your due diligence to understand the challenges and the cons and the pros. Then, if you think you're ready, go for it and don't look back. Doubting yourself will not take you far.

As far as achieving goals in our goal-obsessed society, I am all for setting goals. But I don't want to jinx myself, so I am just thankful every day to be on this planet with the freedom to set my own course.

CHAPTER 7 REVIEW

Becoming an entrepreneur is probably the most exciting (and risky) vocation possible, with a big upside and an equally big downside. Many entrepreneurs have initially failed, like Henry Ford, but many ultimately become enormously successful. While we have seen young entrepreneurs excel at an extremely high level, such as Bill Gates, Steve Jobs, and Mark Zuckerberg, entrepreneurs normally put their company together in their thirties or forties. The lead entrepreneur will initially assemble a small team, designated to focus on three critical areas: operations, marketing, and administration.

Ideally, the entrepreneur will have worked with their partners and will seek raw start-ups, buyouts of exciting companies, or venture-backed projects. The modus operandi for entrepreneurs is to identify a problem, innovate a solution, and then scale the business. Financing the company's growth becomes a major hurdle. The leader of the entrepreneurial team is the driving force, while the others must be committed and persistent.

We know the expression "Failure is part of success," and we see examples of it in the stories of two of our most successful inventors. It took six years of failures before Thomas Edison perfected the light bulb. Edward Land, who invented the enormously successful instant camera, struggled with subsequent products because he refused to release them to the market unless they were perfect, which left other companies the chance to release similar products ahead of Land.

Considering all that we've covered in this chapter, do you see entrepreneurship as a viable option in your future?

Part III

MAKING YOUR MONEY WORK

As we begin the final section of the book, let me remind you of the essence of my message—helping millennials with their financial goals and budgeting techniques. Much of the advice regarding money matters probably has been overlooked by parents and academics, so this message is vital. As a millennial, my granddaughter Katie agrees, and I hope you will concur and make good use of this information.

You will find advice on paying bills on time by utilizing your bank's automated withdrawal system and covering fixed costs, such as mortgage or rent payments, utilities, insurance, and student loans. You will find out about good debt versus bad debt. There is also critical information on budgeting techniques to make your money work, including targeting amounts for an emergency fund or for your retirement savings.

What happens if you default on a student loan? Is there an easy way to check the average real estate purchase or rentals for your town or city? Keep reading, and you will find answers.

Making your money work is a real challenge. The next three chapters should answer some of your questions, as they focus on setting financial goals, budgeting, and dealing with the money aspect of marriage and family. As a millennial nearing thirty, Katie has dealt with all three of these financial challenges.

On setting financial goals, one must start with the top line, which is the annual income from one's job and other sources of revenue. These goals should reflect on whether you will initially be residing with your parents to accumulate your cash reserves or you will expect your parents to help financially with your grad school.

As a top priority, you should be aware of your credit score and how it is calculated, as it will govern the interest rates on your bank loans, car loans, or whether you will be able to get credit at all from an assortment of vendors.

The chapter on budgeting contains one of the most important messages in the entire book, particularly if your parents have not advised you on money management. The core takeaway for budgeting is to adhere to the three categories of allocation: essentials, priorities, and lifestyle. Equally important is saving for emergencies, retirement, and investing.

The chapter on marriage and family finance explains how financial harmony with a partner is a must, whether it's through sharing occupational expenses for an abode or agreeing on the usage of credit cards. Many experts agree that the number one problem in marriages is a result of conflict rising over money matters.

Having children is a blessing, of course, but it can also create a financial burden for some couples. The annual cost of raising a child is steadily rising, and there are many new considerations because of COVID-19 and the increase in millennials working from home.

Chapter 10 may give you a better chance of surviving the "seven-year itch," which is known to be the most frequent period when marriages go astray. Why not do everything you can to ensure a healthy and positive marriage?

8

SETTING REALISTIC
FINANCIAL GOALS

When it comes to imagining and then setting realistic financial goals, the millennial generation has been facing a growing list of challenges for quite some time, and they are to be highly commended for meeting and succeeding in most if not all of them.

Millennials are the most educated generation,[1] yet one-third of these college graduates remain underemployed (or unemployed), which inhibits achieving their financial goals, particularly the majority of the millennials who want to have a positive impact on society and perhaps invent something that will change the world, like Steve Jobs and Bill Gates did when they were of a similar age.

The world has been turned upside down from the immediate effects of the COVID-19 pandemic, especially younger millennials who are now graduating from college at an average age of twenty-three years old, which is delaying by one year their entry into the job market while also postponing their efforts to define and achieve their financial goals.

For example, the most popular scholastic course at Stanford University in recent years has been *Designing Your Life*, open to juniors and seniors of any major. According to instructors Bill Burnett and Dave Evans:

The course uses design thinking to address the "wicked problem" of designing your life and career. This class offers a framework, tools, and most importantly a place and a community of peers and mentors where we'll work on these issues through assigned readings, reflections, and in-class exercises. The course employs a design thinking approach to help students from any major develop a constructive and effective approach to finding and designing their lives and vocations after Stanford.

Topics include the integration of work and worldviews, ideation techniques, a portfolio approach to thriving, designing to increase balance and energy and how to prototype all aspects of your life. We also touch on the realities of engaging the workplace and practices that support vocation formation throughout your life. This is an experiential class that includes seminar-style discussions, personal written reflections, guest speakers, and individual mentoring/coaching. The capstone assignment is the creation of an "Odyssey Plan" focusing on taking action in the three to five years following your Stanford graduation.[2]

Burnett and Evans have penned two *New York Times* best sellers, *Designing Your Life* and *Designing Your Work Life*, both of which I highly recommend.[3]

Their work is inspiring and valuable for all millennials (and others too) and is extremely relevant to the premise of this chapter, which speaks to how you can build the foundation of financial success by starting from "ground zero" without supplemental income or family support. While I don't want to harp on this unfortunate fact, it must be considered in this discussion, as it applies to so many millennials trying to figure out how to make their financial goals a reality. That fact is this: 67 percent of millennials report having credit card debt while 36 percent are facing student loan debt.[4] Perhaps even more disturbing, according to a new Northwestern Mutual survey, 40 percent of millennials say that their biggest source of debt is their credit cards and 22 percent of them do not know the interest rate they are currently paying on their unpaid (and growing) debt.[5]

Sounds like many of these folks, some of them in our own families, could use a little help when it comes to financial awareness and planning, and that begins with setting goals.

GOAL SETTING

As a young millennial, you can strive to become highly proficient in a particular profession by initially working for a large company with generous compensation benefits and a defined career path. Or, upon completing what you believe to be the necessary educational requirements, you can proceed through a progression of jobs by switching your employment from one company to another, based on your emerging skills and competence. Some of you may just "wing it" and not set any goals at all.

There is an expression you might have heard that preparation does not guarantee success, but a lack of preparation will almost always lead to failure. That being said, lifetime careers are no longer the norm. The US Department of Labor's Bureau of Labor Statistics reported in 2020 that wage and salary workers had been with their current employers for an average of 4.1 years, down one-tenth of a percentage point from 2018.[6] According to statistics from Dynamic Signal, 21 percent of millennials have switched jobs in the last twelve months, and Statista reports that 22 percent of millennials expect to stay with the same employers for no more than five years.[7] When we also consider the fact that Americans in general move 11.7 times in their lifetime,[8] how might this affect a person's approach to setting goals, especially among millennials?

When it comes to setting goals, one characteristic that appears to be constant among millennials is an aversion to risk, which means many people of this generation make big life decisions later, and they tend to delay getting married and forming a family or deciding on a long-range career.

Since money is a central part of any relationship and requires prioritizing and discipline when it comes to handling debt payments, credit rating, and a system of savings, it should come as no surprise that millennials are considering all these factors in how they set goals.

BRAGGING ON KATIE

Let me indulge my grandfatherly pride for a moment while also demonstrating the benefits of setting goals. Katie Robb Meehan, my granddaughter (in case you hadn't figured that out by now), is an "almost-thirty" millennial, ambitious on her own and a product of two caring parents who have instilled in her the value of initiative. During her undergraduate studies at Smith College in Northampton, Massachusetts, Katie had paying jobs ranging from summer internships in New York City to working as a camp counselor after her freshman year. Back at Smith, she worked on campus as a lab assistant. After graduation, she worked for the Trustees of Reservations, a large environmental conservation organization in Massachusetts, dedicated to preserving natural and historical places in the Commonwealth. Her experience there transitioned into a role working for The Nature Conservancy, an international nonprofit conservation organization, and later with the Massachusetts Department of Agriculture, overseeing a marketing program promoting local Massachusetts agricultural products on a regional platform. Realizing her career path was limited due to the hierarchy within that organization, she applied for a job at the Kripalu Center for Yoga & Health, a wellness retreat center in Stockbridge, Massachusetts, with more than 500 employees, near to where she lives with her new husband. In a short period of time, at the age of twenty-seven, she was promoted to executive assistant to the CEO. If I say so myself, which I am doing with great admiration, this is a remarkable example of a young millennial who has achieved her ambitious goals.

My personal belief is that many millennials have not been as fortunate as Katie in having parents who help them learn to set realistic financial goals, along with a healthy dose of general financial guidance. All too often, "helicopter parents" undermine their child's ability or even interest in learning to do these things on their own. Couple this with the unwillingness or inability of schools and colleges to substitute relevant financial courses in lieu of other courses. On top of that, we see these problems contributing to a lack of development of these capabilities among millennials, which can only lead to significant delay in learning to set and achieve goals.

Setting realistic financial goals depends on your targeted total annual compensation based on salary, benefits, and bonuses, which governs your basic budget, whether you receive an income of $25,000 or $125,000 or whether you are living with a "significant other" with a dual income stream and/or whether there are dependents involved.

Often, financial goals may be subject to being hired at a generous compensation level, which used to be based on complementary skills, mainly in technological fields, such as engineering, data analysis, copywriting, programming, and accounting. However, we now know that "soft skills" are equally or even more important, such as teamwork, creativity, curiosity, questioning, communication, decision-making, presentations, time management, self-motivation, networking, and listening.

Millennials, for the most part, seem to be doing well in how they are addressing these issues and are to be commended for achieving these attributes to accomplish financial independence. For example, most college graduates do not end up working in careers related to their majors; many are unhappy at their initial jobs, and less than 50 percent have a clear vision of their goals. Yet, despite many of them not feeling passionate about their endeavors, a great deal of these millennials often become successful.

MAKING SENSE OF LOANS

While millennials have lots of excellent personality qualities and worthy talents, in general we could consider them as a group to be financially naive. Whether it's putting their money to work or buying a big-ticket item, like a car, when it comes to knowing how to budget for expenses or finance significant purchases, they are not as savvy as they are navigating their way through the complicated maze of their phones.

Millennials in their twenties, having just graduated from college or grad school, might find their student loans (and repayment plans) overwhelming and be sensible or modest enough to move in with their parents to defray one the largest expenses of renting an apartment. Many millennials either sell their car, use Uber, or carpool to work. As unromantic as it may seem for those contemplating marriage and considering the average cost of a "fancy" wedding, a much smaller ceremony can suffice. These big events and decisions in life can often become an urgent learning curve for millennials facing turning points in their financial situations.

"Millennials are the first generation that will have lower living standards than our parents because of student loans (debt), raising inequality and skyrocketing housing and health costs," said Eric Lesser, the Massachusetts senator from Longmeadow and former Obama aide.[9]

This explains a great deal of why we are currently seeing more millennials occupying garages than automobiles. Of course, I do not have any scientific data to back up this claim, but I'm sure you get the point, especially if you are a parent parking their car on the street or a millennial dreaming of the day when they will have their own garage—and an actual house to call their own—without any more debt than a normal mortgage.

GOOD AND BAD DEBT

Borrowing for the purchase of an automobile is considered "bad debt" because it is categorized as a "depreciating" asset, compared to a mortgage for a house or rental property, which is considered an "appreciating" asset or a "good debt."

Some people believe that good debt translates into using money for education, home improvements, and necessities and taking on bad debt means buying new cars, vacation homes, and luxuries. To each his own, but some rules, or should I say, consequences, do apply.

While everyone has a credit score, there is a misconception that only the wealthy can have good credit, but this is not quite accurate. To build credit, one has to go into some debt, which requires paying all bills on time. With numerous debt obligations, many millennials cannot afford to go into early retirement in their fifties and sixties. Instead, some of them may have to wait until they reach a later age, perhaps even as high as seventy-five.

This is due, in large part, to the escalating use of student loans. A general rule is that total loans should not exceed one's annual salary, which should correspond to the first-year expected salary and what you can afford to pay in that context. If student loans are not paid off by age forty, then the debt limit must equate to two years of your annual salary. One alternative is to spread out your student loans to something like $20,000 over a twenty-year period if those terms are possible.

Debt repayment requires discipline, which can be elevated by utilizing a bank automatic withdrawal system for regular obligations, such as loans, mortgages, and utilities.

Most millennials will require a bank loan at some point, which is usually considered to be a personal loan and which I recommend as a great first step to establish a relationship with a local bank's loan officer. In my case, I befriended a fellow member of the Rotary Club whom I trusted and had known for many years. This made any loan application I needed to file much easier.

Reasons for personal loans can vary. They may be needed for a short duration, triggered by one of many immediate events, such as medical matters, debt consolidation, small business matters, extended vacations, and weddings. A personal loan can extend for an average of thirty-six to forty-five months. The borrower must show employment income records and/or be cosigned by a family member or a reliable person found to be satisfactory by the bank. The loan officer will want to see the borrower with a minimum credit score of 580 to 600 (if you're lucky), but lenders prefer borrowers whose credit scores begin in the range of 690 and above.[10]

Requirements vary from lender to lender, but they generally look at your credit score, your credit history, debt-to-income ratio, and cash flow.[11] The borrower can also secure a personal loan by offering collateral, such as a house, a car, jewelry, an art collection, and even prize box seats for a professional athletic team.

Defaulting on any type of loan, especially a student debt, can be draconian. Usually, the borrower is deemed to be delinquent on the first day they miss a first payment. After ninety days past due, the delinquency is reported to the three major credit bureaus, and after

270 days past due, the loan goes into default. Such action affects the borrower's ability to purchase a car or a home, and the college one attended can even withhold academic transcripts.

Failing to pay federal income taxes can be worse. Years ago, I knew someone of an equivalent who was a successful tennis teaching pro for two decades, running various programs and earning a six-figure annual salary. He was talented and industrious, but then his work was interrupted by two hip replacements. Once he was sufficiently healed, he focused on starting another type of business. For several years, he was unsuccessful in his efforts to develop a self-supporting income that satisfied his previous lifestyle.

The subject had access to an accounting firm to file two years of federal income taxes. However, he failed to engage the firm and did not file his returns himself. In the meantime, through a friend, he applied for a job for which he was qualified. Prior to interviewing with the CEO and owner of the company, the CFO was able to investigate the applicant's financial standings and his tax returns. Not surprisingly, the applicant's records showed a failure to pay his federal income taxes for several years, and he was rejected on the spot!

This just shows that failing to pay your debts is bad enough, but failing to pay taxes may be even worse.

To help you avoid staying out of any bad debt, here is a basic tip for millennials: Do not buy a new car, as it becomes a depreciating asset from the moment you pay for it, so it is not really a growing investment; it's an expense. While some cars hold value longer than others (i.e., Fords, Toyotas, and Hondas), these purchases lose 10 percent of their value as soon as they are driven off the lot and another 10 percent of their yearlong depreciation.

Although it is not recommended, if you insist on buying a car, remember to budget for the down payment, which can vary according to the season, the make and model, the year, your credit rating, and the full set of terms.[12] And when it comes to making a down payment, make it as large as you can because that will help you gain more equity in the car. It will also keep you from going upside down on your loan, which can happen when the initial depreciation reduces your car's value and you end up owing more on the loan than the car is actually worth.[13]

It should be noted that car dealers make more money on the car loan than the dealer makes on the actual car. If your loan is preapproved by your bank, you can negotiate a lower price for the car.

Finally, unless you have a clear-cut business model for doing so, do not lease a car because that may require taking out a loan to pay the down payment. Leasing is usually more expensive in the long run compared to an outright purchase, and there are restrictions on mileage, high insurance costs, and difficulties canceling the lease. Plus, a lease does nothing to build equity in the car.

TIPS ON HOUSING DEBT

Let's assume there is a median price of $270,000 for housing in your desired neighborhood. The mortgage should not exceed 20 percent, plus closing costs of 2 to 5 percent. The quick math means you'll be paying $60,000 (minimum) to get started.[14] Can you swing that? Before you answer, make sure you do your due diligence with your monthly budgeting!

The most common mortgage is a fixed rate of thirty years, but a fifteen-year term will build up equity in the house faster. Be sure to have a mortgage without prepayment penalties. A balloon mortgage refers to when the largest payments are at the end of the life of the mortgage. This kind of arrangement is reasonable if you expect to sell the house in two years. If you are not sure you will occupy the house for several years, then perhaps you should rent. If you are negotiating rent, use Zillow.com for comparisons. Also, negotiate the right to sublet, early termination clauses, and permission to have pets if appliable.

One more factor to consider in owning a house is the property tax, which can vary wildly, depending on where you live and the officially declared value of your home. The national average is 1.07 percent, according to government figures, but it really depends on which state and city or town you live in.[15]

As if you didn't have enough to keep track of and pay for with a new home, don't forget that most lenders require homeowners' insurance and, if your down payment is less than 20 percent, the lender will require private insurance.

So are you sure you're ready to buy a home?

TIPS ON BORROWING/LOANS

For some people, borrowing money is an anathema because it indicates that you are living above your needs (and means) and failing to create a spending plan. In that case, you should consider an alternative to borrowing, with the exception of taking out a mortgage, which is like using the sale of equity in your portfolio.

If you do borrow money, it is recommended to utilize your home equity loan so you do not have to use additional collateral, impact your budget or cash flow, or seriously damage your credit rating, an important criterion for your financial future.[16]

Upon determining the amount needed for the loan, determine how much you can afford to pay back on a timely basis, including any hidden fees (don't worry, they're there), plus structuring a written agreement so there is no misunderstanding.

If you are not satisfied with the response with your regular banker regarding the four types of loans, in other words, unsecured personal loan, secured personal loan, fixed rate, or variable rate, you might work out a better deal with a credit union. If during the time period of the loan there is a surprise obligation, such as a large invoice from a dentist, then you can "arrange" for what is called an overdraft.

Bankers shy away from customers borrowing at the spur of the moment. Bankers will utilize one's credit score. For example, a $5,000 loan will require a credit score of at least 660. Just as a reminder, your household budget should adhere to the following formula: needs (50%), wants (30%), and savings and debt repayments (20%).[17]

Fixed expenses, which are considered "needs," include mortgage and/or rent, property tax and/or state fees, insurance, utility bills, vehicle insurance, or lease (car). Remember, occupational cost for housing should not exceed 30 percent of your gross income.

While this discussion does not include every possible expense you may encounter, it does cover the basics, and if you can get this part of your house in order, you will be in excellent shape as your finances become more interesting and complicated.

KATIE'S KORNER

When it comes to setting financial goals, I have no secret strategies. In fact, I see it as a two-way street between taking jobs that can support your life and adjusting your living expenses to meet your income level. You have to weave together the two to make it work.

Obviously, it's not always up to you how much you get paid, and sometimes you have to take the job that's offered to make *some* amount of money, even if it's not as much as you need or want at the moment. Ideally, as your career progresses, you'll find yourself more and more in the position of being able to be choosy about the job offers you'll accept.

When you do have the option of evaluating job offers, especially for those who want to take jobs that are in the nonprofit sector, where you often forgo some level of compensation because you are "doing good" in the world, make sure it's still enough to cover your basic expenses. Do *not* short change yourself (and your financial reality) simply because you want to change the world. You have to take care of your *own* world first!

The other side of the coin is that, if there is a job you very much want and you have to take a pay cut, money is not everything, of course, so ask yourself whether you can live on the salary that is being offered if it pays enough to cover living expenses, any debts, and then a little for savings and discretionary spending. If it does, then that job may be worth it to you.

This is a personal decision, and your happiness and satisfaction must be considered in the process of deciding whether to take a job offer and why—for the sake of your financial planning and your mental health.

Personally, I have found myself a lot happier when I have taken a small pay cut that did not impact my style of living but did slightly decrease the amount I was putting into savings each month. That choice enabled me to work for a company that I felt aligned with and excited by its prospects.

So, in addition to finding jobs that support your lifestyle, you may need to adjust your lifestyle to meet your earnings, mainly through checking your spending habits or identifying areas where you can make a change to achieve a balance between the two.

CHAPTER 8 REVIEW

Setting financial goals depends on three key points.

To be successful, one has to be disciplined when it comes to adhering to predetermined allocation of expenses, such as rent, student debt payments, 401(k) savings plans, and personal notes with a bank to consolidate payments for such things as credit cards and car payments.

The second point for goal setting is to organize your overall finances to be sure that your income includes your significant other and also covers your total combined expenses.

Last, but not least, is estimating your total income as well as that of your partner.

In summary, one should prioritize the various items according to importance.

The chapter explores the handling of debt payments and reveals the importance of credit ratings, utilizing automatic bank withdrawals, debt consolidation, and various tips on borrowing or mortgages.

As Katie says, it's all about finding balance. Good luck!

9

BUDGETING TECHNIQUES TO KEEP YOU ON TRACK

Many millennials enter adulthood with little advice from their parents regarding the best way to achieve financial independence. While still doing their undergraduates, some receive financial subsidies to carry them through graduation, while others are forced to be financially self-sufficient, which means they must learn the hard way. That process should usually begin with creating a realistic budget and sticking to it.

Schools have the best available platform to start teaching youngsters about financial and economic issues when they are reaching their high school years. Unfortunately, most of our schools have overlooked this important part of our youth's education, and many parents have not taken the time or felt it necessary to teach their teenagers financial literacy. Some may want to but do not have the skills to do so effectively.

Handling money is a life skill, which starts when parents introduce allowances and then expands with random neighborhood jobs, such as babysitting, mowing lawns, and other assorted means of making money. This is the beginning of teaching children the value of money and how it relates to savings and independent purchases, both of which form the pillars of making a budget and managing what is necessary to make it work.

A REFLECTION OF THE TIMES

Millennials are living in an era of constant change, partly as a result of the financial crisis of 2008, when 2.6 million jobs were lost, countless businesses were closed, and unemployment and underemployment reached levels not seen since WWII.[1]

Relatively speaking, millennials (ages twenty-two to thirty-eight) have lower earnings than earlier generations, including Gen Xers (ages thirty-nine to fifty-one) and baby boomers (ages fifty-two to seventy). They are also facing a variety of future financial challenges, such as carrying higher student debt and coping with outdated pension plans and underfunded Social Security accounts. Many are looking at retiring much later than the traditional age of sixty-five, even though they can expect to live a longer life than their predecessors.[2]

Only one out of three students finds a job right out of college, and, as of late 2018, millennials were carrying an average debt of $34,770, up 8 percent from the previous year, which places many of them behind the eight ball. According to Experian data, millennials had an average FICO® Score of 665 in the fourth quarter of 2018. The silent generation, those in their seventies and older, had the highest average FICO® Score of 756, followed by baby boomers, who had an average score of 732. Generation Z—the youngest group, with people between the ages of eighteen and twenty-two—had the same average score as millennials.[3]

"The job search for 2020 graduates is going to be different," says Christine Cruzvergara, vice president of higher education and student success at Handshake. "It's not going to be what their peers had experienced even just a year ago or five years ago."[4]

According to a recent National Association of Colleges and Employers (NACE) salary survey, the average starting salary for graduates with a bachelor of arts degree is approximately $50,000. Those who majored in computer science, engineering, mathematics, health sciences, and business were the highest earners, with salaries ranging from $52,000 to $71,000.[5]

The average starting salary for different jobs can vary, as we see in this sample analysis where NACE explains that the top-paid professions include majors in the following:

Engineering: $69,188
Computer science: $67,539
Math and sciences: $62,177
Business: $57,657
Social sciences: $57,310
Humanities: $56,651
Agriculture: $55,750
Communications: $52,056

A report by Georgetown University says the least-paid professions include majors in:

Drama and theater arts: $44,538
Fine arts: $48,871
Music: $48,686
Studio arts: $41,762
Visual and performing arts: $42,465
Neuroscience: $48,190
Art and music education: $45,613
Early childhood education: $39,097[6]

Since the first item to consider in setting a budget is your gross annual salary, which is what drives the feasibility of your lifestyle, these numbers are important. Interestingly, millennials in general are not necessarily motivated by the highest-paying job offer, but rather a meaningful work–life balance. In any case, numbers don't lie, and they affect our budgets in every way. All these numbers mean that budgeting is necessary, perhaps more than ever before! Budgeting can be difficult for some people because it can feel restricting and depressing, but it works and should not be avoided.

MANAGING YOUR FINANCES

According to Laura L. Carstensen, director of the Stanford Center on Longevity in California:

Millennial poverty is up, and employment is down, college debt is more than five times what it was just 20 years ago, and for those saddled with debt, a more frightening financial picture emerges. Both home owner-ship and participation in retirement savings accounts, the two avenues that Americans follow to secure their financial futures, are starkly down in a generation that needs to prepare for lives of unprecedented length. More than a quarter of millennials report that they could not cover a $3,000 emergency, whether with their own savings or by borrowing from family or friends, and thus live day to day with the knowledge that one mistake or accident could lead to financial ruin.[7]

This unique financial scenario we are seeing with the millennial generation is largely caused by circumstances out of their control. That said, many college graduates today are somewhat disconnected from how much life really costs. This has only been exacerbated by the circumstances surrounding the pandemic.

For example, a renter in an urban location can spend 30 percent of their income on a median-priced apartment and 10 percent on food. These graduates are advised to start saving 10 percent of their income for an emergency fund and eventually even more on a retire-ment fund. For an emergency fund, the general rule is as follows: Save three months of living expenses if you have a 401(k) fund or you can seek family support. Save six months of living expenses if you have no other resources, and save twelve months of living expenses if your income fluctuates widely, such as it often does when it comes to irregular sales commissions.

One should establish and adhere to a budget. A common formula on one's net monthly income after deductions, such as Social Security, for allocations to expenses is as follows:

50 percent for essentials (e.g., rent, food, and utilities)
20 percent for priorities (e.g., loans and savings)
30 percent for lifestyle (e.g., health clubs, restaurants, and vacations)

As part of the priorities stated above, one should set aside an "emergency fund" equivalent to three to six months of expenses. Until this is fully funded, then the lifestyle part of the budget should be reduced to 25 percent, not 30, of the allocation.

For many millennials, managing one's budget can be overwhelming because on the one hand millennials are advised to get out of debt, and on the other hand they are advised to start saving as early as twenty-five years old. It is difficult for millennials to achieve success in both areas of budgeting at the same time (e.g., paying down debt and implementing a savings program).

On top of that, they must be aware of any credit card debt, unless they can meet their obligations promptly, because "compound interest," which can vary but is approximately 13 percent of the unpaid portion, really adds up and is considered by some as usurious.[8]

According to Paul Dodd of Infinity Financial Solutions, the benefits of starting a $500 per month savings program at age twenty-five can be enormous. With a 6 percent annual return using ETFs or mutual funds as an investment vehicle, by age thirty-five one's nest egg should be $60,000 and by sixty-five the nest egg should be worth $481,000. The importance of saving is accentuated because most companies in today's world do not provide pensions and many citizens feel that the Social Security system will be bankrupt in the future. Therefore, it is essential for those benefiting in their company's 401(k) program to provide matching contributions and to implement an individual retirement plan (IRA), which allows tax contributions up to $5,500 annually, which is subject to change in the future.

DEBT

While any debt is undesirable, there is such a thing as "good debt" for education, real estate, or your own business. Bad debt would be for vacations, luxury, or impulse items.

Credit card debt or large monthly payments for big-ticket items, such as automobile purchases, is where most people get into trouble. Unfortunately, generous credit terms by retailers and interest-only credit instruments with balloon payments continue to entice buyers into overleveraged financial situations.

When it comes to payables, it is advisable to prioritize on the most important payables, normally your rent and credit cards. Actually, you should use your credit cards to simplify your payables unless you are tapped out on your credit limits. Paying off the credit card invoice first is advisable because it has the highest interest charges, between 13 and 15 percent or higher, in some cases, and it greatly affects your credit score negatively if your credit card balance starts to accumulate. At least pay the monthly minimum, which may be 3 percent of the total, but beware of this habit, as the balance will take a *long* time to come down.

According to *Investor's Business Daily*, the average credit card balance is $7,000,[9] but its analysis does not specify millennial averages. For those seeking guidance, it is acceptable to have one's total credit card debt equivalent to 10 percent of one's gross annual income, or simply stated, a $5,000 debt on $50,000 gross annual income. If your credit card debt is 25 percent of your gross annual income, you are in trouble, and if it is 50 percent, you are in very serious trouble. Paying minimal monthly credit card debt is critical but beware of credit card companies that charge high annual interest rates on the balance. Most of them do and it is very expensive!

Many people forget that, while businesses have balance sheets in addition to income statements, individuals should have a balance sheet as well. Let's assume the following:

Your condo is worth $200,000. Your savings (401(k) or mutual fund) is worth $50,000.
Your total assets add up to $250,000.

Consider you have a mortgage of $100,000. All your other debts (e.g., student loan and credit cards) add up to $50,000. Your total debt is $150,000, which means your total net assets amount to $100,000.

A total debt of $150,000 equates to a 60 percent debt/equity, with total assets of $250,000. Therefore, your debt to equity of 60 percent is acceptable. If it accelerates to 80 percent, or $200,000 of debt on $250,000 of assets, then you will be in dangerous territory.

How much total debt can you reasonably expect to safely carry in relation to your total income? Your banker will probably tell you that your debt-to-income ratio should be 35 percent or less. So, if your annual income is $50,000, your total debt should not be over $17,500.

An alternative is to make a concerted effort to secure a higher-paying job.

According to Michelle Singletary of the *Washington Post*, "The earlier you start saving, the less you'll have to save over time. Easier said than done. The youth are so overwhelmed with debt that they feel they can't afford to save. The nonprofit Investor Protection Institution did an online poll of more than 1,000 millennials and not surprisingly found 49 percent had student loans, and 34 percent of those surveyed said that their debt is delaying their ability to start saving for retirement."[10]

Making and saving money are not guarantees for financial success, as one must choose sound investments. It is almost imperative to invest some of your savings in a 401(k) program with your employer, mutual funds, and ETFs, especially if you would like to retire at age sixty-five. Once again, saving 10 percent of your annual income should be your goal.

RENT

Spending 30 percent, or preferably less, of your income on rent, including utilities, is a good but optimistic target. By searching online for *Zillow Rent Affordability Calculation*, you can plug in your monthly net income and monthly essential expenses in the town or city in which you are seeking to rent. Arbitrarily selecting $6,000 net monthly income, $3,000 monthly expenses, and the town of Concord, Massachusetts, the Zillow program states that, based on a 33 percent factor, you can afford to pay $2,475 per month, with $3,525 left over for taxes and spending money. In this case, the program also described fifteen matching rentals in the Concord area.

Zillow also has a formula for buying a house in which you plug in your annual income and how much you are willing to put down as a down payment (e.g., $20,000) and Zillow will state what price you can afford for a house and the monthly mortgage payments plus suggested houses for sale in the town of choice.[11]

CREDIT RATING

You should check your own credit ratings with the three major credit reporting companies, Equifax, TransUnion, and Experian. Your credit rating is calculated with a formula based on variables, including payment history, length of credit history, credit mix, amount of debt, and amount of new debt owed. Your credit score may affect the interest rate you pay to a lender and even make the difference between a loan being approved or declined.

The FICO Company (originally named Fair Isaac Company) determines one's credit score. Its determination is used by 90 percent of lenders to assess one's risk, how much to lend, and at what rate of interest. You can obtain your credit score online through FICO, through some credit card companies that provide free scores with your account, or by tracking it by going to www.annualcreditreport .com. It is believed that 60 percent of borrowers do not know their own credit score. The range is between 300 and 850 points. Only one out of nine people has 800+ credit points, and 1 percent of the population has a score of 850 points.

450 points = poor credit rating
680 points = good credit
750–800 points = excellent credit
850 points = exceptional credit.[12]

It may be surprising to you that your salary and net worth have little bearing on your credit score. The credit analysis is not exact with the three agencies, but the general FICO considerations in the scoring are as follows:

Payment on time = 35%
Available credit versus credit used = 30%
Good mix of accounts (e.g., installment, mortgage, car, student loans) = 10%
Accounts with five or more years = 15%
Limited new accounts = 10%
Total = 100%[13]

AUTOMATIC WITHDRAWAL SYSTEMS

Create and stringently adhere to an achievable budget and start saving for the future, especially if your employer contributes to your 401(k) plan. Set up an automatic withdrawal system with your bank so that, when you deposit your weekly/monthly paycheck, certain regular payments are dispersed accordingly, such as your rent, car loan, student loan, and 401(k) savings plan. This ensures that you consistently pay off your fixed costs.

GENERAL RULES TO FOLLOW

Be patient, pragmatic, and analytical when contemplating large purchases, such as a car or home. If you are buying a vehicle, try to adhere to the 20/4/10 rule, which means, if you decide to finance the purchase, plan on placing a 20 percent deposit with a four-year payout on the loan for which you will spend no more than 10 percent of your gross income.

A formula like this keeps you from spending more than you can afford, and ideally the 10 percent is meant to cover your transportation costs of gasoline, maintenance, and insurance. Therefore, if you make $60,000 gross income, your annual costs, including depreciation over four years, adds up to $6,000 per year to own and operate the automobile. If you own your car outright without any loans associated with the purchase, the general rule for the cost of owning a car over a five-year period is to double the price tag of the car and divide by sixty.

For example, if the car is purchased at $10,000, times two equals $20,000, divided by sixty equals $333 per month for operating expenses, depreciation, and insurance. Naturally, if you have the necessary cash to pay for the automobile up front, do so as long as you can pay for your other obligations on time.

Regarding homeownership, the norm is to place a deposit of 20 percent of the price of the house or condo, which will help to restrain you from spending more than you can afford and will give you a better chance of receiving the bank's approval for your mortgage, while also maintaining some deposits to your savings account.

Based on the affordability of buying a house, the general rule to follow is three times the gross annual income of you and your spouse. So, if the combined income with your spouse is $200,000, then the limit for a purchase would be $600,000. Also, factor in closing costs of 2 to 5 percent of the purchase price. The closing costs could include house inspection, appraisals, title insurance, attorneys' fees, and land survey. It may be prudent to delay the purchase of a home until you have paid off a substantial amount of your debt, particularly if your job is dependent on sales commissions or you work for a "start-up" company.

One of the greatest financial challenges for the millennial generation is the dual obligation of paying down college debt and contributing approximately 10 percent of one's annual income to a retirement fund, either through mutual funds, ETFs, or stocks/bond investments.

The rule goes like this: determine the equity and fixed income (bonds) portion based on your age, deducted from the number 120. For example, if you are thirty years old, deduct it from 120, which equates to ninety, which means that 90 percent of your portfolio should be invested in equities. By way of comparison, a person eighty years old would deduct that figure from 120, which equates to forty, which means 40 percent should be invested in equities and the balance in bonds or an equivalent.

To estimate your potential future returns, based on your equity investment, you should expect that over ten years your equities in total should double; otherwise change your selection of funds or advisors.

SETTING GOALS

Addressing your financial future is critical because millennials cannot be confident that Social Security, as we now know it, will be around when they retire, and with fewer employees depending on employee-based 401(k) programs, millennials must focus on both short- and long- term obligations.

While it may seem like a long time in the future for most millennials, retirement is not an eternity away, and this part of your future requires serious consideration. It's never too early to have concerns about savings, liquidity, debt, net worth, cash flow, and investment strategies.

According to 2019 estimates by the US Government Accountability Office (GAO), nearly half (48 percent) of households headed by someone fifty-five and older lack some form of retirement savings. The good news is that this represents a slight uptick from a survey conducted a few years earlier. On the other hand, the study shows that 29 percent of those who are retired or nearing the traditional retirement stage of life still have no retirement savings or a defined benefit plan, such as a job-based pension, and will need to rely on Social Security. Retirement experts have been warning about underfunded retirements for many years. IRAs and work-based 401(k) savings plans have helped compensate for a sizeable decline in pensions. But many Americans have not taken advantage of these ways to save or lack the resources to do so.[14]

One way to feel confident that you have saved enough for retirement, including your 401(k) plan, your IRA, and any pension, is to aim to save one times your annual salary by age thirty-five, two times your annual salary by age forty, and three times your annual salary by age forty-five.

While your goal may be to retire when you are sixty-five years old (give or take), that may be too optimistic, considering the uncertainty of future Social Security payments, taxes, savings, and expenses. It may be more realistic to plan on retirement around the age of seventy-five unless you can secure a secondary source of income.

What is a "normal" amount of retirement savings? If you are asking this question, you may be one of the 63 percent of Americans who either don't think their savings are on track or simply are not sure if they have enough put away. This is according to the findings of the Federal Reserve's Report on the Economic Well-Being of U.S. Households in 2019. It found that, among all adults, median retirement savings was $60,000 and that, by the time of retirement, this number is estimated to grow to a median of $228,900.[15]

WHAT YOU CAN DO NOW

Debt payments, but not mortgage, should be less than 20 percent of your take-home pay. Occupation or housing costs (rent or mortgage) should be less than 30 percent. Savings should be around 10 to 15 percent of your monthly take-home pay.

It's wise to raise your deductible for your homeowner's insurance to at least $500 or $1,000 per claim.

Refinance your $100,000 fifteen-year mortgage if current mortgage rates drop substantially.

Go to the supermarket with a specified list of items needed. Take discounts wherever possible and buy store brands at 20 to 40 percent less than branded products. Eating at home can cost as little as $5 per person, compared to $25 per person at a restaurant. Buy generic drugs when at the drugstore.

If receiving a tax refund, don't spend it; rather, deposit it in your savings account. If you receive a bonus, deposit it in your savings account as well.

Reduce your transportation costs to work by carpooling or using public transportation.

If your bank is charging you ATM fees or for a low deposit balance, switch to another bank without those charges.

Invest in the stock market over time, using dollar cost averaging in mutual funds or ETFs. Historically, such investments have an average rate of return of 9 percent so that a $10,000 investment will be worth $86,231 in twenty-five years and $314,094 in forty years.

Negotiate your rental increases. State your case, such as you are a reasonable tenant or comparable rentals are going for less. As a last resort, you can try to wrangle some improvements to the place to save you money on doing it on your own.

RETIREMENT CONSIDERATIONS

Older millennials, those ages twenty-six to thirty-eight years old, should consider implementing retirement savings to their overall budget. For example, retirement advisors have determined that, if millennials wait until thirty years old to start saving for retirement instead of starting as a twenty-five-year-old, the result will be a 20 percent differential by retirement age because of value appreciation.

With company pensions disappearing, shrinking support from Social Security, increasing health care costs, life expectancy growing, and lifetime employment with employers in jeopardy, there is much to be concerned about when it comes to your financial retirement prospects.

According to Fidelity Investments Retirement Saving Assessments, 55 percent of households in America risk not being able to cover essential expenses in retirement, such as health care and food. The biggest misconception people have about retirement is that their expenses will go down, but they tend to stay the same. The perception is that workers will retire at sixty-five and die at eighty-five years old, but life expectancies are advancing, especially for those who have been privileged to live in comfortable circumstances.

To put the challenge in perspective for the millennial generation, the necessary retirement savings can be equated as follows:

Savings at age thirty-five = two times their annual salary
Savings at age forty-five = four times their annual salary
Savings at age fifty-five = eight times their annual salary
Savings at age sixty-five = twelve times their annual salary

This means that, if a millennial aimed to save $1 million by age sixty-five, the formula would play out to an 8 percent annual return on one's investments. For a twenty-five-year-old, this would require saving $286 per month, or, for a forty-five-year-old, it would translate to saving $1,700 per month. That's a big difference![16]

The unfortunate truth is that most millennials are taught subjects such as art, music, and physical fitness but not critical topics, such as budgeting and financial planning. Instead, these critical aspects of life are left to parents to teach. Financial planning is an ongoing process, like annual medical checkups, and this type of literacy should be taught in schools.

INVESTMENTS

The millennial financial challenge is not only to adhere to a doable operating budget, and to do it consistently, but to create a savings account equivalent to three to six months of living expenses and to contribute to your 401(k) retirement funds, which should be an automatic bank deduction, as we previously discussed.

The most popular 401(k) matching plan is modeled from Fidelity's 401(k) plan in which the firm matches 100% of 3% of the employees' salary and then 50% for the next 2% of the employees' annual salary. Pretax 401(k) contributions are exempt from federal income taxes, state income taxes, and local income taxes. Instead, you defer paying those taxes until you withdraw the money, such as you do with a ROTH IRA plan. There are limits to the total amount one can contribute per year.[17]

For investing in the future, an index fund with stocks in Standard & Poor's 500 selection would be recommended without any investments in bonds. Over the past twenty years, the S&P 500, which is the benchmark of the stock market, has appreciated approximately 10 to 11 percent annually, minus adjustments for inflation.[18]

If you are a millennial contemplating marriage in the near future, it is advisable to be financially transparent with your partner to determine whether you will be fiscally compatible. By disclosing all debts and obligations and sources of income and assets, you will determine whether such a union is workable. One of the major reasons that marriages fail is a disconnect on financial matters with one's spouse.

If you are recently married or cohabitating, then it is advisable to separate each spouse's investment portfolio, savings account, and legal documents. Pooling for assets can be risky, so precaution is in order. The good news is that the median age for marriage is now twenty-eight years old, compared with couples in 1970 who averaged twenty-two years old, which indicates a greater maturity and possible sounder judgment for those choosing to embark on this path together.

Whether you choose to abide by traditional means of calculating a personal budget or have in mind to carve out your own individual path, I encourage you to consider all the elements presented in this chapter and set realistic goals for your short- and long-term future.

It's not a matter of setting up an "I told you so moment," but I'm pretty sure you will thank me later.

KATIE'S KORNER

This is an area where I cannot claim to have much useful advice. I won't bore you with the details, but for a number of reasons I tend not to budget, so I am really not in a position to lecture on the subject.

What I can say is this: I do not spend money that I do not have.

I do not have a credit card (not a single one), and whatever money I have left over each month from spending my paycheck on living expenses I divide up: half goes to a savings account and half goes to discretionary spending.

There's no real science behind this strategy; it's just what has worked for me over the years, and I have no plans to change it any time soon.

For millennials who are still in the process of finding their career path and a well-paying job, are carrying debt from student loans, and are up against high living costs, this may not be an approach to budgeting that works for you.

I suggest you follow my grandfather's advice and seek out your own peers who are managing the budgeting challenges of the modern day in a healthy way.

CHAPTER 9 REVIEW

Millennials are facing unprecedented college debt burdens; a highly competitive job market; stagnant wages; and rising rents, all of which continually eat up their income.

This chapter has focused on financial budgeting. Many millennials have been unfairly accused of being financially illiterate and/or fragile due to their lack of monetary reserves.

They should be reminded that there is a light at the end of the tunnel. In addition to implementing the advice in this chapter, millennials should delay large purchases, such as a house or a new car to strive for financial savings and a superior credit rating.

Budgeting is a life skill, which for some begins in their childhood. If millennials are planning on having children of their own, they better start saving because the burden of financing a college education is only growing bigger each year. This also means that more and more college graduates are delaying marriages and creating families while they target future retirement for age sixty-eight, seventy, or seventy-two (at least) instead of the traditional sixty-five or sixty-six. All of this adds pressure on millennials to plan wisely and save better.

There are three key metrics in budgeting:

1. The total debt to total assets should be no more than one to three, and total credit card debt should be no more than 10 percent of total income.
2. Income allocation should be in the following categories:
   Essential 50%
   Priorities 20%
   Lifestyle 30%
3. A credit card rating will determine interest rates with creditors, mortgage rates, and subsequent financing. Use the Zillow Rent Affordable Calculation app to determine the rent you should pay in a designated location based on affordability.

10

MARRIAGE AND FAMILY FINANCES

Money is an integral part of any marriage, whether the couple is legally married or living together. Getting on the same page financially is crucial, especially since many couples, millennials included, do not discuss their finances nearly enough. Actually, this age group is not as bad as some others, especially those in older groups who tend to remain more tight-lipped about their money.

According to a survey by TD Bank of more than 1,700 adults, 75 percent of millennials in committed relationships said they discuss money on a weekly basis. That's considerably more than Gen X couples and *way* more than baby boomers.[1]

Dr. Jane Greer, a psychotherapist and relationship expert, told CNBC's *Make It*, "We're in a better place than we used to be because younger couples are more willing and open to talk about their money—and to address it directly, right out of the gate."[2]

One of the financial culprits most couples must deal with is their credit card debt, which they often use independently, sometimes with no mutual discussion or planning. According to American Consumer Credit Counseling, a not-for-profit credit counseling service, a general rule is that 10 percent of your entire debt (minus your mortgage) is credit card debt is acceptable, while as much as 30 percent indicates that you are in trouble.[3]

MARRIAGE: THE ULTIMATE TRANSACTION

There is an old proverb that states that you don't marry someone you can live with; you marry someone you can't live without.

I have been twice blessed because I married someone whom I love but who was also a municipal accountant and head of finance for King City, California. She has not only been totally financially responsible; she has also always been aware of the critical importance of an excellent credit rating. This may not sound terribly romantic, but I wouldn't suggest arguing with my wife's expertise either.

To put this in further context, 40 percent of families do not even know their credit score, which is published by the three major credit agencies, and many families live paycheck to paycheck.[4] Does this bode well for married couples who are hesitant or even resistant to communicating about financial matters? Each of us may answer that differently, depending on our experience. How couples handle money is as important as how much they earn. For example, generally speaking, millennials must maintain a six-figure salary to "service" a six-figure loan debt.[5] How many of them know this and are willing to follow the rules for the benefit of their pocketbooks *and* their marriage?

LIVING UP TO EXPECTATIONS

In some respects, millennials live in conflict, as they are expected to pay their bills on time and and also expected to save for emergency funds, retirement, and education costs for their children. Discipline is paramount and saying no to purchasing peripheral items, spending on an assortment of expectations and social standards is entirely acceptable.

There is an expression we've heard for quite some time, which can only be attributed to a wise person named Anonymous. It states the first generation makes the money, the second generation preserves it, the third spends it, and the fourth must recreate it.

We could match that with a pithy quote by the legendary baseball player and New York Yankee icon Yogi Berra, who once said, "If you don't know where you are going, you end up somewhere else."[6]

The Pew Research Center reported in 2020 that "a majority of millennials are not currently married, marking a significant change from past generations. Only 44% of Millennials were married in 2019, compared with 53% of Gen Xers [39–52], 61% of Boomers [53–71] and 81% of Silents [72+] at a comparable age."[7]

Millennials are also getting married later in life than previous generations. In 2019, the men on average got married (for the first time) at age thirty, while women tied the knot on average at age twenty-eight. This is a few years later than it was for both genders just fifteen years earlier.[8]

As marriages occur later for this generation, many still live with a "significant other." Pew reports that in 2019, 12 percent of millennials were living with an unmarried partner, while Gen Xers did so at a rate of 8 percent. Cohabitation is more common among millennials than Gen Xers across most racial and ethnic categories, as well as educational attainment.[9]

MOTIVATIONS

Historically, marriage is the most prestigious way of life for those wishing to raise a family. Millennials seem to be delaying marriage more and more, though, until they feel financially secure and vocationally established and finish their educational endeavors, including grad school.

CNBC, using a Pew analysis of Census Bureau data, reported that as of July 2020, 52 percent of millennials were living in their parents' home, up from 47 percent earlier in the same year, which surpassed the previous high reached in 1940, when 48 percent of young adults lived with their parents.

"In a very short space of time, we are now at levels last seen during the Great Depression," said Richard Fry, a senior researcher at Pew.

Pew also found that the number and share of young adults living with their parents jumped for men and women of all racial and ethnic groups and throughout every geographic region of the country.[10]

This raises a question: does living at home lessen the odds for millennials to get married because it could weaken their social ties with siblings and aging parents? There is no exact data on this topic, but it seems to be a worthwhile perspective to consider. And it does raise additional questions about why millennials might choose to leave the nest and venture out on their own with a new partner.

Money differences can be a potential area of disagreement for a couple living together, especially when it comes to a decision about marriage. For many prospective couples, the wedding event alone can be a stressful event to consider, let alone the actual years of marriage that follow it.

The cost of marriage starts with the price tag for the wedding, which may or may not be prudent if done in any sort of extravagant way, especially when the couple wishes to start off their married life by establishing a sound financial footing. Of course, it all depends on their resources and perhaps the bank accounts of their parents.

The average cost of a wedding (ceremony and reception) in 2020, as reported by The Knot, was estimated to be $19,000, markedly less than the $28,000 it cost in 2019. This, of course, was due to COVID-19 and the limitations on how many could attend a wedding and the size of the spaces a smaller event required. Prices in 2021 seem to already be rising, possibly on their way to returning to previous levels. The prices vary from state to state, with New Jersey being the highest at an average of $53,400 and Utah the lowest at $19,700.[11]

When you add on the typical costs of engagement rings and honeymoons, the calculator just keeps inching higher and higher toward its final totals. One has to wonder, based on habitual spending habits, if a big wedding is needed; is it needed now, and what will happen if it doesn't happen right away?

One of the deep motivations for marriage is the equal trust two people develop for each other, the need to spend time together, and the desire to share experiences as a devoted couple. Millennials in their thirties who are single may often question whether they will meet someone and start a family or they will remain in an inclusive relationship for too long. Having a family together is part of the *raison d'etre* and frequently takes six months to decide whether the other partner is in fact "the one." From an economic point of view, marriage is often leveraging two incomes and combining costs with each other. It's tricky to balance the love and the checkbook, and while this does not sound terribly romantic, it's a vital element of the partnership.

COSTS OF FAMILY

According to the US Department of Agriculture (USDA) in its 2015 *Expenditures on Children by Families* report, also known as "The Cost of Raising a Child," it is estimated that

> a family will spend approximately $12,980 annually per child in a middle-income ($59,200–$107,400), two-child, married-couple family. Middle-income, married-couple parents of a child born in 2015 may expect to spend $233,610 (plus more based on inflation costs) for food, shelter, and other necessities to raise a child through age 17. This includes costs for childcare, education, transportation, healthcare, clothing, etc., but does not include the cost of a college education.[12]

For working mothers, we can add in the cost of maternity leave, and if the wife returns to work, then she and her spouse must consider the cost of nannies, babysitters, or au pairs. The annual comprehensive minimum cost for hosting an au pair is estimated to be $19,550, including fees for applications and placement.[13]

Problems sometimes arise with families when, after years of marriage, the husband leaves the family as the principal bread winner, leaving the wife to not only bring up their children but to also earn the necessary income to support the family. This usually changes the entire calculus for how a family can live and children raised.

FINANCIAL HARMONY IN MARRIAGE

The number one reason for a family breakup and divorce are money problems. The success of a marriage and subsequent family matter is often dependent on financial priorities, the uneven spouses' corporate income and the lack of transparent communication.

Insider.com conducted a study in 2019, with the help of the National Center for Biotechnology Information (NCBI), which showed that 36 percent of the couples questioned said that financial problems were the primary reason for their marriage failing, leading to an eventual divorce. They cited the increased stress and tension within their relationship as the reason things went south.[14]

According to an article in *Forbes*, conflicting money styles can signal trouble for couples. For example, if one party tends to be a "spender" while their spouse is more of a "saver," then tensions can come to the surface and create real and lasting riffs.[15]

In those cases, the couple should try their best to use each other's strengths to their mutual benefit and avoid the weaker tendencies each one has.

By the way, the other reasons marriages did not work out, according to the NCBI survey, included little or no premarital education and religious differences, lack of support from family, health problems, domestic violence, substance abuse, getting married too young, too much conflict and arguing, infidelity or extramarital affairs, and lack of commitment.[16]

The first (financial) step for a newly married couple is to agree on a joint budget, which mirrors a single person's budget of 50 percent attributed to "needs," 30 percent attributed to "wants," and 20 percent to savings and debt repayments.[17]

A number of other items should be addressed too, including the following:

1. Merge all credit accounts under one name.
2. Inform the three major credit reporting companies of your new joint name.
3. File taxes jointly (not separately).
4. Change names on Social Security, driver's license, life insurance, creditors, and student loans to reflect any new name choices.
5. Track your finances, using a software program to keep track of your deductions.

There are three segments to consider when it comes to one's spending power:

Long-term goals, including children
Home expenses
Retirement

Consider hiring a financial advisor to figure all of this out. Even a one-time consultation can be valuable and get you started on the right track.

Marriage will frequently cost one party a piece of their former financial independence in the sense that "my money is now *our* money." Handling money starts with the family influence, and I have seen that talking about money is often taboo around a family setting.

A friend of mine admitted that money matters were never discussed in his family, especially around the dining room table. As a result, none of three male siblings had careers that dealt with money. Ironically, one of the brothers took a job as a financial planner, and, while well qualified, the employee resigned almost immediately.

This should remind you of the importance of hiring a financial planner, especially for certain millennial couples in their thirties who are focused on retirement planning and may have businesses and investments. There are tax benefits of a spouse to consider, such as tax rules of an IRA and estate planning issues. Selecting the right financial planner depends on compatibility, credentials, and their specialty.

PRENUPTIALS

While no one likes to talk about divorce, but about one of two marriages ends up that way. The prevailing issues for divorce include lack of commitment, infidelity, and excessive arguing. While only 5 to 10 percent of marriages resort to prenups, they establish the terms of a breakup and can often help to avoid a lengthy divorce process.

Prenups often are used when there is a significant imbalance of wealth or larger inheritance forthcoming. Sunset agreements can be written into the prenup so that the agreement terminates in a certain number of years. Certain states, like California, require reaffirmation of a prenup in ten years. Prenups have become more prevalent in recent years, usually based on certain red flags, such as children from a previous marriage, ownership of a profitable business, or a recently received large inheritance.[18]

In lieu of drafting a prenuptial, a couple should be fully transparent in divulging how much money they make individually, their credit score, and their individual debt. If Partner A earns $100,000 and Partner B makes $50,000 annually, then they might agree that the rental apartment charge is allocated two to one for the man in comparison to the woman.

A separation agreement is not enforceable, so the next step is to draw up an uncontested divorce in writing for the judge to approve. However, if there are ancillary complications, such as children, past ownership of a family business or part ownership of a family summer cottage, the divorced person with kids intends to move 100 miles away, or the divorced person cohabitates with another person, then a prenup becomes more necessary.

If one party has a significantly larger source of assets or income, then a setup of a trust controlled by trustees is a source of protection for the wealthier marriage partner. While being married is better for your wallet, given the deductions on your tax returns, getting a divorce cancels these benefits.

In any case, since a marriage includes the signing of a legal contract, signing a prenuptial can be viewed as a logical part of that process.

According to Russell D. Knight, a divorce lawyer in Florida, "people want a prenup so they can keep what they brought into the marriage, which the law typically already protects—it's when financial assets get commingled that things get complicated, and that happens easier than you think."[19]

FAMILY GOALS

With so much financial and economic turmoil happening because of COVID-19, job layoffs, high college costs, higher taxes, and general anxiety, more married millennials are keeping their financials somewhat separate. A Bank of America study shows that 37 percent of millennials keep separate bank accounts with separate credit cards and investment portfolios, but they maintain joint savings accounts for shared goals.[20]

Sample Goals

1. Establish an emergency expense fund to hold you for a year.
2. Maximize your 401(k) plan and other retirement funds (10 to 15 percent of income).
3. Pay off credit card debt within four months.
4. Pay off student debt and car loans faster than required.
5. Receive at least one credit report regularly.
6. Cut back on the usual purchases.
7. Review your insurance policy needs (e.g., life, health, property, car, and disability).
8. Be sure you adhere to 50/30/20 budget (essentials, priorities, wants).
9. Set up automatic deductions for payments that are critical from a checking account.

FINANCIAL PRUDENCE

Successful money management boils down to financial prudence and personal discipline. Financial planners almost all agree that the key to budgeting is to allocate 50 percent of one's income to essentials (food, utilities, shelter, transportation), 30 percent to discretionary spending, and 20 percent for debt repayment and savings.

The other side of the coin is one's spending habits.

Back in the 1950s, there were very few supermarkets, so people tended to shop only for those items on their shopping list, not fancy packaged items that lured customers into unnecessary purchases. Nowadays, we see many chain stores that feature private label products instead of more expensive branded items.

Prudence means that one doesn't spend $25 each week on lattes, but rather drinks the office coffee, saving $100 per month, or $1,200 per year. The cost of keeping credit cards, especially store credit cards, can cost a lot too, especially when you calculate the interest on one's unpaid balance

In *Know Yourself, Know Your Money*, personal finance expert Rachel Cruze writes that 78 percent of the American population lives paycheck to paycheck. [21]

According to a survey conducted by Credit Karma, "When it comes to partnership, most millennials want to make sure they're on the same financial page as their 'Significant Other' before they say 'I do.' This involves knowing how much debt their partner has and openly discussing their salary, among other things. Our survey also suggests millennials value maintaining financial independence once they're paired up. Almost two-thirds (62 percent) keep at least one separate personal bank account while in a relationship, and many think it keeps their relationship alive."[22]

With that in mind, it's pretty safe to say that financial prudence is critical for individuals and especially in the context of building a successful marriage. Transparency is also vital to ensure a healthy partnership. Open communication should always be encouraged. And though it may sound old-fashioned, don't ever forget Valentine's Day and your anniversary! It's worked for me for many decades, and I recommend it for millennials everywhere.

KATIE'S KORNER

We often hear the joking reference that "opposites attract," which can be good for many aspects of a marriage, but finances is not an area that benefits from opposites attracting.

In my experience, it's less important how much money each partner makes. Instead, it's about how you each view finances and manage your money and the habits you've developed over the years. In practice, if you both have a similar relationship and outlook on money, saving and spending, you are less likely to squabble over these issues.

My husband and I share a similar mentality about how to spend our hard-earned money. I trust his judgment and respect how he chooses to spend money, so it never becomes a sticking point in our relationship.

During the time when we were dating, one way that we learned about each other's spending habits was by going grocery shopping together, even though we lived apart, because it showed us how we each planned for the weekly grocery shop, how we made decisions about our purchases, how we responded to temptations, and how we evaluated the value of products. This was one way of getting a sense of a potential future partner's spending habits early on before we were in a serious relationship.

Besides grocery shopping together, there are other ways to check a potential partner's spending, like taking a trip together. When we were about a year away from getting married, well into a committed relationship at that point, we bought a car together. Some people told me I was crazy and to wait until we were married, but for me it was an opportunity to see how we would approach making a large purchase together and taking on debt. If our relationship ended, figuring out how to deal with the car would've been a solvable problem.

Instead, I put to the test our ability to navigate making a big financial decision and we passed! The understanding and trust we gained for each other through the process of finding a car and taking out a loan together was what I needed to feel sure that we could get married and handle our finances together successfully.

Experiences like this force you to address the money conversation head-on, and it's a real benefit when you do. Eight years later, we are still completely open with our finances and discuss money on a weekly if not daily basis. For us, it is a source of stability, not division, because we have worked hard to stay on the same page with our approach to spending, saving, and goal setting as it relates to our shared finances.

CHAPTER 10 REVIEW

A harmonious marriage will probably not endure unless the two parties agree on money matters. It is well documented that schisms in marriages and families are often a result of financial conflicts and arguments.

When it comes to money matters, discipline is paramount, when both parties are willing to live by a mutually agreed upon budget instead of living paycheck to paycheck. The culprit can be an independent use of credit cards, which should never exceed 10 percent of a couple's combined income.

Hiring a financial planner can help if you can afford it. Working out budgets, cash flow, debt/income ratios, estate planning issues, and investments is a wise thing to do and highly recommended. Starting a family presents another set of expenses, reducing the cushion of living with dual incomes.

Since traditional financial advisors may be expensive to hire, may I recommend seeking out retired financial planners who offer their expertise as volunteers? You can often find them online or through your local library or community center.

I suggest you do whatever it takes to create and maintain a happy and healthy life at home for you, your spouse, and your children. Managing your money well will go a long way toward establishing a harmonious life.

CONCLUSION

Hopefully, the advice I have imparted in this book, along with Katie's, will help you find a healthy measure of success in your life.

Determining one's future career and successfully obtaining the "right" job is critical when it comes to having enough cash flow and net worth to become financially independent, which means meeting your debt obligations and budgeting requirements.

A lot of your choices depend on your particular talents or interests and how you apply them in the arena of advanced education, relevant internships, and job opportunities. Of course, there is always the possibility of serendipity playing a role in your life and your willingness and courage to move out of your comfort zone.

One of the myths for millennials to deal with is branding, whether it's in the field of education or a career. Except for prestigious name-brand graduate schools in law, medicine, and engineering, what's most important is what you *do* at these postgraduate schools, not where you go and the name you can wave around, as if it's a ticket to success all by itself.

Millennials have become more independent financially, not relying as much on corporate pensions, 401(k)s, Social Security, and other retirement plans, but then again, to build wealth on any level they will have to be hired by well-established companies and usually avoid the gig economy, especially on a long-term basis. That said, there are many exceptions to this, and I wave the white flag when it comes to understanding, let alone living, the life of a gig worker. All I can say is good luck!

We see trends among millennials in how they change jobs so frequently. This may work well for some and not so well for others, especially those looking to enjoy the security of benefits, such as a retirement plan and/or health insurance. But these days, there are other options to acquire them on your own, even if they may be more expensive.

Many millennials feel financially stressed these days partly because their fixed costs are high and the labor market is not fully stable. I hope the advice I've offered, for example, on budgeting, which urges millennials to utilize the automatic deduction method for banks on fixed costs with their depositors, will be helpful, among many other tips and suggestions.

Whether you are a millennial or someone who cares about one, if you are to remain motivated in your life, you will need to make positive financial gains at a rate that is relevant to your living conditions. I hope that this book has achieved its mission by providing you with the tools to accomplish your dreams. The rest is up to you.

NOTES

INTRODUCTION

1. https://iveybusinessjournal.com/publication/the-millennials-a-new-generation-of-employees-a-new-set-of-engagement-policies/.
2. https://www.business.com/articles/tech-savvy-millennials-at-work/.
3. https://www.bls.gov.
4. https://www.forbes.com/sites/neilhowe/2017/01/16/millennials-a-generation-of-page-turners/?sh=527a4d1f1978.
5. https://www.libraryjournal.com/?detailStory=Reading-Through-the-Ages-Generational-Reading-Survey.
6. https://www.mentalfloss.com/article/578177/surprising-millennial-reading-habits.
7. https://educationdata.org/number-of-college-graduates.
8. https://www.pewresearch.org/social-trends/2019/02/14/millennial-life-how-young-adulthood-today-compares-with-prior-generations-2/.
9. https://www.businessinsider.com/average-american-millennial-net-worth-student-loan-debt-savings-habits-2019-6.

PART I

1. https://www.cnbc.com/2020/02/27/82percent-of-college-grads -believe-their-degree-was-a-good-investment.html.
2. https://beam.stanford.edu/careertruths.
3. https://designingyour.life/the-book/.

CHAPTER 1

1. Sherrie Bourg Carter, "The Art and Value of Good Listening," *Psychology Today*, September 28, 2012, https://www.psychologytoday.com/us/ blog/high-octane-women/201209/the-art-and-value-good-listening.
2. Michael Nichols, *The Lost Art of Listening* (New York: The Guilford Press, 2009), XX.
3. Ibid, XX.
4. Jeanne Segal et al., "Nonverbal Communication and Body Language," *HelpGuide*, October 2020, https://www.helpguide.org/articles/relationships -communication/nonverbal-communication.htm.
5. Corine Jansen, "Sex Differences in Listening," *Global Listening Centre*, https://www.globallisteningcentre.org/sex-differences-in-listening/.
6 . *GulfNews*, "Women Are Better Listeners, Study Says," February 13, 2014, https://gulfnews.com/world/europe/women-are-better-listeners-study-says -1.1290574.
7. Akane Otani, "These Are the Skills You Need If You Want to Be Headhunted," *Bloomberg*, January 5, 2015, https://www.bloomberg.com/news/ articles/2015-01-05/the-job-skills-that-recruiters-wish-you-had.
8. Travis Bradberry, "10 Ways to Spot a Truly Exceptional Employee," *World Economic Forum*, May 2, 2019, https://www.weforum.org/ agenda/2019/05/ten-ways-to-spot-a-truly-exceptional-employee.
9. Amy Adkins, "Millennials: The Job-Hopping Generation," *Gallup*, https:// www.gallup.com/workplace/231587/millennials-job-hopping-generation .aspx.
10. Anjuli Sastry, "The Right Mentor Can Change Your Career. Here's How to Find One," *NPR*, September 3, 2020, https://www.npr.org/ 2019/10/25/773158390/how-to-find-a-mentor-and-make-it-work.
11. Ibid.
12. Indeed Editorial Team, "Hard Skills vs. Soft Skills," *Indeed.com*, November 25, 2020, https://www.indeed.com/career-advice/resumes-cover -letters/hard-skills-vs-soft-skills.

13. Jon Shields, "What Do Corporate Recruiters Look For? We Asked Them," *Jobscan*, November 16, 2017, https://www.jobscan.co/blog/what-corporate-recruiters-want/.

14. Mark Murphy, "Leadership Styles Are Often Why CEOs Get Fired," *Forbes*, July 16, 2015, https://www.forbes.com/sites/markmurphy/2015/07/16/leadership-styles-are-often-why-ceos-get-fired/?sh=4f0f914b4988.

15. Richard Weissbourd et al., "Turning the Tide II: How Parents and High Schools Can Cultivate Ethical Character and Reduce Distress in the College Admissions Process," *Harvard Graduate School of Education*, March 2019, https://mcc.gse.harvard.edu/reports/turning-the-tide-2-parents-high-schools-college-admissions.

16. Adam Bryant, "Gary Smith of Ciena: Build a Culture on Trust and Respect," *New York Times*, October 4, 2015, https://www.nytimes.com/2015/10/04/business/gary-smith-of-ciena-build-a-culture-on-trust-and-respect.html.

17. Ibid.

18. Ibid.

19. Jory MacKay, "The Weird Science of First Impressions," *Medium*, November 19, 2014, https://medium.com/swlh/the-weird-science-of-first-impressions-f2daf99043ec.

20. Michelle Trudeau, "You Had Me at Hello: The Science Behind First Impressions," *NPR*, May 5, 2014, https://www.npr.org/sections/health-shots/2014/05/05/308349318/you-had-me-at-hello-the-science-behind-first-impressions.

21. Ibid.

22. Body Language Project.com, "The Six Most Common Types of Smiles and Their Hidden Meaning," http://bodylanguageproject.com/tiny-book-of-body-language/the-six-most-common-types-of-smiles-and-their-hidden-meaning/.

23. Vanessa Van Edwards, "16 Essential Body Language Examples and Their Meanings," *Science of People*, https://www.scienceofpeople.com/body-language-examples/.

24. Jayson Demers, "10 Reasons You're Not Getting Hired," *Inc.com*, March 10, 2015, https://www.inc.com/jayson-demers/10-reasons-you-re-not-getting-hired.html.

25. *Business Insider India*, "25 Super-Successful People Share Their Best Career Advice for 20-Somethings," https://www.businessinsider.in/careers/25-super-successful-people-share-their-best-career-advice-for-20-somethings/slidelist/48089213.cms.

26. *Quote Investigator*, "It Is Not the Strongest of the Species That Survives But the Most Adaptable: Charles Darwin? Leon C. Megginson? Clarence Darrow? Apocryphal?" May 4, 2014, https://quoteinvestigator .com/2014/05/04/adapt/.

CHAPTER 2

1. Richard Fry, "Millennials Overtake Baby Boomers as America's Largest Generation," *Pew Research Center*, April 28, 2020, https://www.pew research.org/fact-tank/2020/04/28/millennials-overtake-baby-boomers-as -americas-largest-generation/.

2. http://crouchnet.com/Reference%20Docs/Bio%20&%20Bibliography .pdf.

3. Nicholas Kristof, "The Four Secrets of Success," *New York Times*, December 7, 2019, https://www.nytimes.com/2019/12/07/opinion/sunday/ student-success-advice.html.

4. Arwa Mahdawi, "Why Are Thirtysomethings Lonely? Because Society Doesn't Value Friendship," *The Guardian*, August 7, 2019, https://www.the guardian.com/commentisfree/2019/aug/07/why-are-thirtysomethings-lonely -because-society-doesnt-value-friendship.

5. Ibid.

6. David S. Rose, *The Startup Checklist: 25 Steps to a Scalable, High-Growth Business* (Hoboken, NJ: Wiley, 2016), xx.

7. "A Real Gem: HP's Audio Oscillator Patent Turns 60," HP.com, January 22, 2002, http://www.hp.com/hpinfo/abouthp/histnfacts/museum/early instruments/0002/0002history.html.

8. "Who Was William Arthur Ward?" *Reference*, April 6, 2020, https:// www.reference.com/world-view/william-arthur-ward-c469181241df9d41.

9. Adam Markel, *Pivot: The Art and Science of Reinventing Your Life* (New York, NY: Atria Books, 2016), xx.

10. James Kwantes, "Robert Friedland and Steve Jobs: How One Billionaire Influenced Another," *CEO.CA*, September 14, 2012, http://blog.ceo.ca/ 2012/09/14/robert-friedland-and-steve-jobs-how-one-billionaire-influenced -another/.

11. Jack Welch, "Importance of Having a Mentor" [video], Jack Welch Management Institute, Strayer, https://jackwelch.strayer.edu/winning/ importance-of-having-a-mentor/.

12. Nicole Lyn Pesce, "Why Millennials Make Great Mentors," January 17, 2019, https://www.marketwatch.com/story/why-gen-z-and-millennial -workers-make-great-mentors-2018-10-24-1388139.

13. Ibid.

14. Eliza Collins, "Alexandria Ocasio-Cortez, a Social Media Star, to School House Democrats on Twitter Use," *USA Today*, January 16, 2019, https://www.usatoday.com/story/news/politics/2019/01/16/alexandria-ocasio -cortez-lawmakers-tap-new-members-twitter-expertise/2592539002/.

15. Carrie Blazina and Drew Desilver, "Boomers, Silents Still Have Most Seats in Congress, though Number of Millennials, Gen Xers Is Up Slightly," *Pew Research Center*, February 12, 2021, https://www.pewresearch.org/fact -tank/2021/02/12/boomers-silents-still-have-most-seats-in-congress-though -number-of-millennials-gen-xers-is-up-slightly/.

16. Beatrice Jin, "Congress' Incoming Class Is Younger, Bluer, and More Diverse than Ever," *Politico*, November 23, 2018, https://www.politico .com/interactives/2018/interactive_116th-congress-freshman-younger-bluer -diverse/.

17. Pesce, "Why Millennials Make Great Mentors."

CHAPTER 3

1. Nikki Graf, "Today's Young Workers Are More Likely than Ever to Have a Bachelor's Degree," *Pew Research Center*, May 16, 2017, https:// www.pewresearch.org/fact-tank/2017/05/16/todays-young-workers-are-more -likely-than-ever-to-have-a-bachelors-degree/.

2. Stephanie Marken, "Half in U.S. Now Consider College Education Very Important," *Gallup*, December 30, 2019, https://www.gallup.com/education/ 272228/half-consider-college-education-important.aspx.

3. National Center for Education Statistics, "Use the Data," https://nces .ed.gov/ipeds/use-the-data.

4. Ben Miller, "It's Time to Worry about College Enrollment Declines among Black Students," *Center for American Progress*, September 28, 2020, https://www.americanprogress.org/issues/education-postsecondary/ reports/2020/09/28/490838/time-worry-college-enrollment-declines-among -black-students/.

5. Kristen Bialik and Richard Fry, "Millennial Life: How Young Adulthood Today Compares with Prior Generations," *Pew Research Center*, January 30, 2019, https://www.pewresearch.org/social-trends/2019/02/14/millennial-life -how-young-adulthood-today-compares-with-prior-generations-2/.

6. "Millennials: The Overqualified Workforce," *Deloitte Insights*, January 2019, https://www2.deloitte.com/us/en/insights/economy/spotlight/economics -insights-analysis-01-2019.html.

7. "Number of People with Master's and Doctoral Degrees Doubles since 2000," US Census Bureau, https://www.census.gov/library/stories/ 2019/02/number-of-people-with-masters-and-phd-degrees-double-since -2000.html.

8. Sandy Baum and Adam Looney, "Who Owes the Most in Student Loans: New Data from the Fed," *Brookings*, October 9, 2020, https://www .brookings.edu/blog/up-front/2020/10/09/who-owes-the-most-in-student -loans-new-data-from-the-fed/.

9. Anthony Cilluffo, "5 Facts about Student Loans," *Pew Research Center*, August 13, 2019, https://www.pewresearch.org/fact-tank/2019/08/13/facts -about-student-loans/.

10. Terri Williams, "Advice for Prospective Business School Students from Successful MBA Grads," *The Economist GMAT Tutor*, https://gmat .economist.com/gmat-advicebusiness-school-admissions/application-advice/ advice-prospective-business-school-students-successful-mba-grads.

11. Ibid.

12. "Stand and Deliver," *IMDB*, 1988, https://www.imdb.com/title/ tt0094027/.

13. Zac Auter and Stephanie Marken, "Professors Provide Most Valued Career Advice to Grads," *Gallup*, November 16, 2018, https://news.gallup .com/poll/244811/professors-provide-valued-career-advice-grads.aspx.

14. Ibid.

15. Anthony P. Carnevale, Artem Gulish, and Jeff Strohl, "Educational Adequacy in the Twenty-First Century," *The Century Foundation*, May 2, 2018, https://productiontcf.imgix.net/app/uploads/2018/04/01160741/TCF _EducationalAdequacyReport.pdf.

16. Jeffrey Selingo and Matt Sigelman, "The Crisis of Unemployed College Graduates," *Wall Street Journal*, February 4, 2021, https://www.wsj .com/articles/the-crisis-of-unemployed-college-graduates-11612454124.

17. Ibid.

18. Angela Duckworth, *Grit: The Power of Passion and Perseverance* (New York, NY: Scribner, 2016).

19. "Setbacks Quotes," *BrainyQuote.com*, https://www.brainyquote.com/ topics/setbacks-quotes_2.

20. Selingo and Sigelman, "The Crisis of Unemployed College Graduates."

PART II

1. Jeff Goins, *The Art of Work* (Nashville, TN: Nelson Books, 2015), XX.

2. "Deloitte Global Millennial Survey 2019," *Deloitte*, https://www2. deloitte.com/content/dam/Deloitte/global/Documents/About-Deloitte/ deloitte-2019-millennial-survey.pdf.

3. J. P. Box, "Unlocking the Talents of the Millennial Lawyer," *Law Practice Today*, April 13, 2018, https://www.lawpracticetoday.org/article/unlock -talents-millennial-lawyer/.

4. "Deloitte Global Millennial Survey 2019."

5. Maggie Overfelt, "Millennial Employees Are a Lot More Loyal than Their Job-Hopping Stereotype," *CNBC*, updated May 11, 2017, https:// www.cnbc.com/2017/05/10/90-of-millennials-will-stay-in-a-job-for-10-years -if-two-needs-met.html.

6. Ryan Avery and James Goodnow, *Motivating Millennials* (City, State: AveryToday, 2017), xx.

7. https://www.gallup.com/workplace/238073/millennials-work-live.aspx.

8. Ilana Kowarski, "How to Become a Doctor: A Step-by Step Guide," *U.S. News*, November 30, 2020, https://www.usnews.com/education/best -graduate-schools/top-medical-schools/articles/how-to-become-a-doctor-a -step-by-step-guide.

9. Leslie Kane, "Physician Compensation Overview, 2020," *Medscape*, May 14, 2020, https://www.medscape.com/slideshow/2020-compensation -overview-6012684.

10. "Engineering Careers and the Education You'll Need," *All Engineering Schools*, https://www.allengineeringschools.com/engineering-careers/article/ become-engineer/.

11. "2021 Engineering Salary Statistics," *Michigan Tech*, https://www.mtu .edu/engineering/outreach/welcome/salary/.

12. "Becoming an Army Officer," US Army, https://www.goarmy.com/ careers-and-jobs/become-an-officer/how-to-become-an-officer-in-the-army .html.

13. "Become an Officer: Frequently Asked Questions," US Army, https:// www.goarmy.com/careers-and-jobs/become-an-officer/army-officer-faqs .html#live.

14. "Master of Business Administration," *College Choice*, June 25, 2021, https://www.collegechoice.net/faq/what-are-the-requirements-for-an-mba/.

15. https://www.careerbuilder.com.

16. "Family Business Facts," Johnson Cornell, https://www.johnson.cornell.edu/smith-family-business-initiative-at-cornell/resources/family-business-facts/.

17. "America's Economic Engine," *Conway Center for Family Business*, https://www.familybusinesscenter.com/resources/family-business-facts/.

18. "The 100 Largest Global and U.S. Family Businesses and the 100 Oldest U.S. Family Businesses," *Family Business*, https://www.familybusinessmagazine.com/100-largest-global-and-us-family-businesses-and-100-oldest-us-family-businesses.

CHAPTER 4

1. Darian Somers and Josh Moody, "10 College Majors with the Best Starting Salaries," *U.S. News*, September 14, 2020, https://www.usnews.com/education/best-colleges/slideshows/10-college-majors-with-the-highest-starting-salaries.

2. Ibid.

3. Anthony P. Carnevale et al., "The Economic Value of College Majors," Georgetown University Center on Education and the Workforce, 2015, https://1gyhoq479ufd3yna29x7ubjn-wpengine.netdna-ssl.com/wp-content/uploads/The-Economic-Value-of-College-Majors-Full-Report-web-FINAL.pdf.

4. Somers and Moody, "10 College Majors with the Best Starting Salaries."

5. https://www.naceweb.org/job-market/compensation/starting-salary-projections-for-top-earning-degrees-lev.

6. https://www.boston.com/author/elaine-varelas.

7. Adam Grant, "The One Question You Should Ask about Every New Job," *New York Times*, December 20, 2015, https://www.nytimes.com/2015/12/20/opinion/sunday/the-one-question-you-should-ask-about-every-new-job.html.

8. Ibid.

9. "Internships by the Numbers," *Chegg Internships*, September 8, 2020, https://www.internships.com/career-advice/basics/internships-by-the-numbers.

10. Lola Fadulu, "Why Aren't College Students Using Career Services?" *The Atlantic*, January 20, 2018, https://www.theatlantic.com/education/archive/2018/01/why-arent-college-students-using-career-services/551051/.

11. Peter Vogt, "Seven Not-So-Obvious Reasons to Take Advantage of Your Campus Career Center," *LiveCareer*, https://www.livecareer.com/resources/jobs/search/campus-career-centers.

12. "Walt Disney (DIS)," *Forbes*, https://www.forbes.com/companies/walt-disney/?sh=4912bb7a5730.

13. "Employees' Choice Awards 2021 Best Places to Work," *Glassdoor*, https://www.glassdoor.com/Award/Best-Places-to-Work-LST_KQ0,19.htm.

14. "How to Write a Successful College Graduate Resume (With Job-Winning Sample)," *Indeed.com*, May 17, 2021, https://www.indeed.com/career-advice/resumes-cover-letters/college-graduate-resume.

15. "Hard Skills vs. Soft Skills," *Indeed.com*, November 25, 2020, https://www.indeed.com/career-advice/resumes-cover-letters/hard-skills-vs-soft-skills.

16. Ibid.

17. Heather Long, "The New Normal: 4 Job Changes by the Time You're 32," *CNN Business*, April 12, 2016, https://money.cnn.com/2016/04/12/news/economy/millennials-change-jobs-frequently/.

18. Olivia Allen, "Millennials: 5 Ways We're Reinventing the Workplace," *Kforce*, https://www.kforce.com/articles/millennials-5-ways-were-reinventing-the-workforce.

19. Monica Rodriguez, "Is This the End of the Unpaid Internship?" *Fortune*, July 2, 2018, https://fortune.com/2018/07/02/unpaid-internships-ending/.

20. Nick Morrison, "You Don't Need to Be an Intern to Get a Job," *Forbes*, May 13, 2019, https://www.forbes.com/sites/nickmorrison/2019/05/13/you-dont-need-to-be-an-intern-to-get-a-job/?sh=498fe58742ce.

21. Ibid.

22. Eric Woodward, *The Ultimate Guide to Internships* (New York: All-worth, 2015), xx.

23. Noah Parsons, "What Is a SWOT Analysis and How to Do It Right (with Examples)," *LivePlan*, February 2, 2021, https://www.liveplan.com/blog/what-is-a-swot-analysis-and-how-to-do-it-right-with-examples/.

CHAPTER 5

1. Jennifer Burrowes et al., "Bridge the Gap: Rebuilding America's Middle Skills," *Harvard Business School*, https://www.hbs.edu/competitiveness/Documents/bridge-the-gap.pdf.

2. Ilana Kowarski, "4 Reasons to Delay Applying to Business School," *U.S. News & World Report*, July 6, 2017, https://www.usnews.com/education/best-graduate-schools/top-business-schools/articles/2017-07-06/4-reasons-to-delay-applying-to-business-school.

3. Ibid.

4. Bethany Garner, "Should I Get My MBA Right After Undergrad? Ask Yourself These 5 Questions First," *Business Because*, January 11, 2020, https://www.businessbecause.com/news/admissions-stories/6566/should-i -get-my-mba-right-after-undegrad-ask-these-5-questions-first?sponsored.

5. "Top MBA Programs Where You Can Apply as a College Senior," *Ivy-Wise*, https://www.ivywise.com/ivywise-knowledgebase/resources/article/top -mba-programs-where-you-can-apply-as-college-senior/.

6. Brian DeChesare, "Management Consulting vs Investment Banking: The Eternal Battle," *Mergers & Acquisitions*, https://www.mergersand inquisitions.com/management-consulting-vs-investment-banking/.

7. "Should You Go to Grad School Right After Undergrad?" *The Princeton Review*, https://www.princetonreview.com/grad-school-advice/should-you -go-to-grad-school-right-after-undergrad.

8. Ananya Bhatt, "120 John Wooden Quotes to Motivate You to Succeed," *The Random Vibez*, March 22, 2021, https://www.therandomvibez.com/ john-wooden-quotes/.

9. Amy Adkins, "Millennials: The Job-Hopping Generation," *Gallup*, https:// www.gallup.com/workplace/231587/millennials-job-hopping-generation .aspx.

10. "Internships by the Numbers," *Chegg Internships*, September 8, 2020, https://www.internships.com/career-advice/basics/internships-by-the -numbers.

11. Onicia Muller, "Should You Take a Gap Year? Here's What Experts Say," *Today*, September 16, 2020, https://www.today.com/tmrw/ should-you-take-gap-year-here-s-what-experts-say-t190699.

12. Ibid.

13. Ibid.

14. Ibid.

15. Ibid.

16. Colin Murchison, "The Pros & Cons of Taking a Gap Year," *Go Overseas*, November 25, 2020, https://www.gooverseas.com/blog/ pros-and-cons-taking-gap-year.

17. "Gap Year Benefits," Gap Year Association, https://www.gapyear association.org/data-benefits.php.

18. Samantha Subin, "Millennials, Gen Z Are Job-Hopping, But Contrary to Popular Belief, Maybe Not Enough," *CNBC.com*, February 28, 2021, https://www.cnbc.com/2021/02/28/millennials-gen-z-are-job-hopping-but -maybe-not-enough.html.

CHAPTER 6

1. "Gig," *Merriam-Webster.com*, https://www.merriam-webster.com/dictionary/gig.

2. https://www.macdonaldlaurier.ca/experts/linda-nazareth/.

3. Elka Torpey and Andrew Hogan, "Working in a Gig Economy," US Bureau of Labor Statistics, May 2016, https://www.bls.gov/career outlook/2016/article/what-is-the-gig-economy.htm.

4. Ibid.

5. "Gig economy," *Merriam-Webster.com*, https://www.merriam-webster.com/dictionary/gig%20economy.

6. Josh Zumbrun, "How Estimates of the Gig Economy Went Wrong," *Wall Street Journal*, January 7, 2019, https://www.wsj.com/articles/how-estimates-of-the-gig-economy-went-wrong-11546857000.

7. Robin Madell, "What Is the Gig Economy? Definition, Pros & Cons, Jobs," *Flexjobs*, January 17, 2020, https://www.flexjobs.com/blog/post/what-is-the-gig-economy-v2/.

8. "AAPSS Fellows Alan Krueger and Lawrence Katz Reconsider the 'Gig Economy,'" *American Academy of Political & Social Science*, February 8, 2019, https://www.aapss.org/news/category-fellows-fellows-alan-krueger-and-lawrence-katz-reconsider-the-gig-economy/.

9. "People at Work 2021: A Global Workforce View," *ADP Research Institute*, April 27, 2021, https://www.adpri.org.

10. Samantha Subin, "Millennials, Gen Z Are Job-Hopping, But Contrary to Popular Belief, Maybe Not Enough," *CNBC.com*, February 28, 2021, https://www.cnbc.com/2021/02/28/millennials-gen-z-are-job-hopping-but-maybe-not-enough.html.

11. http://www.marciapledger.com.

12. "Gig Economy," *Investopedia*, February 4, 2021, https://www.investopedia.com/terms/g/gig-economy.asp.

13. Gabriel San Roman, "Cal State Fullerton Professor Co-Edits New Anthology on Unemployment," *OC Weekly*, April 12, 2017, https://www.ocweekly.com/csuf-professor-co-edits-new-book-on-unemployment-8031418/.

14. Julian Zelizer, "'It's the Economy, Stupid' All Over Again," *CNN.com*, May 8, 2020, https://www.cnn.com/2020/05/08/opinions/economy-2020-election-trump-biden-zelizer/index.html.

15. Gregory Daco, "The Economic Outlook under President Biden," *Oxford Economics*, https://blog.oxfordeconomics.com/the-economic-outlook-under-president-biden.

16. Marion McGovern, *Thriving in the Gig Economy: How to Capitalize and Compete in the New World of Work* (Newburyport, MA: Weiser, 2017), xx.

17. Diane Mulcahy, *The Gig Economy: The Complete Guide to Getting Better Work, Taking More Time Off, and Financing the Life You Want* (New York: AMACOM, 2016).

18. Annie Nova, "The Real Reason So Many People Are Working 'Side Hustles,'" *CNBC.com*, May 17, 2018, https://www.cnbc.com/2018/05/17/the-real-reason-so-many-people-are-working-side-hustles.html.

19. "Betterment's 2018 Report: Gig Economy and the Future of Retirement," *Betterment*, https://www.betterment.com/uploads/2018/05/The-Gig-Economy-Freelancing-and-Retirement-Betterment-Survey-2018_edited.pdf.

20. Jonathan Rothwell and Jessica Harlan, "Self-Employment and Gig Economy Trends in the U.S.," *Quickbooks*, 2019, https://quickbooks.intuit.com/self-employed/report/.

21. Kelly Monahan et al., "Decoding Millennials in the Gig Economy: Six Trends to Watch in Alternative Work," *Deloitte*, May 1, 2018, https://www2.deloitte.com/us/en/insights/focus/technology-and-the-future-of-work/millennials-in-the-gig-economy.html.

22. Ibid.

23. Katy Steinmetz, "Exclusive: See How Big the Gig Economy Really Is," *Time*, January 6, 2016, https://time.com/4169532/sharing-economy-poll/.

24. https://staffingindustry.com/?region=site.

25. Chiradeep BasuMallick, "15 Top Gig Economy Companies," *Gigonomy*, July 3, 2020, https://gigonomy.info/15-top-gig-economy-companies/.

26. "Through the Lens of Students: How Perceptions of Higher Education Influence Applicants' Choices," *UCAS*, July 2016, https://www.ucas.com/sites/default/files/through-the-lens-of-students.pdf.

27. "Underemployment: Research on the Long-Term Impact on Careers," *Burning-Glass Technologies*, https://www.burning-glass.com/research-project/underemployment/.

28. Shelly Steward, "JPMorgan Chase Institute Report Shows Continued Growth in Platform Work," *Gig Economy Data Hub*, September 24, 2018, https://www.gigeconomydata.org/blog/jpmorgan-chase-institute-report-shows-continued-growth-platform-work.

29. https://www.pewresearch.org/2015/?category_name=survey-report.

30. "68% of U.S. Consumer Products Companies Use Outsourcing," *Noria Corporation*, https://www.reliableplant.com/Read/1716/68-of-us-consumer-products-companies-use-outsourcing.

31. Matt Witschel, "Union Organizing and Gig-Economy Workers," *Wall Street Journal*, September 13, 2020, https://www.wsj.com/articles/union-organizing-and-gig-economy-workers-11600018191.
32. Charles Duhigg et al., "What Makes a 'Good Job' Good?" *New York Times Magazine*, January 1, 2019, xx.

CHAPTER 7

1. Peter Brooke obituary, *Wall Street Journal*, https://www.wsj.com/articles/peter-brooke-remembered-as-founding-father-of-private-equity-11586469840.
2. Roger Thompson, "Ten Rules for Entrepreneurs," *Harvard Business School*, December 2, 2010, https://www.alumni.hbs.edu/stories/Pages/story-bulletin.aspx?num=1690.
3. "Team," *Swift River Capital*, http://swiftrivercapital.com/team.html.
4. "#1317 Herb Chambers," *Forbes*, https://www.forbes.com/profile/herb-chambers/?sh=2328883b2483.
5. "Thomas Edison," *Biography.com*, updated April 2, 2021, https://www.biography.com/inventor/thomas-edison.
6. Marina I. Jokic, "The Story of Edwin Land," *The Harvard Gazette*, December 7, 2016, https://news.harvard.edu/gazette/story/2016/12/the-story-of-edwin-land/.
7. Malcolm Gladwell, "The Art of Failure," *New Yorker*, August 13, 2000, https://www.newyorker.com/magazine/2000/08/21/the-art-of-failure.
8. Samra Khawaja, "The Art of Failure," *National Endowment for the Arts*, April 18, 2016, https://www.arts.gov/stories/blog/2016/art-failure.
9. Courtney Connley, "Suzy Welch: 3 Signs You've Got What It Takes to Be a Successful Entrepreneur," *CNBC.com*, January 15, 2019, https://www.cnbc.com/2019/01/14/suzy-welch-here-are-the-3-things-you-need-to-start-and-build-a-business.html.
10. Zach Bulygo, "12 Business Lessons You Can Learn from Amazon Founder Jeff Bezos," *Neil Patel*, https://neilpatel.com/blog/lessons-from-jeff-bezos/.
11. Hayley Peterson, "Jeff Bezos Shares His Best Advice for Anyone Starting a Business," *Business Insider*, June 6, 2019, https://www.businessinsider.com/amazons-jeff-bezos-shares-advice-for-entreprenuers-2019-6.
12. Peter Cohan, "This Survey of 1,300 Harvard Business School Alumni Reveals the 5 Skills You Need to Succeed as an Entrepreneur," *Inc.com*, October 8, 2018, https://www.inc.com/peter-cohan/this-survey-of-1300

-harvard-business-school-alumni-reveals-5-skills-you-need-to-succeed-as-an -entrepreneur.html.

13. Ibid.

14. Mary Ellen Biery, "6 Things to Know About Buy-Sell Agreements," *Forbes*, October 11, 2015, https://www.forbes.com/sites/sageworks/2015/10/11/6 -things-to-know-about-buy-sell-agreements/?sh=60c86c7f75b8.

15. "About," *Shark Tank*, https://abc.com/shows/shark-tank/about-the -show.

16. "Disruptive Innovation," *Christensen Institute*, https://www.christensen institute.org/disruptive-innovations/.

17. David S. Rose, *The Startup Checklist: 25 Steps to a Scalable, High-Growth Business* (Hoboken, NJ: Wiley, 2016), xx.

18. "Write Your Business Plan," *Small Business Administration*, https:// www.sba.gov/starting-business/write-your-business-plan%20.

19. Bulygo, "12 Business Lessons You Can Learn from Amazon Founder Jeff Bezos."

CHAPTER 8

1. Suzanne Morrison-Williams, "Millennials—Changing the Face of Higher Education," *Education Initiative*, https://educationinitiative.thepacific institute.com/articles/story/millennials-changing-the-face-of-higher -education.

2. "ME104B: Designing Your Life," *Stanford Life Design Lab*, http://life designlab.stanford.edu/dyl.

3. Bill Burnett and Dave Evans, *Designing Your Life: How to Build a Well-Lived, Joyful Life* (New York, NY: Knopf, 2016); and Bill Burnett and Dave Evans, *Designing Your Work Life: How to Thrive and Change and Find Happiness at Work* (New York: Knopf, 2020).

4. Zack Friedman, "Student Loan Debt Statistics in 2019: A $1.5 Trillion Crisis," *Forbes*, February 25, 2019, https://www.forbes.com/sites/zack friedman/2019/02/25/student-loan-debt-statistics-2019/?sh=4581902f133f.

5. "Millennials and Credit Card Debt," *Harvester Financial Credit Union*, https://www.harvesterfcu.org/millennials-and-credit-card-debt/.

6. "Employee Tenure in 2020," *US Bureau of Labor Statistics*, September 22, 2020, https://www.bls.gov/news.release/pdf/tenure.pdf.

7. Branka Vuleta, "30 Remarkable Stats About Millennials in the Workplace," *What to Become*, March 30, 2021, https://whattobecome.com/blog/ millennials-in-the-workplace/.

8. "How Many Times Does the Average Person Move in a Lifetime?" *Steinway Moving & Storage*, July 10, 2018, https://www.steinwaymovers.com/news/how-many-times-does-the-average-person-move-in-a-lifetime.

9. "Sen. Lessor Recommits to Passing Student Loan Bill of Rights, Unveils Expanding Coalition Backing Effort," *Senatorlessor.com*, March 6, 2019, https://www.senatorlesser.com/news/2019/3/8/sen-lesser-recommits-to-passing-student-loan-bill-of-rights-unveils-expanding-coalition-backing-effort.

10. Annie Millerbernd, "What Credit Score Do You Need for a Personal Loan?" *Nerdwallet*, October 15, 2020, https://www.nerdwallet.com/article/loans/personal-loans/credit-score-need-get-personal-loan.

11. Sarah Brodsky, "What Credit Scores Do I Need to Get a Personal Loan?" *CreditKarma.com*, November 3, 2020, https://www.creditkarma.com/personal-loans/i/personal-loan-credit-score.

12. Rick Kranz, "How Much Is the Typical Car Down Payment?" *Kelley Blue Book*, March 26, 2019, https://www.kbb.com/car-news/what-is-the-best-down-payment/.

13. Lance Cothern, "How Much Should Your Car Down Payment Be?" *Money Under 30*, October 19, 2020, https://www.moneyunder30.com/car-down-payment.

14. "Mortgage Calculator," *Nerdwallet*, https://www.nerdwallet.com/mortgages/mortgage-calculator/calculate-mortgage-payment.

15. "Property Tax Calculator," *Smart Asset*, https://smartasset.com/taxes/property-taxes.

16. Jeanne Lee, "What Is Home Equity?" *Bankrate*, April 15, 2021, https://www.bankrate.com/home-equity/what-is-home-equity/.

17. Jim Akin, "What Credit Score Is Needed for a Personal Loan?" *Experian*, April 23, 2020, https://www.experian.com/blogs/ask-experian/what-credit-score-is-needed-for-a-personal-loan/.

CHAPTER 9

1. David Goldman, "Worst Year for Jobs since '45," *CNN Money*, January 9, 2009, https://money.cnn.com/2009/01/09/news/economy/jobs_december/.

2. "Millennials: Coming of Age," *Goldman Sachs*, https://www.goldmansachs.com/insights/archive/millennials/.

3. Stefan Lembo Stolba, "Millennials and Credit: The Struggle Is Real," *Experian*, April 2, 2019, https://www.experian.com/blogs/ask-experian/taking -a-look-at-millennial-credit-scores/.

4. Adedayo Akala, "This Could Be the Worst Job Market for New College Grads since the Financial Crisis," *CNBC.com*, March 29, 2020, https:// www.cnbc.com/2020/03/29/new-grads-may-face-worst-job-market-since -2008-financial-crisis.html.

5. "What Is the Average Salary for College Graduates?" *Indeed.com*, February 22, 2021, https://www.indeed.com/career-advice/pay-salary/average -salary-for-college-graduates.

6. Ibid.

7. Laura Carstensen, "What Millennials Already Know About Growing Old," *Time*, June 16, 2016, https://time.com/4371185/what-millennials -already-know-about-growing-old/.

8. Eric Rosenberg, "What Is Compound Interest?" *CreditKarma.com*, June 1, 2021, https://www.creditkarma.com/savings/i/compound-interest.

9. Michael Molinski, "3 Most Trusted Credit Card Companies," *Investor's Business Daily*, June 9, 2021, https://www.investors.com/news/most -trusted-credit-card-issuers/.

10. Michelle Singletary, "In Your 20s?" *Washington Post*, https://www .washingtonpost.com/business/get-there/in-your-20s-dont-squander-your -biggest-financial-asset-time/2015/09/18/59e1ba04-5b19-11e5-9757-e 49273f05f65_story.html.

11. "Rent Affordability Calculator," *Zillow.com*, https://www.zillow.com/ rent-affordability-calculator/.

12. "Credit Rating," *Bankrate*, https://www.bankrate.com/glossary/c/ credit-rating/.

13. "What's in My FICO® Scores?" *MyFICO.com*, https://www.myfico .com/credit-education/whats-in-your-credit-score.

14. William E. Gibson, "Nearly Half of Americans 55+ Have No Retirement Savings," *AARP*, March 28, 2019, https://www.aarp.org/retirement/ retirement-savings/info-2019/no-retirement-money-saved.html.

15. Amelia Josephson, "Average Retirement Savings: Are You Normal?" *Smart Asset*, December 15, 2020, https://smartasset.com/retirement/average -retirement-savings-are-you-normal.

16. "Retirement Savings Assessment 2020," *Fidelity Investments*, https://www.fidelity.com/bin-public/060_www_fidelity_com/documents/ about-fidelity/2020-rsa-executive-summary.pdf.

17. https://nb.fidelity.com/public/nb/401k.

18. J. B. Maverick, "What Is the Average Annual Return for the S&P 500?" *Investopedia*, June 1, 2021, https://www.investopedia.com/ask/answers/042415/what-average-annual-return-sp-500.asp.

CHAPTER 10

1. "One-Third of Consumers Live Paycheck to Paycheck, TD Survey Finds," *PR Newswire*, July 26, 2018, https://www.prnewswire.com/news-releases/one-third-of-consumers-live-paycheck-to-paycheck-td-survey-finds-300687134.html.

2. Megan Leonhardt, "75% of Millennial Couples Talk About Money at Least Once a Week—And It Seems to Be Working for Them," *CNBC.com*, July 27, 2018, https://www.cnbc.com/2018/07/27/75-percent-of-millennial-couples-talk-about-money-at-least-once-a-week.html.

3. "How Much Credit Card Debt Is Okay?" *ComsumerCredit.com*, https://www.consumercredit.com/how-much-credit-card-debt-is-okay/.

4. Joel Anderson, "Survey: Nearly 40% of Americans Don't Know Their Credit Score—Do You?" *Yahoo! Money*, November 14, 2019, https://money.yahoo.com/survey-nearly-40-americans-don-053700667.html.

5. Wesley Whistle, "Millennials and Student Loans: Rising Debts and Disparities," *New America*, https://www.newamerica.org/millennials/reports/emerging-millennial-wealth-gap/millennials-and-student-loans-rising-debts-and-disparities.

6. Michele Gorman, "Yogi Berra's Most Memorable Sayings," *Newsweek*, September 23, 2015, https://www.newsweek.com/most-memorable-yogi-isms-375661.

7. Amanda Barroso et al., "As Millennials Near 40, They're Approaching Family Life Differently than Previous Generations," *Pew Research Center*, May 27, 2020, https://www.pewresearch.org/social-trends/2020/05/27/as-millennials-near-40-theyre-approaching-family-life-differently-than-previous-generations.

8. Frank Olito, "The Average Age People Get Married in Every State," *Insider*. February 4, 2019, https://www.insider.com/when-people-get-married-every-state-2019-1.

9. Barroso et al., "As Millennials Near 40, They're Approaching Family Life Differently than Previous Generations."

10. Jessica Dickler, "Pandemic Sends the Majority of Young Adults Back to Living with Mom and Dad," *CNBC.com*, September 8, 2020, https://www

.cnbc.com/2020/09/08/majority-of-young-adults-now-live-with-mom-and -dad-due-to-coronavirus.html.

11. Esther Lee, "This Was the Average Cost of a Wedding in 2020," *The Knot*, February 11, 2021, https://www.theknot.com/content/average-wedding -cost.

12. Mark Lino, "The Cost of Raising a Child," *USDA*, February 18, 2020, https://www.usda.gov/media/blog/2017/01/13/cost-raising-child.

13. "How Much Does It Cost to Host an Au Pair?" *Cultural Care Au Pair*, https://culturalcare.com/pricing/.

14. Gabbi Shaw, "These Are the 11 Most Common Reasons People Get Divorced, Ranked," *Insider*, January 31, 2019, https://www.insider.com/why -people-get-divorced-2019-1.

15. Nancy L. Anderson, "5 Financial Mistakes That Ruin Your Marriage," *Forbes*, November 10, 2011, https://www.forbes.com/sites/financial finesse/2011/11/10/5-financial-mistakes-that-ruin-your-marriage-2/?sh =b7b9b9bafa50.

16. Shaw, "These Are the 11 Most Common Reasons People Get Divorced, Ranked."

17. Elizabeth Renter, "Budgeting for Newlyweds: A Guide to Family Finance," *Nerdwallet*, May 4, 2017, https://www.nerdwallet.com/article/ finance/budgeting-for-newlyweds.

18. "What You Need to Know About Prenuptial Agreements," *Nationwide*, https://www.nationwide.com/lc/resources/personal-finance/articles/ prenuptial-agreement-basics.

19. Nicole Spector, "Prenuptial Agreements: What Is a Prenup and Should I Get One?" *NBC News*, April 12, 2019, https://www.nbcnews.com/better/ lifestyle/prenuptial-agreements-what-prenup-should-i-get-one-ncna993616.

20. "Better Money Habits Millennial Report," Bank of America, Winter 2020, https://about.bankofamerica.com/assets/pdf/2020-bmh-millennial -report.pdf.

21. Rachel Cruze, *Know Yourself, Know Your Money* (Franklin, TN: Ramsey Press, 2021).

22. Paris Ward, "Over 50% of Dating Millennials Don't Want to Marry Until Their Finances Are in Order," *CreditKarma.com*, July 16, 2020, https://www.creditkarma.com/insights/i/millennials-delaying-marriage-to-get -finances-in-order.

BIBLIOGRAPHY

Adkins, Amy. "Millennials: The Job-Hopping Generation." *Gallup*. https://
www.gallup.com/workplace/231587/millennials-job-hopping-generation
.aspx.

ADP Research Institute. "People at Work 2021: A Global Workforce View."
April 27, 2021. https://www.adpri.org.

Akala, Adedayo. "This Could Be the Worst Job Market for New College
Grads since the Financial Crisis." *CNBC.com*. March 29, 2020. https://
www.cnbc.com/2020/03/29/new-grads-may-face-worst-job-market-since
-2008-financial-crisis.html.

Akin, Jim. "What Credit Score Is Needed for a Personal Loan?" *Experian*.
April 23, 2020. https://www.experian.com/blogs/ask-experian/what-credit
-score-is-needed-for-a-personal-loan/.

Allen, Olivia. "Millennials: 5 Ways We're Reinventing the Workplace." *Kforce*.
https://www.kforce.com/articles/millennials-5-ways-were-reinventing
-the-workforce.

All Engineering Schools. "Engineering Careers and the Education You'll Need."
https://www.allengineeringschools.com/engineering-careers/article/
become-engineer/.

American Academy of Political & Social Science. "AAPSS Fellows Alan
Krueger and Lawrence Katz Reconsider the 'Gig Economy.'" February
8, 2019. https://www.aapss.org/news/category-fellows-fellows-alan-krueger
-and-lawrence-katz-reconsider-the-gig-economy/.

Anderson, Joel. "Survey: Nearly 40% of Americans Don't Know Their Credit Score—Do You?" *Yahoo! Money*. November 14, 2019. https://money.yahoo.com/survey-nearly-40-americans-don-053700667.html.

Anderson, Nancy L. "5 Financial Mistakes That Ruin Your Marriage." *Forbes*. November 10, 2011. https://www.forbes.com/sites/financial finesse/2011/11/10/5-financial-mistakes-that-ruin-your-marriage-2/?sh =b7b9b9bafa50.

Auter, Zac, and Stephanie Marken. "Professors Provide Most Valued Career Advice to Grads." *Gallup*. November 16, 2018. https://news.gallup.com/poll/244811/professors-provide-valued-career-advice-grads.aspx.

Avery, Ryan, and James Goodnow. *Motivating Millennials*. New York: Avery Today, 2017.

Bank of America. "Better Money Habits Millennial Report." Winter 2020. https://about.bankofamerica.com/assets/pdf/2020-bmh-millennial-report .pdf.

Bankrate. "Credit Rating." https://www.bankrate.com/glossary/c/credit -rating/.

Barroso, Amanda, Kim Parker, and Jesse Bennett. "As Millennials Near 40, They're Approaching Family Life Differently than Previous Generations." *Pew Research Center*. May 27, 2020. https://www.pewresearch.org/social -trends/2020/05/27/as-millennials-near-40-theyre-approaching-family-life -differently-than-previous-generations.

BasuMallick, Chiradeep. "15 Top Gig Economy Companies." *Gigonomy*. July 3, 2020. https://gigonomy.info/15-top-gig-economy-companies/.

Baum, Sandy, and Adam Looney. "Who Owes the Most in Student Loans: New Data from the Fed." *Brookings*. October 9, 2020. https://www.brookings .edu/blog/up-front/2020/10/09/who-owes-the-most-in-student-loans-new -data-from-the-fed/.

Betterment. "Betterment's 2018 Report: Gig Economy and the Future of Retirement." https://www.betterment.com/uploads/2018/05/The-Gig -Economy-Freelancing-and-Retirement-Betterment-Survey-2018_edited .pdf.

Bhatt, Ananya. "120 John Wooden Quotes to Motivate You to Succeed." *The Random Vibez*. March 22, 2021. https://www.therandomvibez.com/john-wooden-quotes/.

Biography.com. "Thomas Edison." Updated April 2, 2021. https://www .biography.com/inventor/thomas-edison.

Bialik, Kristen, and Richard Fry. "Millennial Life: How Young Adulthood Today Compares with Prior Generations." *Pew Research Center*. January 30, 2019. https://www.pewresearch.org/social-trends/2019/02/14/

millennial-life-how-young-adulthood-today-compares-with-prior
-generations-2/.

Biery, Mary Ellen. "6 Things to Know About Buy-Sell Agreements." *Forbes*. October 11, 2015. https://www.forbes.com/sites/sageworks/2015/10/11/6 -things-to-know-about-buy-sell-agreements/?sh=60c86c7f75b8.

Blazina, Carrie, and Drew Desilver. "Boomers, Silents Still Have Most Seats in Congress, though Number of Millennials, Gen Xers Is Up Slightly." *Pew Research Center*. February 12, 2021. https://www.pewresearch.org/ fact-tank/2021/02/12/boomers-silents-still-have-most-seats-in-congress -though-number-of-millennials-gen-xers-is-up-slightly/.

Body Language Project.com. "The Six Most Common Types of Smiles and Their Hidden Meaning." ttp://bodylanguageproject.com/tiny-book -of-body-language/the-six-most-common-types-of-smiles-and-their -hidden-meaning/.

Box, J. P. "Unlocking the Talents of the Millennial Lawyer." *Law Practice Today*. April 13, 2018. https://www.lawpracticetoday.org/article/unlock -talents-millennial-lawyer/.

Bradberry, Travis. "10 Ways to Spot a Truly Exceptional Employee." *World Economic Forum*. May 2, 2019. https://www.weforum.org/agenda/2019/05/ ten-ways-to-spot-a-truly-exceptional-employee.

BrainyQuote.com. "Setbacks Quotes." https://www.brainyquote.com/topics/ setbacks-quotes_2.

Brodsky, Sarah. "What Credit Scores Do I Need to Get a Personal Loan?" *CreditKarma.com*. November 3, 2020. https://www.creditkarma.com/ personal-loans/i/personal-loan-credit-score.

Bryant, Adam. "Gary Smith of Ciena: Build a Culture on Trust and Respect." *New York Times*. October 4, 2015. https://www.nytimes.com/2015/10/04/ business/gary-smith-of-ciena-build-a-culture-on-trust-and-respect.html.

Bulygo, Zach. "12 Business Lessons You Can Learn from Amazon Founder Jeff Bezos." *Neil Patel*. https://neilpatel.com/blog/lessons-from-jeff-bezos/.

Burnett, Bill, and Dave Evans. *Designing Your Life: How to Build a Well-Lived, Joyful Life*. New York: Knopf, 2016.

Burnett, Bill, and Dave Evans. *Designing Your Work Life: How to Thrive and Change and Find Happiness at Work*. New York: Knopf, 2020.

Burning-Glass Technologies. "Underemployment: Research on the Long-Term Impact on Careers." https://www.burning-glass.com/research-project/ underemployment/.

Burrowes, Jennifer, Alexis Young, Dan Restuccia, Joseph Fuller, and Manjari Raman. "Bridge the Gap: Rebuilding America's Middle Skills." *Harvard Business School*. https://www.hbs.edu/competitiveness/Documents/bridge -the-gap.pdf.

Business.com. "From Texting to Tweeting: Tech-Savvy Millennials Changing the Way We Work." March 4, 2020. https://www.business.com/articles/tech-savvy-millennials-at-work/.

Business Insider India. "25 Super-Successful People Share Their Best Career Advice for 20-Somethings." https://www.businessinsider.in/careers/25-super-successful-people-share-their-best-career-advice-for-20-somethings/slidelist/48089213.cms.

Carnevale, Anthony P., Ban Cheah, and Andrew R. Hanson. "The Economic Value of College Majors." Georgetown University Center on Education and the Workforce. 2015. https://1gyhoq479ufd3yna29x7ubjn-wpengine.netdna-ssl.com/wp-content/uploads/The-Economic-Value-of-College-Majors-Full-Report-web-FINAL.pdf.

Carnevale, Anthony P., Artem Gulish, and Jeff Strohl. "Educational Adequacy in the Twenty-First Century." *The Century Foundation.* May 2, 2018. https://productiontcf.imgix.net/app/uploads/2018/04/01160741/TCF_EducationalAdequacyReport.pdf

Carstensen, Laura. "What Millennials Already Know About Growing Old." *Time.* June 16, 2016. https://time.com/4371185/what-millennials-already-know-about-growing-old/.

Carter, Sherrie Bourg. "The Art and Value of Good Listening." *Psychology Today.* September 28, 2012. https://www.psychologytoday.com/us/blog/high-octane-women/201209/the-art-and-value-good-listening.

Chegg Internships. "Internships by the Numbers." September 8, 2020. https://www.internships.com/career-advice/basics/internships-by-the-numbers.

Christensen Institute. "Disruptive Innovation." https://www.christensen institute.org/disruptive-innovations/.

Cilluffo, Anthony. "5 Facts about Student Loans." *Pew Research Center.* August 13, 2019. https://www.pewresearch.org/fact-tank/2019/08/13/facts-about-student-loans/.

Cohan, Peter. "This Survey of 1,300 Harvard Business School Alumni Reveals the 5 Skills You Need to Succeed as an Entrepreneur." *Inc.com.* October 8, 2018. https://www.inc.com/peter-cohan/this-survey-of-1300-harvard-business-school-alumni-reveals-5-skills-you-need-to-succeed-as-an-entrepreneur.html.

College Choice. "Master of Business Administration." June 25, 2021. https://www.collegechoice.net/faq/what-are-the-requirements-for-an-mba/.

Collins, Eliza. "Alexandria Ocasio-Cortez, a Social Media Star, to School House Democrats on Twitter Use." *USA Today.* January 16, 2019. https://www.usatoday.com/story/news/politics/2019/01/16/alexandria-ocasio-cortez-lawmakers-tap-new-members-twitter-expertise/2592539002/.

Connley, Courtney. "Suzy Welch: 3 Signs You've Got What It Takes to Be a Successful Entrepreneur." *CNBC.com.* January 15, 2019. https://www.cnbc.com/2019/01/14/suzy-welch-here-are-the-3-things-you-need-to-start-and-build-a-business.html.

ConsumerCredit.com. "How Much Credit Card Debt Is Okay?" https://www.consumercredit.com/how-much-credit-card-debt-is-okay/.

Conway Center for Family Business. "America's Economic Engine." https://www.familybusinesscenter.com/resources/family-business-facts/.

Cothern, Lance. "How Much Should Your Car Down Payment Be?" *Money Under 30.* October 19, 2020. https://www.moneyunder30.com/car-down-payment.

Crouch, Clark. http://crouchnet.com/Reference%20Docs/Bio%20&%20 Bibliography.pdf.

Cruze, Rachel. *Know Yourself, Know Your Money.* Franklin, TN: Ramsey Press, 2021.

Cultural Care Au Pair. "How Much Does It Cost to Host an Au Pair?" https://culturalcare.com/pricing/.

Daco, Gregory. "The Economic Outlook under President Biden." *Oxford Economics.* https://blog.oxfordeconomics.com/the-economic-outlook-under-president-biden.

DeChesare, Brian. "Management Consulting vs Investment Banking: The Eternal Battle." *Mergers & Acquisitions.* https://www.mergersand inquisitions.com/management-consulting-vs-investment-banking/.

Deloitte. "Deloitte Global Millennial Survey 2019." https://www2.deloitte.com/content/dam/Deloitte/global/Documents/About-Deloitte/deloitte-2019-millennial-survey.pdf.

Deloitte Insights. "Millennials: The Overqualified Workforce." January 2019, https://www2.deloitte.com/us/en/insights/economy/spotlight/economics-insights-analysis-01-2019.html.

Demers, Jayson. "10 Reasons You're Not Getting Hired." *Inc.com.* March 10, 2015. https://www.inc.com/jayson-demers/10-reasons-you-re-not-getting-hired.html.

Dickler, Jessica. "Pandemic Sends the Majority of Young Adults Back to Living with Mom and Dad." *CNBC.com.* September 8, 2020. https://www.cnbc.com/2020/09/08/majority-of-young-adults-now-live-with-mom-and-dad-due-to-coronavirus.html.

Dodd, Paul. *InfinitySolutions.com.* https://www.infinitysolutions.com/author/paul-dodd/.

Duckworth, Angela. *Grit: The Power of Passion and Perseverance.* New York: Scribner, 2016.

Duhigg, Charles, Emily Bazelon, and John Legend. "What Makes a 'Good Job' Good?" *New York Times Magazine*, January 1, 2019.

Fadulu, Lola. "Why Aren't College Students Using Career Services?" *The Atlantic*. January 20, 2018. https://www.theatlantic.com/education/archive/2018/01/why-arent-college-students-using-career-services/551051/.

Family Business. "The 100 Largest Global and U.S. Family Businesses and the 100 Oldest U.S. Family Businesses." https://www.familybusiness magazine.com/100-largest-global-and-us-family-businesses-and-100 -oldest-us-family-businesses.

Fidelity Investments. "Retirement Savings Assessment 2020." https:// www.fidelity.com/bin-public/060_www_fidelity_com/documents/about -fidelity/2020-rsa-executive-summary.pdf.

Forbes. "#1517 Herb Chambers." https://www.forbes.com/profile/herb -chambers/?sh=2328883b2483.

Forbes. "Walt Disney (DIS)." https://www.forbes.com/companies/walt -disney/?sh=4912bb7a5730.

Friedman, Zack. "Student Loan Debt Statistics in 2019: A $1.5 Trillion Crisis." *Forbes*. February 25, 2019. https://www.forbes.com/sites/zackfriedman/2019/02/25/student-loan-debt-statistics-2019/?sh=4581902f133f.

Fry, Richard. "Millennials Overtake Baby Boomers as America's Largest Generation." *Pew Research Center*. April 28, 2020. https://www.pew research.org/fact-tank/2020/04/28/millennials-overtake-baby-boomers-as -americas-largest-generation/.

Gap Year Association. "Gap Year Benefits." https://www.gapyearassociation .org/data-benefits.php.

Garner, Bethany. "Should I Get My MBA Right After Undergrad? Ask Yourself These 5 Questions First." *Business Because*. January 11, 2020. https://www.businessbecause.com/news/admissions-stories/6566/should-i -get-my-mba-right-after-undegrad-ask-these-5-questions-first?sponsored.

Gibson, William E. "Nearly Half of Americans 55+ Have No Retirement Savings." *AARP*. March 28, 2019. https://www.aarp.org/retirement/retirement -savings/info-2019/no-retirement-money-saved.html.

Gilbert, Jay. "The Millennials: A new generation of employees, a new set of engagement policies." *Ivey Business Journal*. September/October 2011. https://iveybusinessjournal.com/publication/the-millennials-a-new -generation-of-employees-a-new-set-of-engagement-policies/.

Gladwell, Malcolm. "The Art of Failure." *New Yorker*. August 13, 2000. https://www.newyorker.com/magazine/2000/08/21/the-art-of-failure.

Glassdoor. "Employees' Choice Awards 2021 Best Places to Work." https:// www.glassdoor.com/Award/Best-Places-to-Work-LST_KQ0,19.htm.

Goins, Jeff. *The Art of Work*. Nashville, TN: Nelson Books, 2015.

Goldman, David. "Worst Year for Jobs since '45." *CNN Money*. January 9, 2009. https://money.cnn.com/2009/01/09/news/economy/jobs_december/.

Goldman Sachs. "Millennials: Coming of Age." https://www.goldmansachs .com/insights/archive/millennials/.

Gorman, Michele. "Yogi Berra's Most Memorable Sayings." *Newsweek*. September 23, 2015. https://www.newsweek.com/most-memorable-yogi -isms-375661.

Graf, Nikki. "Today's Young Workers Are More Likely than Ever to Have a Bachelor's Degree." *Pew Research Center*. May 16, 2017. https://www .pewresearch.org/fact-tank/2017/05/16/todays-young-workers-are-more-lik ely-than-ever-to-have-a-bachelors-degree/.

Grant, Adam. "The One Question You Should Ask about Every New Job." *New York Times*. December 20, 2015. https://www.nytimes.com/2015/12/20/ opinion/sunday/the-one-question-you-should-ask-about-every-new-job .html.

Gulf News. "Women Are Better Listeners, Study Says." February 13, 2014. https://gulfnews.com/world/europe/women-are-better-listeners-study-says -1.1290574.

Harvester Financial Credit Union. "Millennials and Credit Card Debt." https://www.harvesterfcu.org/millennials-and-credit-card-debt/.

Hess, Abigail Johnson. "82% of College Grads Believe Their Bache- lor's Degree Was a Good Investment—But Most Would Make This One Change." *CNBC.com*. February 27, 2020. https://www.cnbc.com/ 2020/02/27/82percent-of-college-grads-believe-their-degree-was-a-good -investment.html.

Hoffower, Hillary. "Meet the Average American Millennial, Who Has an $8,000 Net Worth, Is Delaying Life Milestones Because of Student-Loan Debt, and Still Relies on Parents for Money." *Business Insider*. February 27, 2020. https://www.businessinsider.com/average-american-millennial -net-worth-student-loan-debt-savings-habits-2019-6.

Howe, Neil. "Millennials: A Generation of Page-Turners." *Forbes*. January 16, 2017. https://www.forbes.com/sites/neilhowe/2017/01/16/millennials-a -generation-of-page-turners/?sh=527a4d1f1978.

HP.com. "A Real Gem: HP's Audio Oscillator Patent Turns 60." January 22, 2002. http://www.hp.com/hpinfo/abouthp/histnfacts/museum/earlyinstruments/ 0002/0002history.html.

IMDB. "Stand and Deliver." 1988. https://www.imdb.com/title/tt0094027/.

Indeed.com. "Hard Skills vs. Soft Skills." November 25, 2020. https://www .indeed.com/career-advice/resumes-cover-letters/hard-skills-vs-soft-skills.

Indeed.com. "How to Write a Successful College Graduate Resume (With Job-Winning Sample)." May 17, 2021. https://www.indeed.com/career-advice/resumes-cover-letters/college-graduate-resume.

Indeed.com. "What Is the Average Salary for College Graduates?" February 22, 2021. https://www.indeed.com/career-advice/pay-salary/average-salary-for-college-graduates.

Investopedia. "Gig Economy." February 4, 2021. https://www.investopedia.com/terms/g/gig-economy.asp.

IvyWise. "Top MBA Programs Where You Can Apply as a College Senior." https://www.ivywise.com/ivywise-knowledgebase/resources/article/top-mba-programs-where-you-can-apply-as-college-senior/.

Jansen, Corine. "Sex Differences in Listening." *Global Listening Centre*. https://www.globallisteningcentre.org/sex-differences-in-listening/.

Jin, Beatrice. "Congress' Incoming Class Is Younger, Bluer, and More Diverse than Ever." *Politico*. November 23, 2018. https://www.politico.com/interactives/2018/interactive_116th-congress-freshman-younger-bluer-diverse/.

Johnson Cornell. "Family Business Facts." https://www.johnson.cornell.edu/smith-family-business-initiative-at-cornell/resources/family-business-facts/.

Jokic, Marina I. "The Story of Edwin Land." *The Harvard Gazette*. December 7, 2016. https://news.harvard.edu/gazette/story/2016/12/the-story-of-edwin-land/.

Josephson, Amelia. "Average Retirement Savings: Are You Normal?" *Smart Asset*. December 15, 2020. https://smartasset.com/retirement/average-retirement-savings-are-you-normal.

Kane, Leslie. "Physician Compensation Overview, 2020." *Medscape*. May 14, 2020. https://www.medscape.com/slideshow/2020-compensation-overview-6012684.

Khawaja, Samra. "The Art of Failure." *National Endowment for the Arts*. April 18, 2016. https://www.arts.gov/stories/blog/2016/art-failure.

Kowarski, Ilana. "4 Reasons to Delay Applying to Business School." *U.S. News & World Report*. July 6, 2017. https://www.usnews.com/education/best-graduate-schools/top-business-schools/articles/2017-07-06/4-reasons-to-delay-applying-to-business-school.

Kowarski, Ilana. "How to Become a Doctor: A Step-by Step Guide." *U.S. News & World Report*. November 30, 2020. https://www.usnews.com/education/best-graduate-schools/top-medical-schools/articles/how-to-become-a-doctor-a-step-by-step-guide.

Kranz, Rick. "How Much Is the Typical Car Down Payment?" *Kelley Blue Book*. March 26, 2019. https://www.kbb.com/car-news/what-is-the-best-down-payment/.

Kristof, Nicholas. "The Four Secrets of Success." *New York Times*. December 7, 2019. https://www.nytimes.com/2019/12/07/opinion/sunday/student-success-advice.html.

Kwantes, James. "Robert Friedland and Steve Jobs: How One Billionaire Influenced Another." *CEO.CA*. September 14, 2012. http://blog.ceo.ca/2012/09/14/robert-friedland-and-steve-jobs-how-one-billionaire-influenced-another/.

Lee, Esther. "This Was the Average Cost of a Wedding in 2020." *The Knot*. February 11, 2021. https://www.theknot.com/content/average-wedding-cost.

Lee, Jeanne. "What Is Home Equity?" *Bankrate*. April 15, 2021. https://www.bankrate.com/home-equity/what-is-home-equity/.

Leonhardt, Megan. "75% of Millennial Couples Talk About Money at Least Once a Week—And It Seems to Be Working for Them." *CNBC.com*. July 27, 2018. https://www.cnbc.com/2018/07/27/75-percent-of-millennial-couples-talk-about-money-at-least-once-a-week.html.

Lino, Mark. "The Cost of Raising a Child." *USDA*. February 18, 2020. https://www.usda.gov/media/blog/2017/01/13/cost-raising-child.

Long, Heather. "The New Normal: 4 Job Changes by the Time You're 32." *CNN Business*. April 12, 2016. https://money.cnn.com/2016/04/12/news/economy/millennials-change-jobs-frequently/.

MacKay, Jory. "The Weird Science of First Impressions." *Medium*. November 19, 2014. https://medium.com/swlh/the-weird-science-of-first-impressions-f2daf99043ec.

Madell, Robin. "What Is the Gig Economy? Definition, Pros & Cons, Jobs." *Flexjobs*. January 17, 2020. https://www.flexjobs.com/blog/post/what-is-the-gig-economy-v2/.

Mahdawi, Arwa. "Why Are Thirtysomethings Lonely? Because Society Doesn't Value Friendship." *The Guardian*. August 7, 2019. https://www.theguardian.com/commentisfree/2019/aug/07/why-are-thirty-somethings-lonely-because-society-doesnt-value-friendship.

Markel, Adam. *Pivot: The Art and Science of Reinventing Your Life*. New York: Atria Books, 2016.

Marken, Stephanie. "Half in U.S. Now Consider College Education Very Important." *Gallup*. December 30, 2019. https://www.gallup.com/education/272228/half-consider-college-education-important.aspx.

Maverick, J. B. "What Is the Average Annual Return for the S&P 500?" *Investopedia*. June 1, 2021. https://www.investopedia.com/ask/answers/042415/what-average-annual-return-sp-500.asp.

McGovern, Marion. *Thriving in the Gig Economy: How to Capitalize and Compete in the New World of Work*. Newburyport, MA: Weiser, 2017.

Merriam-Webster.com. "Gig." https://www.merriam-webster.com/dictionary/gig.

Merriam-Webster.com. "Gig economy." https://www.merriam-webster.com/dictionary/gig%20economy.

Michigan Tech. "2021 Engineering Salary Statistics." https://www.mtu.edu/engineering/outreach/welcome/salary/.

Miller, Ben. "It's Time to Worry about College Enrollment Declines among Black Students." *Center for American Progress*. September 28, 2020. https://www.americanprogress.org/issues/education-postsecondary/reports/2020/09/28/490838/time-worry-college-enrollment-declines-among-black-students/.

Miller, Celia. "College Graduation Statistics." *Educationdata.org*. June 8, 2019. https://educationdata.org/number-of-college-graduates.

Millerbernd, Annie. "What Credit Score Do You Need for a Personal Loan?" *Nerdwallet*. October 15, 2020. https://www.nerdwallet.com/article/loans/personal-loans/credit-score-need-get-personal-loan.

Molinski, Michael. "3 Most Trusted Credit Card Companies." *Investor's Business Daily*. June 9, 2021. https://www.investors.com/news/most-trusted-credit-card-issuers/.

Monahan, Kelly, Jeff Schwartz, and Tiffany Schleeter. "Decoding Millennials in the Gig Economy: Six Trends to Watch in Alternative Work." *Deloitte*. May 1, 2018. https://www2.deloitte.com/us/en/insights/focus/technology-and-the-future-of-work/millennials-in-the-gig-economy.html.

Morrison, Nick. "You Don't Need to Be an Intern to Get a Job." *Forbes*. May 13, 2019. https://www.forbes.com/sites/nickmorrison/2019/05/13/you-dont-need-to-be-an-intern-to-get-a-job/?sh=498fe58742ce.

Morrison-Williams, Suzanne. "Millennials—Changing the Face of Higher Education." *Education Initiative*. https://educationinitiative.thepacificinstitute.com/articles/story/millennials-changing-the-face-of-higher-education.

Mulcahy, Diane. *The Gig Economy: The Complete Guide to Getting Better Work, Taking More Time Off, and Financing the Life You Want*. New York: AMACOM, 2016.

Muller, Onicia. "Should You Take a Gap Year? Here's What Experts Say." *Today*. September 16, 2020. https://www.today.com/tmrw/should-you-take -gap-year-here-s-what-experts-say-t190699.
Murchison, Colin. "The Pros & Cons of Taking a Gap Year." *Go Overseas*. November 25, 2020. https://www.gooverseas.com/blog/pros-and-cons -taking-gap-year.
Murphy, Mark. "Leadership Styles Are Often Why CEOs Get Fired." *Forbes*. July 16, 2015. https://www.forbes.com/sites/markmurphy/2015/07/16/ leadership-styles-are-often-why-ceos-get-fired/?sh=4f0f914b4988.
MyFICO.com. "What's in My FICO® Scores?" https://www.myfico.com/ credit-education/whats-in-your-credit-score.
National Association of Colleges and Employers. "Starting Salary Projections for Top Earning Degrees." https://www.naceweb.org/search results.aspx?searchtext=starting+salary+projections+for+top+earning +degrees.
National Association of Colleges and Employers. "Trends & Predictions." https://www.naceweb.org/career-development/trends-and-predictions/.
National Center for Biotechnology Information. https://www.ncbi.nlm.nih .gov.
National Center for Education Statistics. "Use the Data." https://nces.ed.gov/ ipeds/use-the-data.
Nationwide. "What You Need to Know About Prenuptial Agreements." https://www.nationwide.com/lc/resources/personal-finance/articles/ prenuptial-agreement-basics.
Nerdwallet. "Mortgage Calculator." https://www.nerdwallet.com/mortgages/ mortgage-calculator/calculate-mortgage-payment.
New York Times Magazine. "What Makes a 'Good Job' Good?" February 24, 2019. https://www.amazon.com/Ellery-Queens-Mystery-Magazine-April/ dp/B002FLACBO.
Nichols, Michael P. *The Lost Art of Listening*. Second ed. New York: The Guilford Press, 2009.
Noria Corporation. "68% of U.S. Consumer Products Companies Use Outsourcing." https://www.reliableplant.com/Read/1716/68 -of-us-consumer-products-companies-use-outsourcing.
Nova, Annie. "The Real Reason So Many People Are Working 'Side Hustles.'" *CNBC.com*. May 17, 2018. https://www.cnbc.com/2018/05/17/the -real-reason-so-many-people-are-working-side-hustles.html.
Olito, Frank. "The Average Age People Get Married in Every State." *Insider*. February 4, 2019. https://www.insider.com/when-people-get-married-every -state-2019-1.

Otani, Akane. "These Are the Skills You Need If You Want to Be Head-hunted." *Bloomberg*. January 5, 2015. https://www.bloomberg.com/news/articles/2015-01-05/the-job-skills-that-recruiters-wish-you-had.

Overfelt, Maggie. "Millennial Employees Are a Lot More Loyal than Their Job-Hopping Stereotype." *CNBC*. Updated May 11, 2017. https://www.cnbc.com/2017/05/10/90-of-millennials-will-stay-in-a-job-for-10-years-if-two-needs-met.html.

Parsons, Noah. "What Is a SWOT Analysis and How to Do It Right (with Examples)." *LivePlan*. February 2, 2021. https://www.liveplan.com/blog/what-is-a-swot-analysis-and-how-to-do-it-right-with-examples/.

Pesce, Nicole Lyn. "Why Millennials Make Great Mentors." *MarketWatch*. January 17, 2019. https://www.marketwatch.com/story/why-gen-z-and-millennial-workers-make-great-mentors-2018-10-24-1388139.

Peterson, Hayley. "Jeff Bezos Shares His Best Advice for Anyone Starting a Business." *Business Insider*. June 6, 2019. https://www.businessinsider.com/amazons-jeff-bezos-shares-advice-for-entreprenuers-2019-6.

Petsko, Emily. "Millennial Reading Habits Are Surprisingly Traditional." *Mental Floss*. March 27, 2019. https://www.mentalfloss.com/article/578177/surprising-millennial-reading-habits.

Pew Research Center. Survey Report. https://www.pewresearch.org/2015/?category_name=survey-report.

Pledger, Marcia R. http://www.marciapledger.com.

The Princeton Review. "Should You Go to Grad School Right After Under-grad?" https://www.princetonreview.com/grad-school-advice/should-you-go-to-grad-school-right-after-undergrad.

PR Newswire. "One-Third of Consumers Live Paycheck to Paycheck, TD Survey Finds." July 26, 2018. https://www.prnewswire.com/news-releases/one-third-of-consumers-live-paycheck-to-paycheck-td-survey-finds-300687134.html.

Quote Investigator. "It Is Not the Strongest of the Species That Survives But the Most Adaptable: Charles Darwin? Leon C. Megginson? Clarence Dar-row? Apocryphal?" May 4, 2014. https://quoteinvestigator.com/2014/05/04/adapt/.

Rea, Amy. "Reading through the Ages: Generational Reading Sur-vey." *Library Journal*. January 6, 2020. https://www.libraryjournal.com/?detailStory=Reading-Through-the-Ages-Generational-Reading-Survey.

Reference. "Who Was William Arthur Ward?" April 6, 2020. https://www.reference.com/world-view/william-arthur-ward-c469181241df9d41.

Renter, Elizabeth. "Budgeting for Newlyweds: A Guide to Family Finance." *Nerdwallet*. May 4, 2017. https://www.nerdwallet.com/article/finance/budgeting-for-newlyweds.

Rodriguez, Monica. "Is This the End of the Unpaid Internship?" *Fortune*. July 2, 2018. https://fortune.com/2018/07/02/unpaid-internships-ending/.

Rose, David S. *The Startup Checklist: 25 Steps to a Scalable, High-Growth Business*. Hoboken, NJ: Wiley, 2016.

Rosenberg, Eric. "What Is Compound Interest?" *CreditKarma.com*. June 1, 2021. https://www.creditkarma.com/savings/i/compound-interest.

Rothwell, Jonathan, and Jessica Harlan. "Self-Employment and Gig Economy Trends in the U.S." *Quickbooks*. 2019. https://quickbooks.intuit.com/self-employed/report/.

San Roman, Gabriel. "Cal State Fullerton Professor Co-Edits New Anthology on Unemployment." *OC Weekly*. April 12, 2017. https://www.ocweekly.com/csuf-professor-co-edits-new-book-on-unemployment-8031418/.

Sastry, Anjuli. "The Right Mentor Can Change Your Career. Here's How to Find One." *NPR*. September 3, 2020. https://www.npr.org/2019/10/25/773158390/how-to-find-a-mentor-and-make-it-work.

Segal, Jeanne, Melinda Smith, Lawrence Robinson, and Greg Boose. "Nonverbal Communication and Body Language." *HelpGuide*. October 2020. https://www.helpguide.org/articles/relationships-communication/nonverbal-communication.htm.

Selingo, Jeffrey, and Matt Sigelman. "The Crisis of Unemployed College Graduates." *Wall Street Journal*. February 4, 2021. https://www.wsj.com/articles/the-crisis-of-unemployed-college-graduates-11612454124.

Senatorlessor.com. "Sen. Lessor Recommits to Passing Student Loan Bill of Rights, Unveils Expanding Coalition Backing Effort." March 6, 2019. https://www.senatorlesser.com/news/2019/3/8/sen-lesser-recommits-to-passing-student-loan-bill-of-rights-unveils-expanding-coalition-backing-effort.

Shark Tank. "About." https://abc.com/shows/shark-tank/about-the-show.

Shaw, Gabbi. "These Are the 11 Most Common Reasons People Get Divorced, Ranked." *Insider*. January 31, 2019. https://www.insider.com/why-people-get-divorced-2019-1.

Shields, Jon. "What Do Corporate Recruiters Look For? We Asked Them." *Jobscan*. November 16, 2017. https://www.jobscan.co/blog/what-corporate-recruiters-want/.

Singletary, Michelle. https://www.washingtonpost.com/people/michelle-singletary/.

Small Businees Administration. "Write Your Business Plan." https://www.sba
.gov/starting-business/write-your-business-plan%20.

Smart Asset. "Property Tax Calculator." https://smartasset.com/taxes/
property-taxes.

Somers, Darian, and Josh Moody. "10 College Majors with the Best Starting Salaries." *U.S. News*. September 14, 2020. https://www.usnews.com/
education/best-colleges/slideshows/10-college-majors-with-the-highest
-starting-salaries.

Spector, Nicole. "Prenuptial Agreements: What Is a Prenup and Should I Get
One?" *NBC News*. April 12, 2019. https://www.nbcnews.com/better/lifestyle/
prenuptial-agreements-what-prenup-should-i-get-one-ncna993616.

Staffing Industry Analysts. https://staffingindustry.com/?region=site.

Stanford Life Design Lab. "ME104B: Designing Your Life." http://lifedesign
lab.stanford.edu/dyl.

Stanford University. "Career Truths." https://beam.stanford.edu/careertruths.

Steinmetz, Katy. "Exclusive: See How Big the Gig Economy Really Is." *Time*.
January 6, 2016. https://time.com/4169532/sharing-economy-poll/.

Steinway Moving & Storage. "How Many Times Does the Average Person
Move in a Lifetime?" July 10, 2018. https://www.steinwaymovers.com/
news/how-many-times-does-the-average-person-move-in-a-lifetime.

Steward, Shelly. "JPMorgan Chase Institute Report Shows Continued
Growth in Platform Work." *Gig Economy Data Hub*. September 24, 2018.
https://www.gigeconomydata.org/blog/jpmorgan-chase-institute-report
-shows-continued-growth-platform-work.

Stolba, Stefan Lembo. "Millennials and Credit: The Struggle Is Real."
Experian. April 2, 2019. https://www.experian.com/blogs/ask-experian/
taking-a-look-at-millennial-credit-scores/.

Subin, Samantha. "Millennials, Gen Z Are Job-Hopping, But Contrary to
Popular Belief, Maybe Not Enough." *CNBC.com*. February 28, 2021.
https://www.cnbc.com/2021/02/28/millennials-gen-z-are-job-hopping-but
-maybe-not-enough.html.

Swift River Capital. "Team." http://swiftrivercapital.com/team.html.

Thompson, Roger. "Ten Rules for Entrepreneurs." *Harvard Business
School*. December 2, 2010. https://www.alumni.hbs.edu/stories/Pages/
story-bulletin.aspx?num=1690.

Torpey, Elka, and Andrew Hogan. "Working in a Gig Economy." US Bureau
of Labor Statistics. May 2016. https://www.bls.gov/careeroutlook/2016/
article/what-is-the-gig-economy.htm.

Trudeau, Michelle. "You Had Me at Hello: The Science Behind First
Impressions." *NPR*. May 5, 2014. https://www.npr.org/sections/health

-shots/2014/05/05/308349318/you-had-me-at-hello-the-science-behind
-first-impressions.

UCAS. "Through the Lens of Students: How Perceptions of Higher Education Influence Applicants' Choices." July 2016. https://www.ucas.com/sites/default/files/through-the-lens-of-students.pdf.

US Army. "Becoming an Army Officer." https://www.goarmy.com/careers-and-jobs/become-an-officer/how-to-become-an-officer-in-the-army.html.

US Army. "Become an Officer: Frequently Asked Questions." https://www.goarmy.com/careers-and-jobs/become-an-officer/army-officer-faqs.html#live.

US Bureau of Labor Statistics. https://www.bls.gov.

US Bureau of Labor Statistics. "Employee Tenure in 2020." September 22, 2020. https://www.bls.gov/news.release/pdf/tenure.pdf.

US Census Bureau. "Number of People with Master's and Doctoral Degrees Doubles since 2000." https://www.census.gov/library/stories/2019/02/number-of-people-with-masters-and-phd-degrees-double-since-2000.html.

Van Edwards, Vanessa. "16 Essential Body Language Examples and Their Meanings." Science of People. https://www.scienceofpeople.com/body-language-examples/.

Varelas, Elaine. Boston.com. https://www.boston.com/author/elaine-varelas.

Vogt, Peter. "Seven Not-So-Obvious Reasons to Take Advantage of Your Campus Career Center." LiveCareer. https://www.livecareer.com/resources/jobs/search/campus-career-centers.

Vuleta, Branka. "30 Remarkable Stats About Millennials in the Workplace." What to Become. March 30, 2021. https://whattobecome.com/blog/millennials-in-the-workplace/.

Ward, Paris. "Over 50% of Dating Millennials Don't Want to Marry Until Their Finances Are in Order." CreditKarma.com. July 16, 2020. https://www.creditkarma.com/insights/i/millennials-delaying-marriage-to-get-finances-in-order.

Weissbourd, Richard, Trisha Ross Anderson, Brennan Barnard, Alison Cashin, and Alexis Ditkowsky. "Turning the Tide II: How Parents and High Schools Can Cultivate Ethical Character and Reduce Distress in the College Admissions Process." Harvard Graduate School of Education. March 2019. https://mcc.gse.harvard.edu/reports/turning-the-tide-2-parents-high-schools-college-admissions.

Welch, Jack. "Importance of Having a Mentor" [video]. Jack Welch Management Institute, Strayer. https://jackwelch.strayer.edu/winning/importance-of-having-a-mentor/.

Whistle, Wesley. "Millennials and Student Loans: Rising Debts and Disparities." *New America*. https://www.newamerica.org/millennials/reports/emerging-millennial-wealth-gap/millennials-and-student-loans-rising-debts-and-disparities.

Williams, Terri. "Advice for Prospective Business School Students from Successful MBA Grads." *The Economist GMAT Tutor*. https://gmat.economist.com/gmat-advicebusiness-school-admissions/application-advice/advice-prospective-business-school-students-successful-mba-grads.

Witschel, Matt. "Union Organizing and Gig-Economy Workers." *Wall Street Journal*. September 13, 2020. https://www.wsj.com/articles/union-organizing-and-gig-economy-workers-11600018191.

Woodward, Eric. *The Ultimate Guide to Internships*. New York: Allworth, 2015.

Zelizer, Julian. "'It's the Economy, Stupid' All Over Again." *CNN.com*. May 8, 2020. https://www.cnn.com/2020/05/08/opinions/economy-2020-election-trump-biden-zelizer/index.html.

Zillow.com. "Rent Affordability Calculator." https://www.zillow.com/rent-affordability-calculator/.

Zumbrun, Josh. "How Estimates of the Gig Economy Went Wrong." *Wall Street Journal*. January 7, 2019. https://www.wsj.com/articles/how-estimates-of-the-gig-economy-went-wrong-11546857000.

INDEX

ABOUT THE AUTHORS

Russell Robb is a seasoned financial professional who has navigated more than six decades of economic environments and has a vast understanding of financial matters pertinent to every stage of life. A highly respected and established member of the financial community, Robb's background spans a wealth of areas, particularly mergers and acquisitions, and he has held top positions at highly prestigious firms, including Tully & Holland, Inc. (managing director), Atlantic Management Company, Inc. (managing director), O'Conor, Wright Wyman Inc. (vice president), and Benchmark Consulting Group (principal). His specialty has been in M&A for midmarket businesses, with sales between 10 and 100 million.

Robb's notable deals include successfully negotiating a full-price sale of Data Industrial Corporation, a leader in the liquid flow sensor industry, to Badger Instrument Company, an AMEX public company from Milwaukee. He was hired to find synergistic acquisitions for Ken's Foods, a multibillion-dollar branded producer of salad dressings and sauces for retail and restaurant customers. Drew's Company in Vermont hired Robb to sell their company. He attracted potential buyers and negotiated the final sale to Gertrude Hawk Chocolate Company of Pennsylvania. In five years, this acquisition has increased Drew's sales by five times what they were prior to the acquisition.

In addition, Robb's first book, *Buying Your Own Business*, sold more than 30,000 copies worldwide. He also edited and published a successful monthly newsletter, called *M&A Today*.

Robb is the recipient of several service awards in the business and finance world. He is the former president of The Hamilton Trust (established 1882), the oldest investment club in the country, and he received its Lifetime Achievement Award in 2019. He also served as president for the Association for Corporate Growth (ACG), the largest international M&A organization, which now counts 14,500 members. It awarded him the Meritorious Service Award in 1995. He was also awarded the Distinguished Alumni Award from Fenn School.

Robb continues to serve and advise younger generations in matters relating to business and personal finance.

As a former lance corporal with the US Marine Corps, Robb has a deep respect for men and women in uniform. He has four children and seven grandchildren, whom he regularly advises on financial matters. He and his wife live in Massachusetts.

Katharine Robb Meehan is a millennial with a career as an executive-level administrator. Having graduated from Smith College with a BA in Environmental Science & Policy, she turned her education in natural and social sciences into a career highlighting her ability to blend the operational with the strategic while working for nonprofit organizations and government agencies. Committed to deploying her skills to support organizations with impact, she served the Massachusetts Department of Agricultural Resources, the US Department of Agriculture, The Nature Conservancy, and the Trustees of Reservations. Most recently, she supported the leadership team at the Kripalu Center for Yoga & Health, a wellness retreat center in the Berkshires of Massachusetts, where she acted as thought partner to the CEO in her role as executive assistant. She is also married and a mother, using those well-honed operational and strategic skills to achieve the always elusive work–life balance as best as possible.

David Tabatsky is a writer, editor, and performing artist, based in New York City. He received his bachelor's degree in communications and a master's degree in theater education, both from Adelphi University.

Among his more than fifty book projects, he was consulting editor for Marlo Thomas and her *New York Times* best seller, *The Right Words at the Right Time, Volume 2: Your Turn*; coauthor of Chicken Soup for the Soul's, *The Cancer Book: 101 Stories of Courage, Support and Love*; coauthored with Dr. Mark Banschick *The Intelligent Divorce—Books One and Two*; and coauthored with Dr. Randy Wright *The Wright Choice: Your Family's Guide to Healthy Eating, Modern Fitness and Saving Money*. He has written essays for *The Forward*, *Parenting*, and *Sesame Street Parent*, among others.

He is the also the coauthor of several books about cancer, including *Rx for Hope*, *Reimagining Women's Cancers*, and *Reimagining Men's Cancers*, and the author of *Write for Life: Communicating Your Way Through Cancer*.

His memoir, *American Misfit*, was released in 2017.

Please visit www.tabatsky.com.

CPSIA information can be obtained
at www.ICGtesting.com
Printed in the USA
BVHW091638070122
624438BV00002B/2

9 781538 149485

.